NO LOST CAUSES

ÁLVARO URIBE VÉLEZ

NO LOST CAUSES

A CELEBRA BOOK

CELEBRA
Published by New American Library, a division of
Penguin Group (USA) Inc., 375 Hudson Street,
New York, New York 10014, USA
Penguin Group (Canada), 90 Eglinton Avenue East, Suite 700, Toronto,
Ontario M4P 2Y3, Canada (a division of Pearson Penguin Canada Inc.)
Penguin Books Ltd., 80 Strand, London WC2R 0RL, England
Penguin Ireland, 25 St. Stephen's Green, Dublin 2,
Ireland (a division of Penguin Books Ltd.)
Penguin Group (Australia), 250 Camberwell Road, Camberwell, Victoria 3124,
Australia (a division of Pearson Australia Group Pty. Ltd.)
Penguin Books India Pvt. Ltd., 11 Community Centre, Panchsheel Park,
New Delhi - 110 017, India
Penguin Group (NZ), 67 Apollo Drive, Rosedale, Auckland 0632,
New Zealand (a division of Pearson New Zealand Ltd.)
Penguin Books (South Africa) (Pty.) Ltd., 24 Sturdee Avenue,
Rosebank, Johannesburg 2196, South Africa

Penguin Books Ltd., Registered Offices:
80 Strand, London WC2R 0RL, England

First published by Celebra,
a division of Penguin Group (USA) Inc.

First Printing, October 2012
10 9 8 7 6 5 4 3 2 1

LIBRARY OF CONGRESS CATALOGING-IN-PUBLICATION DATA:

Uribe Vélez, Álvaro, 1952-
No lost causes / Álvaro Uribe Vélez.
p.   cm.
ISBN 978-0-451-41381-9
1. Uribe Vélez, Álvaro, 1952–   2. Presidents—Colombia—Biography.
3. Colombia—Politics and government—1974–   I. Title.
F2279.22.U78A3 2012
986.106'34092—dc23   2012014078
[B]

Set in Adobe Garamond Pro
Designed by Alissa Amell

Printed in the United States of America

PUBLISHER'S NOTE
Penguin is committed to publishing works of quality and integrity. In that spirit, we are proud to offer this
book to our readers; however the story, the experiences and the words are the author's alone.
      While the author has made every effort to provide accurate telephone numbers and Internet addresses
at the time of publication, neither the publisher nor the author assumes any responsibility for errors, or for
changes that occur after publication. Further, publisher does not have any control over and does not
assume any responsibility for author or third-party Web sites or their content.

For Lina,
who represents my whole family

SECTION ONE

Love

"The only regret I will have in dying is if it is not for love."
—GABRIEL GARCÍA MÁRQUEZ

1

"The troops are ready, Mr. President."

"Then proceed," I said. "Proceed under my responsibility."

I closed my eyes. I said a prayer.

And then I saw their faces.

2

Guillermo Gaviria Correa and Gilberto Echeverri were friends of mine, men who were willing to sacrifice everything for their love of country. Men of peace, like so many Colombians, men of faith. And when they ventured into a hazardous stretch of coffee country in our shared home state of Antioquia on April 17, 2002, they fully expected that faith to be returned in kind.

Gaviria, the scion of an influential publishing family from Medellín, a deeply spiritual man who counted Gandhi and Martin Luther King, Jr. among his heroes, had organized the "March of Reconciliation and Solidarity"—a five-day, thirty-mile peace march to the town of Caicedo. The purpose: to show that a nonviolent solution to Colombia's decades of mayhem and bloodshed was possible. Gaviria had considerable national clout as the governor of Antioquia state, a job I had held a few years before him. According to media reports, Gaviria instructed the police and army to stay clear of the march, not to protect him, and, above all, not to retaliate if he was kidnapped or killed.

This was brave. The terrorist group known as the Revolutionary Armed Forces of Colombia, the FARC, had tormented the area around Caicedo for too many years, perpetrating kidnappings, civilian massacres, and other innumerable horrors. Gaviria was by no means blind to the dangers of our country: His mother, Doña Adela Correa, had been kidnapped some years before by a separate armed group, the EPL. Our army had warned Gaviria against staging the march, saying the area was too hazardous. Yet Gaviria was young and charismatic, a poet and a dancer, with all the zeal of a true believer. The town of Caicedo had recently grabbed the whole country's attention by declaring itself "neutral" in Colombia's violence, and Gaviria was certain that this pacifist approach illuminated the path to peace nationwide. He wanted to show other Colombian politicians—including me, it was said—that armed confrontation was not the answer to our ills.

The march was meant to be a turning point in Colombian history—our

Selma. To those who warned him of the dangers, Gaviria replied: "I'm more afraid of the cowardice of not going." I must say, I know exactly what he meant.

Gaviria was joined on the road to Caicedo by almost a thousand people. Among them was Gilberto Echeverri, a widely admired elder statesman and former defense minister and ambassador, an extraordinary Colombian whose family I had known since childhood. The other marchers included the president of the Colombian Episcopal Conference; the bishops of Medellín and several other cities; and even an American who had marched with Dr. King in Alabama in 1965: Bernard Lafayette, a university professor and peace activist who had, like so many others, been inspired by the purpose of Gaviria's mission.

For five days the demonstrators, clad in white T-shirts and waving white flags, marched indefatigably along the highway, singing peace songs and handing out rosary beads to passersby. At several points, villagers spontaneously spilled out onto the road, chanting, "No to violence!" and waving homemade white flags of their own. It was a beautiful sight, an earnest, heartwarming demonstration of how the vast majority of Colombians, no matter their politics or creed, yearned for normalcy and peace.

Had the FARC been honorable, or even minimally rational, they would have embraced these good-hearted people—or at least left them alone. But it was not to be. On the march's final day, April 21, just two miles from Caicedo, the procession was stopped on the highway by a group of terrorists from the so-called 34th Front of the FARC. They were led by Aicardo de Jesús Agudelo Rodríguez, a.k.a. "El Paisa," a career criminal—a bona fide monster—who, according to the Colombian National Police, was responsible for more than four hundred kidnappings and five hundred homicides, including the murder of the mother of Cecilia María Vélez, education minister during our administration.

El Paisa asked Gaviria to accompany them to a meeting with guerilla leaders, and when Gaviria balked, they lied and told him they wanted only to learn more about the march's goals. Accompanied by several other protesters, including Gilberto Echeverri—who had joined him out of solidarity—and the American professor, he followed them.

Hours later, those who awaited the governor were met by a group of his companions. Gaviria and Echeverri were missing. The FARC had kidnapped him and had spirited them away on horseback into the deepest reaches of the Colombian jungle. Two new hostages were added to the more than twenty-eight hundred others who were taken captive that year, the helpless casualties of a dark and infamous era.

3

Oh, how we worked to find them!

When I became president of Colombia four months later, in August 2002, I dedicated myself fully to the liberation of Guillermo Gaviria Correa, Gilberto Echeverri, and all of our hostages. Every day, without fail, I spoke to my skilled team of military commanders and reminded them of the importance of the issue. We flew special reconnaissance planes high over Antioquia, searching for any sign of them. We offered rewards to informants who could provide us with their location. And, through it all, we never stopped planning for a possible military rescue. On Friday nights, I often stayed at my desk in the presidential palace until very late at night, calling my generals, colonels, and officials to discuss our progress on security issues and on our anti-kidnapping operations. With the exception of mandatory acts of protocol (hosting foreign dignitaries or important figures), there were no social gatherings, no vacations, no days off. Our sole mission was to restore security and to liberate every Colombian hostage.

We worked non-stop because our country was in crisis. While we did not share their opinion, many analysts were saying that Colombia was a lost cause. As I took office, as much as half of our national territory was under the effective control of a vast and bewildering constellation of outlaws: drug kingpins, murderous paramilitary groups, and nominally Marxist terrorists such as the FARC, who murdered and pillaged at will. In just the previous months, the criminals had firebombed a church, killing forty-eight children; hijacked a Colombian commercial airliner; and kidnapped one of my opponents in the 2002 presidential campaign, whom they would hold hostage in the jungle for the next six years. The FARC had even attempted to sabotage my inauguration by firing more than a dozen mortars at the presidential palace as the ceremonies got started—most of them missed, and hit a cluster of humble homes nearby. Nineteen innocent people died.

This was not some passing crisis. For decades, Colombia had been under the spell of illegal drug trafficking and terrorists. Village massacres and urban bombings often appeared before the world's eyes. All told, we suffered from

the world's highest murder rate, with more than twenty-eight thousand homicides a year. The violence had forced more than two million Colombians
from their homes. Only Sudan and Angola had more displaced people. It
wasn't even possible to drive between most major Colombian cities anymore—the armed groups set up roadblocks on major highways, kidnapping
helpless car passengers and holding them for ransom for months at a time.
Meanwhile, the cumulative effect of all this chaos had a disastrous effect on
our economy—we had just endured our worst recession since the 1930s,
unemployment was stuck at 16 percent, and future generations were bur-
dened with large budget deficits that seemed to stretch into eternity. Shortly
after I took office, my finance minister told me that, without radical solutions, we could run out of cash to pay our soldiers within just six weeks.

Yes—it was an exhausting, almost interminable list of problems. Some
people had simply given up: they believed that Colombia somehow defied
solutions. Previous governments had seemingly tried everything: peace negotiations, military crackdowns, states of emergency, foreign mediators, amnesty deals, prisoner swaps . . . and yet our problems only grew worse. Anyone
who showed the courage to try to change Colombia's status quo faced a real
risk of death—senators, mayors, labor union leaders, and priests had all been
struck down in the previous decade. I myself had survived at least fifteen
assassination attempts during my career.

We live in a cynical era, one in which many people around the world have
lost faith in the ability of their leaders, and their governments, to change their
lives for the better. Maybe I was an incorrigible romantic; maybe all those
bullets and bombs had made me stubborn. But I refused to accept that
Colombia was a lost cause. I passionately believed in the power of leadership
to solve any problem, no matter how dire. I believed that, if we set our sights
on an audacious vision and worked tirelessly toward it, we could indeed
take back our country. With the dedication and teamwork of our ministers,
military and police commanders, and thousands of other dedicated public
servants, we would show our teeth to the violent ones and overcome them,
without compromising our values. This was always the purpose of our administration: We would bring security, prosperity, and the rule of law to
Colombia, while strengthening our democracy and human rights.

None of this would be easy—there would be many failures, and much heartbreak, during our journey. But our government would spare no effort, and I was willing to do absolutely anything—big or small—to bring Colombia back from the brink. I publically gave out my personal cell phone number, and did my best to take calls at any hour. I telephoned business leaders around the world and asked them what it would take for them to start investing in Colombia again. Every single Saturday, my ministers and aides and I visited a different city or village, often in the most dangerous corners of the country, and we listened for eight hours at a time or more as the people there told us about their problems—and helped us to brainstorm policy solutions. I was so focused on details that, when we flew into a Colombian city, I would often check the airport bathrooms, garden areas, and hallways to make sure they were clean—and alert the management if they were not. Some people called this micromanaging—others thought it was just strange—and maybe they were right on both counts. But I believed that we had to combine the big picture with the small details, and dedicate our lives totally to executing the kind of transformative change that Colombia needed. Anything less just wouldn't do.

Encouraged by some very early victories in the first few months of my government, Colombians had tentatively begun to believe in their country again. People began to remember that, when the sun shone brightly and the dragons were kept at bay, our country could seem like a heaven without parallel. We were blessed with a vibrant people, an embarrassment of natural riches, and breathtaking God-given beauty. Colombia was a country worth dedicating ourselves to, heart and soul. Our potential was limitless. But these early victories did not stop us from searching for the hundreds of kidnap victims, scattered in jungle camps throughout the country, chained to trees or living in small metal cages, while suffering from tropical diseases and separation from their families for years at a time—they were like soldiers who had been left on the battlefield. They were a symbol of everything that was still wrong and unjust about Colombia; their plight was our plight.

It was in this context that the kidnappings of Gaviria Correa and Echeverri took place; this was why they were so devastating not just for their families, but for our entire nation. Here were two of our most beloved political figures—one of them the sitting governor of one of our largest states, the other a supremely dignified statesman—languishing in conditions that could barely be considered human. Their absence tore at my soul, more unbearable with each passing day. I was responsible for their fate; I was the president. For the first six months of my administration, the trail was cold, apart from letters that Gaviria sent his wife, detailing the conditions of their captivity. That was it. We had no clue where they were.

And then, finally, we got a tip.

4

"It seems to me a very grave error of the FARC to have us here, rather than to listen to our ideas," Gaviria wrote in one of dozens of letters he sent his wife during his captivity. He spent his days fishing in the jungle's rivers, giving English classes to his fellow hostages, and reading books, including the Holy Bible. At night, making the arduous journeys between camps by mule, he would often gaze up into the starry sky. "Spectacular," he wrote. And through it all, he remained convinced that he would eventually impress his philosophy upon his captors. "What I do will bear fruit sooner or later," he declared. "It will have been worth it if the FARC opens the opportunity to nonviolence."

Gaviria and his fellow captives showed tremendous courage and resilience, as did virtually all of Colombia's hostages. Inevitably, though, the months of captivity took their toll. Gaviria and Echeverri had been taken to a camp with several other hostages, and two of them developed leishmaniasis—a horrid tropical disease transmitted by biting parasitic sand flies, which results in egg-size, festering open sores on the skin that can spread unless properly treated. One of the men had a sore just above his eye, and there was no appropriate medicine available at the camp. "I'm really afraid that he will lose his eye if it is permitted to worsen," Gaviria wrote. Another hostage, who had just completed six years in captivity, was suffering his nineteenth bout of malaria since being taken prisoner. Gaviria reported that his own health was fine, apart from a fungus that plagued his feet, but he expressed deep concern for Echeverri, who was just a few weeks shy of his sixty-seventh birthday and showing signs of breaking down. "At his age," Gaviria wrote, "he should not be running the risks that we run here."

There were times when the relentless monotony of the rain, the arduous physical demands of jungle life, and the mental anguish of being separated from one's family for an indefinite period could break down even the strongest soul. For emotional sustenance, Gaviria often turned to the radio—and programs such as *The Voices of the Kidnapped*, part of an entire world that had sprung up around the Colombians in captivity and their families. On these radio shows, which usually aired during the predawn hours, the hostages' families and friends would speak directly to their loved ones as the rest of Colombia listened in, offering them tantalizing details of the triumphs and travails at home: a daughter who had been born, a nephew's birthday. These kinds of simple messages could sustain the hostages for weeks or months at a time. "Your voice made my soul rejoice," Gaviria wrote his wife. "It was very beautiful."

Escape was unthinkable. None of the FARC's most prized prisoners—the "high-value" hostages, as they were cynically known—had ever succeeded in getting away. They were kept under constant guard. If somehow they did wriggle out of their chains and evade the armed guards assigned to them, and slipped through the ring of terrorists that patrolled any camp's outer perimeter, they then had to cope with the cruelest warden of all: Mother Nature. The FARC usually held its prisoners in areas of thick jungle populated with snakes and other horrors. Twenty-foot anacondas were rumored to have dragged grown men underwater as they tried to swim away by river. The vegetation was so thick that it could be difficult to hear, much less see, anything more than ten yards away. Seemingly the only people in Colombia who knew how to properly cope with this terrain were the FARC—who had accumulated four decades of experience as jungle nomads—and they were usually able to rekidnap anyone who fled within hours. Those who were caught were often punished with savage beatings, and made to sleep with tight chains around their neck for months at a time. Virtually every prisoner knew all of this; they rarely even tried to leave.

As hard as life was for the prisoners, the stress was often unbearable for their families. The pain of having a relative in endless captivity—in a kind of limbo, not dead, but not fully alive either—was enough to drive people to the brink of reason. Marriages sometimes fell apart while one spouse was in captivity; children often grew up not knowing a parent. These traumas rippled through every strata of Colombian society: The captives ranged from humble Colombians to conscripted soldiers to members of the economic and political elite. By the time I came into office, some of them had been held for nearly a decade.

By early 2003, the FARC's prisoners included Fernando Araújo, a former minister of development; Ingrid Betancourt, a French-Colombian former presidential candidate who had been abducted the previous year; and three

American contractors—Marc Gonsalves, Keith Stansell, and Tom Howes—whose plane had crashed in February 2003 while the men were on a counternarcotics mission and who were then taken prisoner. Kidnapping was, in sum, a tragedy that knew no national, social, or economic boundaries; it held the families hostage, too—they were unable to be with their loved ones but also unable to grieve. Some said it was worse than death.

Gaviria, as was his nature, didn't agree with that at all.

"Kidnapping is like a type of death from which it is possible to return," he wrote. "This is the only difference: It gives us a second chance."

5

They had been right under our noses the whole time.

A young boy of humble means in rural Antioquia was out fishing and hunting one afternoon when he stumbled across a FARC camp. Curious, he skirted around the camp's edges and spotted what appeared to be about a dozen hostages. As luck would have it, this boy had a brother in the armed forces, and the tip made its way quickly up the chain of command. One of our generals took the youth and his brother up in an army airplane and asked them to point out to him where the camp was. And that was how we discovered that the FARC was holding Gaviria, Echeverri, and other prisoners in an isolated area of alpine jungle near the Murrí and Mandé rivers in Antioquia, thirty miles from the town of Urrao—and only about eighty miles in a straight line from Medellín.

That this camp was within a short helicopter flight of one of Colombia's biggest cities spoke volumes. In many other countries, a patrol of army or police based in a city of Medellín's size would surely have detected them already. Yet in Colombia, with our crazy quilt of mountains, valleys, and jungles, plus our legacy of uneven economic and social development, the camp might as well have been a thousand miles away.

We put additional intelligence assets on the case and found there were about a hundred terrorists in the vicinity of the camp. Fifteen to twenty of them were charged with guarding the hostages. In addition to Gaviria and Echeverri, the hostages included ten Colombian soldiers, many of whom had been kept in the jungle for even longer: four years or more—not unusual, sadly, by the standards of the time. We were told that the group's commander—the criminal El Paisa—was present as well, personally supervising the captivity of what the FARC considered to be "high-value" hostages.

We had the facts: Now we needed to decide how to get the hostages out.

I had numerous concerns. Our primary consideration, of course, was the hostages' lives. Many of their families favored the option of a negotiated prisoner swap—in which my government would free hundreds of FARC prisoners from our jails in return for the liberation of the hostages. I never ruled out this possibility, as long as certain conditions were met, such as the former FARC agreeing to desert the terrorist group and leave the country, or consenting to enter a program that would reinsert them into Colombian society. During my government I accepted many proposals from the international community and the Catholic Church to try to negotiate the hostages' release. But all too often the FARC would back away from their proposals, or insist on conditions they knew were impossible. And ultimately, I feared that paying a ransom or engaging in a swap of hostages for imprisoned terrorists would only embolden the FARC to undertake more kidnappings. This was not conjecture; it was exactly what recent Colombian history had demonstrated.

The health problems among the hostages in Gaviria and Echeverri's camp added urgency to our decision making, not solely because of them, but because their condition illuminated the fate of dozens of other prisoners, many of whom had been stranded for a much longer period and were in even worse condition, both physically and psychologically. How many more years would we stand idly by and allow them to languish in the jungle, away from their lives and families? Five? Seven? Ten? No, that passiveness had to end.

With the hostages' location in hand, we needed to act quickly, before the camp moved. So I asked the Colombian military to design a plan for the rescue of Gaviria, Echeverri, and the other ten hostages.

The operation was designed to minimize the risk of casualties as much as possible among both our hostages and the FARC. We would depend heavily on the dual elements of surprise and overwhelming force, having a large amount of troops descend on the area by fast rope to locate the hostages quickly. Our men would be equipped with megaphones to make clear to the FARC that if they handed over the hostages peacefully, no one would be harmed. Instead of its taking place at night, or at dawn, we would conduct the operation around lunchtime, when our intelligence told us the camp would be the most relaxed. Meanwhile, the army unit responsible for the area, the 4th Brigade, temporarily halted the operations of the two battalions that were in the area so the FARC would be as relaxed as possible at the time of our operation. Our military took aerial photos of the area so that our troops would be familiar with the terrain prior to the raid.

I was aware that the mission could, for better or for worse, define my presidency; if it failed, it could potentially derail our entire security plan, which was already generating some controversy. Yet I refused to allow political risks to be a consideration. I had campaigned from the very start on the need to defeat kidnapping and liberate the hostages, by force if necessary. I had a clear mandate to do so.

By early May 2003, the operation was ready to be executed.

I weighed the risks carefully. A mission of this scale had never been attempted in Colombia before, and there were concerns in some quarters about whether our military and information-gathering capabilities were yet up to the task. Yet, in the final balance, I had, and still have, full confidence in our armed forces. The intelligence was deemed excellent. The condition of the hostages—indeed, the condition of Colombia as a whole—demanded urgent action.

The decision was clear.

I gave the order.

6

At five a.m. on the morning of the raid, I woke up, turned to my wife, Lina, and said, "We need to pray."

That day I adhered to our strict policy when covert operations were under way: business as usual, so as not to raise suspicions among the armed groups, some of which had infiltrated our ranks. I flew from Bogotá to Cali aboard FAC-001, our presidential plane, and from there we traveled by helicopter to Los Farallones National Park in the mountains that tower above the city. That morning I was to inaugurate a new High Mountain Battalion named after the late Rodrigo Lloreda Caicedo, who had been a valiant and beloved Colombian defense minister. These battalions were a special kind of outpost that was designed to clear and hold strategic points in the Andes, ensure that we had the advantage of altitude over the FARC, cut off their escape routes, and, perhaps ironically, put an end to the massive kidnappings in Cali and the rest of the valley below.

Moments before I began my speech, I received word from our defense minister, Marta Lucía Ramírez, that the mission was now under way. If it proved successful, she or the senior military official present—General Jorge Enrique Mora Rangel—would almost certainly receive confirmation via cell phone during my speech.

As I addressed the crowd, I thought of my friends and comrades—of Guillermo Gaviria Correa, of Gilberto Echeverri, of the ten captive soldiers, of their families, and all the other hostages across our nation. I thought of the troops who were conducting the operation, and I said a prayer for their safety, too. Once or twice, my eyes flickered over to General Mora Rangel or to Minister Ramírez, to try to gauge their expressions, to see whether they had already received the good news.

Yet the call we all hoped for never came.

7

Twenty years earlier, almost exactly to the day, my father, Alberto Uribe Sierra, woke up agitated. A jovial, charismatic volcano of a man, the very image of health, happiness, and vigor, my father was an accomplished horseman and amateur bullfighter who was strong enough to deliver the final blow from the top of a horse with his sword, the kind of good-humored man who never let himself be unsettled by anything or anyone. Yet on this June morning in 1983, my father rose and immediately began pacing—angry, impetuous, unsettled. Like a bull.

This sort of anguish was unusual for him. He was, in so many ways, a resident of that *other* Colombia: a place of blinding beauty, of horses and music and dancing—a paradise for a self-made man who had left home at the age of fourteen to go seek his fortune and live his life. Alberto Uribe Sierra always had a guitar nearby; he would break into a ballad at the most unexpected moments. His parties were the stuff of legend, often lasting for days at a time. He was a Don Juan of sorts—possessed of extreme charm, a source of joy for those around him.

He was happiest, though, on his ranch, where he worked tirelessly, often accompanied by one of my brothers and sisters or me. My father and I would ride together through the long grass, enveloped in a thousand different shades of green, checking up on cattle and helping mend fences until twilight would finally descend on us. "Ay, Álvaro," he would say with a sigh. "This ranching life, there's not much money in it, I'm afraid to tell you. There's only the romance. You have to be in it for love." And then he would smile, give his horse a swift kick, and we would head for home together.

Indeed, the ranching life meant everything to my father. So we had all been surprised when, three weeks prior, he had made an almost unprecedented concession. "We're not returning to Guacharacas," he told my brothers. "For the moment, we're not going back there."

Guacharacas was my father's favorite property, a gorgeous and productive piece of land in the rolling horse country of Antioquia. He had owned it since 1975 in partnership with a local rancher. During that era, the train to Puerto

Berrío still ran through the property; the house had once been an inn near the train station. Guacharacas had a staff of forty hands, plus a foreman; it was a region characterized by hardworking, honest people who knew how to get the most from the land. It was also, by the early 1980s, starting to become a redoubt of the FARC.

My father was no stranger to such circumstances; violence stalked him always. His early adulthood was marked by *La Violencia*, the civil war of the late 1940s and 1950s between *liberales* and *conservadores* that left more than two hundred thousand Colombians dead. He incurred many great risks during that era, and by 1961 he'd moved to the far north of Antioquia in the hope of settling into a quieter life. As fate would have it, that area—near the town of Montelíbano, Córdoba—became the birthplace of the EPL, the *Ejército Popular de Liberación* or People's Liberation Army, an armed group that operated primarily in rural areas and gained strength with alarming speed. One night in the mid-1960s, when I was twelve or thirteen years old, the EPL came to our property, destroyed the farm equipment, stole the cattle, and set our house on fire. No one from our family was present at the time—but just a few days before, my brother Jaime and I had spent the night there with some friends from school. Surely, if we had been there when they attacked, we would have been kidnapped or killed.

Despite the threats—or, more likely, *because* of them—my father never backed down. Even as the FARC consolidated itself as Colombia's most powerful armed group, and began engaging in ever-bolder extortion of land- and factory owners and ordinary Colombians alike, he refused to make concessions. A year previously, in May of 1982, the FARC's leadership had established its landmark "strategic plan"—a blueprint for building up its forces, inciting class warfare, leading insurrections in major cities, and, ultimately, toppling the government in Bogotá. The group's military strength was bolstered by its growing participation in Colombia's narcotics trade, feeding the era's blossoming and ultimately insatiable appetite for cocaine in the United States and Europe, providing the FARC with revenues to expand their remit even further. When the FARC arrived in a new area, they would typically demand two things: money and silence. My father's reaction? *"No camino un paso, y no doy un peso,"* he said. "I won't walk a step, and I won't give them a cent."

This stubbornness made his sudden edict not to return to Guacharacas all the more puzzling. How could he yield to their pressure now, after all these years of resistance? We still don't know for certain why he told us not to go—perhaps he had received a specific threat; perhaps it was intuition. We also don't know why, on that ill-fated morning in June 1983, after pacing around the house for a good while, he just as abruptly changed his mind.

I suspect that, in the end, Alberto Uribe Sierra just couldn't live with what he saw as a capitulation. This was a man who, at the age of fifty, had gone through life without making compromises; who believed that his generous treatment of his workers somehow placed him above Colombia's bubbling class tensions; who had faith in his country, and his countrymen, to abide by the same code he had.

He picked up the phone and dialed my brother Santiago. "Meet me at the airport," he said. "We're going to Guacharacas."

Before leaving the house, he called my sister María Isabel and invited her along, too. And then he picked up his pistol, a Walther. *"Mejor muerto que secuestrado,"* he once told my brother. "Better dead than kidnapped." With the gun in his holster, and a revitalized spring in his step, he bounded out the door, into the promise of a glorious Colombian morning.

8

"Mr. President?"

The moment I saw the look on the minister's face, I knew.

The first details from the scene were incomplete, and came in spurts:

As planned, five Black Hawk helicopters lifted off from the Urrao airport at about ten a.m., carrying seventy-five soldiers from our *Fuerza de Despliegue Rápido*, the elite rapid-response unit of the Colombian Special Forces. They had the support of two Arpia helicopters, a command-and-control unit, and a plane hovering far overhead for logistical support. The flight time to the three designated drop zones near the FARC encampment was approximately eighteen minutes—a short enough lapse to allow for a degree of surprise, even if word of the operation somehow filtered out.

By the time our troops reached the campsite, the terrorists were gone. Our troops found only the dead bodies of nine of the thirteen hostages. All of the dead had been shot with firearms at close range, execution-style, either behind the ear or in the back of the neck. Guillermo Gaviria Correa and Gilberto Echeverri were among the dead. Three of the captive soldiers had been wounded, while one hostage had emerged unhurt.

From start to finish, our troops had not fired a single shot.

We had no further details, just a thousand unanswered questions: Was the intelligence flawed? Had our troops been spotted? To where had the terrorists fled? What was the condition of the wounded? Was there an informant in our midst?

Heartache gripped me like a vise around my stomach—an old feeling, far too familiar. I knew right away that this tragedy would haunt me for the rest of my days—as has effectively happened. But this was not a time for grieving. We needed to act.

My first instinct was to proceed immediately to Urrao, and from there to the location of the massacre. Always, throughout my career, I have believed in the need to be physically present at the scene of major crises—to better coordinate the response, to transmit authority, and to assume responsibility for the situation. In this case, I needed to honor the fallen and oversee an urgent investigation into what had gone wrong. I needed to examine the site with my own eyes so I could better fathom the challenges of the military operation, see the jungle, and understand the conditions that the hostages had endured.

I gathered my security team for a brief meeting and I gave them my orders. From there, we returned via helicopter to Cali, where we boarded FAC-001, bound for Medellín.

I sat on the plane in silence with my eyes closed, trying to gather my thoughts and fully understand the human, political, and military consequences of this tragedy. All around me, my advisers were discussing whether we should conduct a quick investigation ourselves, or whether we should bring in "neutral" investigators from elsewhere. How much should we tell the victims' relatives, and when? What should we disclose to the Colombian people? What would this mean for the presidency? For our security plan? For the remaining hostages?

I opened my eyes and enumerated the three main principles that would guide our response:

1. We would tell the truth—every single detail, that same day, in a live televised address to the nation.
2. We would accept any and all criticism as valid, and learn from it.
3. We would not yield in our fight against the terrorists, and I would personally take all responsibility for the failed operation.

Of course, we would eventually conduct a full probe into the events near Urrao. But I felt that, under the circumstances, the nation needed to know the truth right away. If confusion, recrimination, and innuendo were our enemies, then transparency was our only friend. The truth might be painful; it might reveal that I had acted hastily, or rashly, or that our government institutions were not yet equal to the challenges that faced us. Yet those were risks I was willing to take. I believed that, at moments of great tragedy such as this, people could disagree with our actions or methods—but the most important thing was for them to *believe* in us.

Without credibility, all faith in our government would vanish. We had already lost the fallen; unless we handled this tragedy with honesty, dignity, and strength, we would lose the nation, too.

9

Geography has always been Colombia's biggest blessing and our biggest curse: a blessing because our country is endowed with stunning natural beauty and resources. We have 1 percent of the world's landmass, but 10 percent of its biodiversity. White-sand beaches along the Caribbean coast give way to unthinkably fertile plains, which then rise into the lush, cool mountain country. Highland states such as Santander and my native Antioquia are like a symphony of terraces, each plateau with its own temperature, ecosystem, and glorious shade of green. Our borders encircle a veritable treasure chest of precious commodities—gold, oil, emeralds, freshwater, and so on. It is sometimes hard to believe that God has endowed one country with so much wealth.

Yet the same extraordinary terrain that yielded these bounties has also made aspects of governing Colombia extraordinarily difficult—politically, economically, and militarily. Throughout our history, it has almost always been so. "A guerrilla's delight," was how a *Time* magazine reporter described it in 1956. Indeed, our geography was one of the main reasons why, in two centuries of history, no government in Bogotá had ever been able to extend full control over our territory. Three distinct chains of mountains cut through the country from south to north, separated by deep valleys. Half of the country was virtually unpopulated—much of it in the Amazon south and east, the Orinoco River basin and its savannas, and also in vast areas such as the Pacific coast. This mix of terrain made Colombia a perfect place for armed groups to operate—and to hold hostages for years at a time.

I have traveled all over Colombia, from the deserts of the Guajira Peninsula, to the Amazon jungle in Leticia near the Peruvian and Brazilian borders, to the soaring peaks of Paramo de las Papas, where the Magdalena River has its origins. And I can say that the terrain near Urrao where the massacre took place was as impenetrable as I have ever seen. As our helicopter approached the site, the ground was totally obscured by the canopy of the trees, each of them forty-five to fifty feet tall, stretching to the horizon in every direction. In a few patches, there were a few soft, barely perceptible depressions in the canopy—which marked the creeks and small rivers bisecting the area. Otherwise we saw just the monotony of a thick, impenetrable jungle.

Dusk was already falling as our helicopter gingerly landed on a small patch of sand on the banks of a river—very near the spot where our special forces had touched down. I was accompanied by General Mora Rangel, General Mario Montoya, Defense Minister Ramírez, and my trusted aide Ricardo Galán, a career journalist whom I had asked to record every detail of our investigation. There was also a small squad of soldiers for our protection. As the helicopter powered down, some on board heard gunfire outside. As we waited for our troops to secure the area, word came via radio that another of the hostages had perished from his wounds. We sat there in silence, sweating, a suffocating sense of grief and vulnerability in the air.

Once we were able to safely disembark from the helicopter and we began to survey the surrounding area, we quickly realized what had gone wrong. Even though the camp with the fallen hostages was only a few hundred yards away, the slope leading up from the landing site was impossibly steep. Almost vertical. Anyone who had landed at this particular spot would have essentially been stuck—even if they had successfully scaled the slope, it would have required so much time that the element of surprise would have been lost. This helped explain why the FARC had so much time to react, and then execute the hostages.

I had seen what I needed to see.

We scampered back down the slope to the helicopter, racing against time to get back to Medellín and complete our investigation. Word of the tragedy started to leak out to the public. It was night by the time we returned to the city—and there, at a public hospital, we were able to speak to the surviving hostages.

One of them was in terrible condition, barely able to talk to us. But he and another soldier were still able to independently confirm to us the events of that day, and provide us with the definitive account of why the mission had gone wrong.

Conditions at the camp had been bleak for weeks; several of the hostages were in deteriorating health. Despite the recent calm in the immediate vicinity, the FARC had been in a state of high alert, possibly because of the military operations that we were conducting elsewhere in the country. On the day of the raid, the helicopters carrying our troops had flown low over the campsite, possibly having miscalculated the exact site of the camp. This, by itself, was not a fatal mistake—the survivors told us that helicopters had been occasionally passing over the region in previous days on medical missions to nearby indigenous communities. But as the copters flew overhead, the terrorists were able to see through the jungle canopy that *the soldiers' feet were dangling out the doors,* in obvious attack position.

Realizing a raid was imminent, the terrorists scattered, at first leaving the hostages alone—bound by ropes, unable to move. About ten minutes later, they reappeared and threw the captives to the ground on their knees. According to the survivors, El Paisa himself then ran through the camp, screaming his orders:

"Don't leave a single one of them alive!" he yelled. "Not a single one!"

Gunfire echoed through the camp and, one by one, the captives dropped lifelessly to the jungle floor.

Those who survived did so by pretending to be dead—by remaining perfectly still, even though they had been shot in the head or legs, until the terrorists fled the camp and our own troops finally arrived.

We stood there respectfully, listening to their accounts. The magnitude and intent of these murders—how these men had been killed in pure cold blood—were fully dawning on us now for the first time. One of my aides then asked the question that was at the front of all of our minds: How could the FARC have abducted, and so heartlessly killed, two men who had done nothing but advocate for reconciliation and peace?

The soldiers told us that, especially toward the end, they had raised this question repeatedly with their captors. Echeverri had been showing signs of illness, they said, and the idea of releasing him had gained some currency among the FARC's rank and file. They insisted, and finally they won an audience with El Paisa himself.

"How can you treat us like this," Echeverri asked, "when we are friends of peace and dialogue with you?"

El Paisa's response encapsulated four decades of Colombian suffering:

"You are not our friends," he retorted. "You are our class enemies. You are our useful idiots."

"Where's the foreman?" my father kept asking, disconsolate. Nobody quite understood why. "Could somebody please tell me where's the foreman?"

Hours earlier, he had departed Medellín, accompanied by my brother Santiago, and my youngest sister, María Isabel. One of my father's best friends disembarked from the helicopter at the very last minute, apologizing profusely, saying he had other commitments. My father shrugged it off: "Next time," he offered jovially. The aircraft, flown as always by the trusted family pilot, Captain Bernardo Rivera, lifted off and banked deep into the lush Antioquian mountains, a hundred different shades of green. After performing a quick sweep of the area, the helicopter touched down at Guacharacas around four in the afternoon, just as the tropical sun was beginning its rapid descent behind the mountains.

As the rotor blades slowed, a crowd of about twenty ranch workers, clearly surprised by the family's arrival, gathered around the copter to welcome them. In the near distance were the stables, the corrals, and a bridge over the River Nus. My father smiled weakly, scanned the crowd, and frowned. Without a word, he walked over to the house, but failed to find what he was looking for. He slumped down on the ground, running his hands through his hair, as Alberto Uribe Sierra was known to do during the moments— exceedingly rare—when he was truly worried.

Captain Rivera finished powering down the helicopter.

"I'm sure the foreman is out with the horses," Santiago offered, disturbed to see my father in such a state. "I'm sure he'll be back soon."

My father sat there, saying nothing, grasping his head.

For one final moment, there was a kind of peace: a glimpse, too fleeting, of what a normal life in the Colombian countryside could—should—have been. The sun was out of view now, and the ranch hands began to return to their evening chores. The horses clattered through the stable, finished for the day. The river churned quietly nearby.

Then, out of the trees, the armed men appeared.

My father jumped to his feet with the agility of a man half his age, pulled the Walther from his belt, and began firing furiously in their direction.

"Don Alberto, no!" Captain Rivera shouted. "There are too many of them! They'll kill you!"

"Así será," my father yelled back as he sought refuge in the kitchen. "So be it! See that everyone else escapes!"

The response from the outlaws came fast: a hail of bullets screaming through the air. Shrapnel pierced the door and the walls; everyone scattered, screaming in utter terror. María Isabel fled into the house, seeking refuge in a bedroom upstairs. Captain Rivera hid in the barn. Santiago took shelter in a bathroom on the back side of the house. Upon realizing that my father was nowhere to be seen, Santiago bravely resolved to try to go find help.

Santiago darted out of the complex and swam across the river, headed in the direction of a nearby road. Then, hearing that the gunfire continued at fevered pitch, he thought better of himself—there was no time for a rescue, he now realized—and he doubled back to try to save our father.

"The police are coming!" Santiago yelled from the other side of the bridge. "The police are coming!"

At that instant, the torrent of merciless gunfire shifted toward my brother, who took off running in a zigzag toward the jungle, desperate to get away. To no avail. A sharp burning sensation exploded in his back, sending him tumbling to the ground—a bullet had punctured his lung.

Santiago lay on the ground, panting, unable to move. After a short while he looked up and saw a tall man, dressed in camouflage fatigues and carrying an assault rifle, standing over him, frowning.

"Why were you screaming and running, eh?"

"Out of fear," Santiago replied, gasping for breath.

"Who are you?" the man asked.

My brother paused, gathering his thoughts. "I'm a trader from the fair," he replied, "and I came to see some cattle."

The man eyed him suspiciously, stroking his rifle.

Just then another, shorter man walked over.

"What's up?" the short one asked.

A long silence.

"Let's go," the taller one finally said. "Nothing happened here, eh?"

Santiago waited, facedown, bleeding, for what seemed like an eternity. Moments after the gunfire stopped, he heard the explosion. The outlaws had blown up the helicopter. Craning his head across the river, he saw nothing— no sign of the men, no sign of our father or sister. Supposing the worst, he decided the only possible path to survival was to seek help. Somehow, despite his wounds, he managed to struggle to his feet and stagger to a nearby road. There he eventually flagged down a cattle truck to plead for help, to beg for someone to please, please come save his family.

11

I was in Medellín, leaving for a meeting of the Instituto de Estudios Liberales, when a phone call came to my office from a hospital in the town of Yolombó. The doctor said that my brother Santiago had been admitted as a patient, that he was seriously hurt and might not live, and that I needed to come to Yolombó with great urgency.

We called the Red Cross to see if they could arrange for a helicopter to bring Santiago back to Medellín, where the medical care might be better. But it was too late in the day, the weather was awful, and the helicopter couldn't land there. Confused, but never imagining what had actually happened, I set out myself by car. It is a journey that takes maybe two hours by paved road in today's Colombia—back then it was over a miserable little stretch of dirt track, and I bounced along for half the night in morbid silence, listening to the local radio station for any news of my brother.

Suddenly:

"In a massacre today near Puerto Berrío, Don Alberto Uribe Sierra was killed. . . ."

My eyes welled with tears. I shook the steering wheel in despair. And in that instant, I became a member of the community—half of all Colombians—who have lost a loved one to violence.

12

On the afternoon of June 14, 1983, my father was murdered during an attempted kidnap attempt by the FARC. He was shot twice—once in the throat, and once in the chest, the latter the blow that killed him. He was just fifty years old. Based on accounts from our neighbors, and from the staff at Guacharacas, the crime was committed by roughly a dozen men from the so-called 36th Front of the FARC. Until midnight that night, we believed that the *sicarios* had kidnapped my sister; to our relief, we discovered that a teacher had protected her, at great personal risk, for several hours because of the immense loyalty she felt toward my father. My brother was in critical condition in the hospital for several days afterward; it was a miracle that he survived. The criminals who carried out the assault were never caught.

The tragedy was felt by countless people around Colombia who had been touched by my father's laughter and generosity: His funeral was attended by ten thousand people. In my family, the consequences of the murder have reverberated through time in heartrending, unpredictable ways. My brother Jaime, whom people often described as the only Uribe child who fully inherited my dad's sense of humor and *joie de vivre*, may have taken his death the hardest. He was never quite the same afterward, and when he died of throat cancer in 2001, some family members whispered that the stress from the tragedy had somehow been responsible. My half brother, Camilo, who was only ten months old at the time, grew up without a father. At my dad's funeral, Lina told me she felt ill; a few days later our second son was born, three months premature—he was given little chance of survival.

The final tragedy at Guacharacas itself would not come for another thirteen years—on February 25, 1996, when I was governor of Antioquia, militants from the National Liberation Army, the ELN, invaded the farm and burned down the house. A few days later, one worker who had grown up on the farm, and adored my father immensely, asked us whether he could stay on the property to take care of what little was left. We agreed. The ELN shot him dead on May 31 of that same year.

I loved my father; I miss him every day. The tragedy at Guacharacas

marked a turning point for me—it has influenced my personal and professional lives to an enormous, perhaps immeasurable extent. But not in the
ways that some people believe.

Over the years, I have occasionally been portrayed as a kind of South
American Bruce Wayne, a child of privilege who set out to avenge the murder
of his father at the hands of criminals. According to this narrative, I entered
politics, and then became president, with the primary purpose of exacting
revenge on the FARC and on other leftist groups. This school of thought
holds that I was willing to cut deals with the devil, and tolerate all manner
of abuses, in order to accomplish my "mission" at any cost.

This narrative is false. Yet I must admit that it is not entirely irrational,
given my country's past. Indeed, many of the saddest chapters of Colombian history have been written with the blood of those seeking revenge. From
the civil wars of the nineteenth century, to *La Violencia* of the 1950s, to the
cocaine-fueled score settling of the modern day, the foot soldiers of our militias and vigilante armies have swelled with the ranks of people who undertook arms to avenge a father who was murdered, a sister who was raped, a
cousin whose land was stolen. Having experienced great tragedy, I have also
experienced the intense emotions that come with it: anger among them. I
suppose everyone who endures such a loss has a decision to make. But I do
believe that, when faced with such a choice, the vast majority of people take
the same path that I did.

In the days after my father's death, I was overcome with immense pain.
We gathered, as a family, and we cried together. We expressed our dismay
that we lived in a country where such awful things could happen. Yet we
knew that we were not alone. Many other friends and acquaintances had also
lost loved ones to kidnappings and shootings: During that same period, the
FARC killed the father of my friend Claudia Blum, a distinguished public
servant from a well-known family in Cali, who served as a senator and whom
I would appoint many years later as Colombia's ambassador to the United
Nations, as well as Jaime Ortíz, a rancher in Urabá. I remember telling my
brothers and sisters: "Look, this pain that we're feeling right now—half the
people in our country are feeling it. What we have here is a personal tragedy, but it's a national problem. We're eventually going to have to face it in
some way."

It was natural for us to see our own tragedy in context—this was how we were raised. I came from a family with a strong civic identity, and some participation in politics. The goal for all of us, always, was not personal advancement or to address our own grievances—but to do anything that would uplift the well-being and prosperity of our fellow citizens. We were taught to put our own feelings aside.

By the time of my father's death in 1983 I was just thirty years old, but had already begun rising in public office myself, holding several positions, including mayor of Medellín. So, once the immediate pain of the murder had passed, the first thing I did was to accept an appointment from President Belisario Betancur to serve on a peace commission in Antioquia. We toured the state, holding forums in several communities, calling for an end to the violence, and holding public conversations with representatives of the armed groups, including the FARC. Was it emotionally difficult to share a room with people from the same organization that killed my father, at a moment when his grave was still fresh in the ground? Yes, it was. But I knew with all my heart that it was necessary.

In the years that followed, as I rose in politics, I tried to discuss my family's tragedy as little as possible. I feared that doing so might create a sensation of martyrdom, or give people the false impression that the tragedy was the core reason for my career. As councilman, governor, and then as president, I only rarely mentioned my father in speeches or in meetings. For example, U.S. President George W. Bush said in an interview after his presidency that, in our multiple meetings over the years, he didn't remember me ever raising the topic. It was sufficient for me to tell President Bush, and others, that I was a member of the community of Colombians who had suffered great loss.

I have met countless other members of this community: wives of fallen soldiers, parents of murdered kidnap victims, the children of senators and ministers who have given their lives to the cause. When I became president, in my original cabinet at least four of the thirteen ministers' families had suffered a kidnapping or a murder at the hands of the violent groups. My vice president, Francisco Santos Calderón, had been kidnapped and held hostage for several months in the 1990s. These travails had nothing to do with why I selected them; the composition of my cabinet was merely representative of the Colombian experience.

In decades of conversations with people from this community, I have found that all of us passed through the same whirlwind of emotion: anger, guilt, recrimination, great sadness . . . but, over time, almost without exception, we were united by one desire alone: to make the killing stop, so that there may be peace.

Revenge solves nothing. Violence in Colombia cannot be interpreted in moral terms, as a confrontation between good and evil. No, the violence is rooted in complex socio-political factors: Poverty, a lack of education, bankrupt ideologies, social inequality, the government's shortcomings, the scourge of narcotics, and numerous other problems have lead to the fact that in two centuries of life, Colombia has only experienced forty seven years of peace. Obviously, none of these things justify the violence, but they do form the backdrop to this long, unbroken chain of tragedies that have touched the lives of so many Colombians. We cannot lash out angrily at this violence and expect it to go away. We must study what causes each and every one of these problems and work hard to create a consensus around a solution—then we must have the strength and wisdom to act.

In truth, my commitment to security-related issues began well before my father's death; as the mayor of Medellín, I had started a program called Metroseguridad, which implemented and collected a special tax to fund our security forces. Over time, my pain evolved. At first it coalesced into an all-encompassing drive to solve these problems, to ensure that future generations of Colombians would not have to experience the heartbreak that mine has. I have given my life over to this cause, to the exclusion of almost everything else. This has come at a cost. I have placed my loved ones—and myself—in constant danger. I have lost many friends and allies. I have not been able to pursue the kind of varied interests that I might have in another lifetime under other circumstances—I do not know how to dance or sing. I am not a good teller of jokes. The last Hollywood movie I saw in a theater was *The Lone Ranger*—back when I was just a kid. I have missed countless birthdays, parties, the milestones of life. But these sacrifices have been necessary so that I could fulfill my vision for Colombia—so that I could honor my father, and so many other fallen compatriots, by ensuring that their deaths were not in vain.

In ensuing years, as I grew as a person and as a leader, my grief continued to transform into something else. I felt it when I visited the front lines and I spoke with our soldiers. I felt it when I visited small towns on our mountains and coasts, and heard stories of how lives had improved, and how families had been able to stay together, because of our government's policies. I felt it when I talked with the thousands of people whom we helped to desert the armed groups and start new lives of peace and responsibility. This sentiment illuminated my heart and guided my actions in countless moments of tragedy and darkness, such as the massacre at Urrao. It was the core truth from which my emotions, beliefs, and decisions flowed. For me, the final stage of all this grief was not hatred, but love: love for my country; love for my countrymen; and love, above all, for a future Colombia where fathers would not be torn away from their daughters and sons.

13

"It's an extraordinarily sad moment for the nation," I began. "Today, the FARC terrorist group committed another enormous massacre, another genocide." And then I read the name and rank, or title, of all who had been killed: Governor Guillermo Gaviria Correa; former defense minister Gilberto Echeverri Mejía; Lieutenant Alejandro Ledesma Ortiz; Lieutenant Wágner Tapias; First Sergeant Héctor Duván Segura; First Corporal Francisco Negrete Mendoza; First Corporal Jairsinio Navarrete; First Corporal Mario Alberto Marín Franco; Second Corporal Jean Peña Guarnizo; and First Corporal Samuel Ernesto Cote, who died en route to the hospital in Medellín.

I talked at length about how we obtained the intelligence for the operation. I described the jungle that I had seen, and how difficult the terrain was. I explained in detail how the operation had been planned and executed—how no shots had been fired, how the soldiers had been equipped with loudspeakers so they could tell the FARC to give themselves up, to hand over the kidnapped, that their lives would be spared, and that there was no need to shoot. I explained why we had decided to address the nation so quickly with the results of our investigation. I said the need for transparency had triumphed over all concerns, political and otherwise.

The camera shifted to General Carlos Ospina, our army commander. He expressed his regrets to the families, and confirmed the army's commitment to pressing ahead with the fight.

We then played videotapes of interviews we had conducted with two of the survivors. The tapes were rough, totally uncut, because there had been no time to edit them, and also because we wanted to show the footage in its natural state, to eliminate any doubts that the footage had somehow been staged or manipulated.

The first interview was conducted by an independent journalist from a local station, Telemedellín. The soldier, Agenor Enrique Vieyar Hernández, told of how the guerrillas had given the order to kill; how he had been next to Gilberto Echeverri at the moment when three shots were fired; how

Echeverri's body had fallen on top of his, making the guerrillas think both of them were dead, a stroke of fate—or an act of God—that had saved his life.

The other "interviewer," by necessity, was me; another surviving soldier, Sergeant Humberto Aranguren González, was being rushed into surgery and so, at his consent, we had time only to make a quick video of my abbreviated conversation with him.

The sight of him wounded by the assault and ravaged by years of jungle captivity saddened me greatly. But I tried to keep our conversation optimistic and crisp.

I smiled and asked: "How are you, *mi sargento?*"

"I'm fine, *mi presidente.*"

"How long had you been there?"

"Four years," he replied. And then he related the story again of how the guerrillas had given the execution order, and how our troops had not fired a shot.

"And your family?" I asked. "Where are they from? Have you talked to them yet?"

At that moment, I could tell the young man was fading fast. As he struggled to form an answer, I decided to cut the conversation off.

"We're going to leave you now, because they're going to perform a little surgery on you here," I said softly. "May it go well, and we ask God that you recover quickly, and we're going to rid the country of this plague, these bandits."

This seemed to rouse him, and the sergeant opened his mouth to speak once more. "Thank God we got out alive," he said, his voice trembling, "so we could tell this story and tell the country what kind of people these are."

"Is there any message that you'd like to give your *compañeros?*" I asked.

"Yes," he replied. "That we should march onward, that we're going to win this war. We will win this war."

There was not much more I could say. Speaking from the heart, and without notes, I concluded the address by explaining to the country again that our offer of peace talks with the FARC and all other illegal armed groups remained on the table, but that first those groups would need to cease all armed action and release all their hostages. In the absence of such a deal, I spoke of the need to defeat the "professional killers"—the armed groups' ringleaders, men such as Pedro Antonio Marín Marín, alias Manuel Marulanda, and Victor Julio Suárez Rojas, alias Mono Jojoy. I spoke of the need to defeat not only terrorism, in all its forms, but corruption as well. I said we had to defend our democracy. And I appealed, not for the first time, to the rank and file of the terrorist groups, urging them to desert their organizations, and assuring them they would be received with "generosity . . . for all those who were on the wrong path, but make the decision to come home and live with us."

I finished my address by saying:

"*Compatriotas*, in the midst of this pain, I want to ask you that we not falter in the task of defeating the terrorists. We're going to reincorporate those who made it out unharmed. And heal those who are injured. And ask those who have been murdered that, from heaven, they may help us to complete this mission.

"Colombia cannot give up. Now is the moment in which we have to strengthen our willpower to defeat terrorism. Let us defeat terrorism. This terrorism that, every day, steals investment from us. This terrorism that, every day, condemns poor people to be more poor, and Colombia to be more backward. I know that we can defeat it.

"A wise man once said that the greatest trait is courage. Because it is from courage that all other traits are derived. In this hour of pain, in this hour when everything is tearing us apart, my compatriots: courage.

"My sincere condolences to the families of those who have died. Our government planned this operation with all due responsibility and all due prudence. General Mora reported to the minister of defense, and she reported to me.

"I cannot elude responsibility," I concluded. "I assume it."

14

In the days after the massacre near Urrao, Colombia mourned. Naturally there was some soul-searching, a kind of national conversation about the path we should take. Some asked whether we should take another, less confrontational approach; others, on the opposite extreme, called for revenge in the form of an even more intensive military campaign against the FARC and other armed groups.

Some of the most vocal opinions came from the families of the hostages who remained in captivity. "Looking at these tragic results, we are going to insist that the government abstain from doing any military operations to rescue Ingrid," Ingrid Betancourt's husband told the media. A spokesman for another group of hostages said, "Instead of rescuing the kidnapped politicians, the only thing those missions do is seal their graves." Some other critics condemned both the FARC and my government equally, accusing both parties of a "warmongering" attitude that had made Colombia's violence even worse.

I listened to and respected these opinions. But there would be no turning back. Colombia had already been down the path of appeasement on numerous occasions throughout our history—it *never* worked. The majority of the nation seemed to realize this. In the days following the tragedy, we saw that Colombians favored pressing ahead with our offensive. Public opinion polls put the FARC's popular support at around 2 percent—statistically insignificant. Those same polls showed that support for the government increased to about 70 percent. Though we took no personal satisfaction in this, we were heartened to see evidence that Colombians' faith had not been shaken in their institutions, or the direction we had chosen.

Condemnation of the FARC poured in from around the world, including a telegram from Pope John Paul II, who expressed his "deep sorrow" over the killings and "yet again, vigorous reprehension for terrorist attacks which threaten peaceful coexistence and offend the deepest sentiments of human beings." One of the most interesting, and relevant, reactions came from Ingrid Betancourt herself. When she heard the news on the radio from her jungle camp, she demanded that her FARC captors allow her to record a message. She wanted to express her ardent wish that the Colombian military not rule out future military rescues just because of the failure at Urrao. "I understood that I could speak only for myself," she later wrote in her memoir. "But I wanted to stress the fact that freedom was a right and any effort to recover that freedom was a duty. . . . The president of the republic himself must bear total responsibility."

Indeed, I was determined to absorb every possible lesson from our failure. Clearly the operation at Urrao pointed to shortcomings in our military's operational ability and our intelligence gathering that we needed to address as soon as possible. I made this a personal priority in the following years.

In the meantime, we began to heal. All of Colombia now knew that our government, and our nation as a whole, would not yield in the face of intimidation or tragedy. If the FARC or the other violent ones tried to strike at us, we would only grow stronger. Our military leaders, in particular, now knew that their president, and their nation, would stand firmly behind them, even in the darkest hours. My generals later said that the confidence and solidarity they felt on that tragic day in 2003 were fundamental in a great many of the victories that would come later.

Even though they had left us, the example of the perished hostages continued to inspire people in Colombia and around the world. Guillermo Gaviria Correa was posthumously nominated for the Nobel Peace Prize by a group of peace advocates in the United States. A book of the letters he wrote to his wife while in captivity was published in Spanish and in English. In coming years, we would endeavor to honor the memory of him, and the others who had fallen, in the best way we knew how.

15

For five long years after the massacre in the jungle near Urrao, we hunted tirelessly for Aicardo de Jesús Agudelo Rodríguez, a.k.a. "El Paisa."

On several occasions, we came very close. We would narrow down his location, and then El Paisa, clever bandit that he was, would escape at the last minute. This was demoralizing to the hundreds of intelligence and military operatives who were tracking him. But we would not be denied justice—not with this case. To quote a popular saying that was a favorite of my mother's, *"La constancia vence lo que la dicha no alcanza:"* "Perseverance conquers what desire does not achieve."

And so we persevered. Ultimately, it was El Paisa's love of prostitutes that proved to be his undoing. Our intelligence services homed in on this weakness after interviewing several former FARC operatives who demobilized in the years following the Urrao massacre, accepting our offer of reinsertion into society in return for their full cooperation with security forces. Based on this information, we were able to put together a full psychological portrait: including El Paisa's daily routine, his weaknesses, his sicknesses, his collaborators, and the prostitutes he brought to his camp at the end of every month from Medellín.

In March 2008, the intelligence agency of Colombia's National Police, the DIPOL, was able to successfully infiltrate an agent in the commercial network that supplied goods—and the girls—to El Paisa's secret camp on the Río Murrí. Over time, this agent was able to gain the confidence of the criminal's favorite prostitute. Soon she told him every detail of the camp where El Paisa lived. The DIPOL was then able to map out the coordinates of the base camp and surrounding areas using cutting-edge GPS-based technology that had not been available to us in 2003.

By August, the DIPOL agent convinced the prostitute to escort him to her usual rendezvous point with El Paisa: a house that was separate from the rest of the camp. On several consecutive visits, our agent hid in the woods behind the house, sometimes just a hundred yards away, casing out the area, waiting for the young woman to leave. She usually did so in the early morning.

On September 21, 2008, El Paisa returned to the house for another rendezvous. That night the DIPOL, acting in concert with our Special Operations Command and the Colombian Air Force, decided to act. Shortly after the prostitute left the house, a precision bomb crashed down upon the site. El Paisa would cause no more suffering for Colombia.

I had a policy in my government: When the news was bad, I went on television and announced it to the nation myself. When the news was good, I generally asked my ministers, generals, and other collaborators to speak instead. That day my defense minister, Juan Manuel Santos, informed a relieved Colombia of El Paisa's demise.

The death of El Paisa in 2008 capped a year of successive, backbreaking disasters for the FARC and all the other outlaws in Colombia. It was a year that saw more than a million Colombians take to the streets in a march demanding an end to the FARC's activities. It was a year that would see several of the FARC's senior leaders brought to justice. It was a year that would see a successful military operation resulting in the rescue of several hostages who had been held in the jungle for years—without shedding a single drop of blood.

By the time our government drew to a close, we had reduced kidnappings in Colombia from more than three thousand a year to just 282—still too many, but a 90 percent decrease. Colombia's murder rate fell by half. Killings of innocent civilians, including labor union leaders and journalists, dropped even more sharply. On the economic front, as investors rushed back to a safer Colombia, we doubled our average rate of GDP expansion and reached growth rates of nearly 7 percent. Foreign investment more than doubled, and our exports tripled. We negotiated new trade deals with the United States, Central America, Canada, the European Union, Mercosur, and other places. Tourism soared as our marvelous country finally began attracting the positive attention it has always deserved. We even started a new advertising campaign for international visitors: "Colombia: The Only Risk Is Wanting to Stay."

The story of how all this was possible has many twists and turns. It involves the sacrifices of many good people.

It begins in a bullring.

SECTION TWO

Courage

"Courage is rightly esteemed the first of human qualities . . .
because it is the quality which guarantees all others."

—WINSTON CHURCHILL

1

"Álvaro!"

I looked up into the crowd and saw my father.

"Be firm, Álvaro!"

I was kneeling in the sand, waiting for the bull to charge out of the gate. This was a bit of *tremendismo* and showmanship, designed to impress the crowd. The move is known as the *farol de rodillas,* literally the "kneeling street-lamp": The matador drops to his knees in front of the bull and, as the beast's horns pass tantalizingly near his neck and face, the matador waves the cape over and around the bull's head. It is considered a particularly beautiful—and hazardous—maneuver in bullfighting.

The gate swung open, and the bull came storming out. But instead of coming toward me right away, it veered away toward the side of the ring. And then the beast spun back around, faced me, stomped impetuously, and prepared to charge.

"Stay down on your knees, Álvaro!" my father yelled above the roar of the crowd. "Stay down!"

In the years since, my mind has occasionally drifted back to that day, back to that moment between father and son, and what it all may have meant. Perhaps it was simply bravado. Perhaps it was a case of paternal one-upmanship run amok. But I have always suspected that there was something much larger, much more important at work.

My father was always trying to teach me—always trying to prepare me for the life that he knew awaited me. He knew, like many others from his generation, that danger was a part of everyday life in Colombia—a constant, an element to be reckoned with, like rain, heat, or hunger. He believed that you could account for it. You could make adjustments, if necessary. You could even retreat, to come back and fight another day. But you could never, ever let the danger intimidate you.

This was an easy thing to say, a much harder thing to live. After all, managing one's emotions in such situations is not easy. Perhaps it is not even natural. There may be some people on this earth who are born with an ability to ignore or suppress their feelings, to look death in the eyes and feel nothing. But my experience certainly suggests otherwise. During my childhood, when our neighbors in Antioquia were assaulted or chased from their homes, I had to summon every last ounce of courage in my bones to stay resilient. The same was true later in life, when the terrorists detonated a bomb that destroyed my room, leaving me shell-shocked and momentarily unable to move; or when my friends and colleagues were ambushed, and I had to use a gun to help them escape. Learning how to control my emotions, and channel them for a constructive purpose, took a lifetime of experience for me.

Many of the episodes that follow I have never discussed in public before; some not even my family is fully aware of. I was loath to dramatize or glorify them; some are too painful to retell more than once. I share them here because they may help explain who I am, and why I governed Colombia the way I did. Perhaps they may also illuminate an imperfect path for those who face similar challenges.

On that day in the bullring, I suspect my father was showing me one way to face a threat: by mocking it, by taunting it, by looking it straight in the eye—and winking, even if your heart was pounding inside. So I dropped down on my knees in front of that bull, and I stayed there, resolute, as it charged. Because, as my father had told me beforehand, there are only two proper ways to leave the bullring: in a coffin, or on the shoulders of the people. In this kind of life, there is no in-between.

2

For as long as I can remember, there has been a paradox at the heart of Colombian life. On the one hand, our country suffers from its well-known maladies and afflictions. On the other, it is a country that is also capable of stunning, almost inconceivable goodness—a place where the laughter seems heartier, the food tastes better, and the sun shines brighter than anywhere else. The overwhelming majority of our lives take place in the latter place. Learning how to reconcile the two worlds was, for most of our history, the very essence of being Colombian.

For me, the most indelible incarnation of the marvelous Colombia has always been the idyll of my parents' farm in Antioquia, the place where I spent my earliest years. I'd rise early every morning, to help with the daily chores. I'd shake off the cold, devour some arepas and coffee or hot chocolate for breakfast, and then sprint to the barn. We would milk the cows and saddle the horses. We'd ride horses, fish and swim in rivers, and recreate in the lush green splendor of rural Antioquia.

Some mornings we would even assist with the collection and processing of the coffee—not easy work, especially for a child. My father was *much* tougher on us than he was on the hands who lived with us on the ranch. Our work, especially, had to be done right and on time, always.

"What ails that mare?" my father would ask.

"Her knee."

"Have you put a medicinal cream on her yet?"

"Yes, sir."

"Have you done it today?"

Finally, an hour later at most, my father would always circle back and check to ensure that the job had been done.

This kind of constant *acompañamiento,* this zeal for observing tasks and then following up to ensure results, was imperative to successfully running a farm of such complexity and size. Over the years, as my father built up his landholdings, we sometimes had several hundred workers at a time, with operations ranging from sugarcane harvesting to coffee to cattle. You could not possibly manage such an operation without constantly overseeing every little detail, and also performing a great deal of the work yourself. To succeed, you had to know everyone else's job even better than they did. You had to teach by setting a good example, and by being a good and industrious member of the team. Twenty-four hours a day, seven days a week, you had to be on guard and ready to act: A filly could be born; a cow could wander off the property. One mistake in one corner of the farm and the crops could spoil; an animal could be left permanently lame; you could very easily lose everything.

Not everyone is cut out for this kind of work. I *loved* it. It was paradise to me. And not just because it permitted me to work alongside my family: I had great zeal for the enterprise itself, the sense of accomplishment, working with people from all different kinds of backgrounds, and being able to see the fruits of my labor (sometimes literally) at the end of the day. Managing a large and complex system such as this, and doing it well, made my head hum with the purest sort of pleasure. It was absolutely instrumental in forming who I am.

Our farm was on a piece of rolling land about a hundred kilometers southwest of Medellín—near the small town of Salgar, but far enough away to seem like a self-contained universe of its own. It was an isolated corner of an isolated state within an isolated country, especially in the 1950s, with a rural lifestyle that had probably changed very little during the previous century. Once my siblings and I had finished our chores and the sun was fully up, we would ride our horses to our one-room school, the Escuela Rural Integrada de la Liboriana, three times a week, since the boys and girls alternated days. My first schoolteacher, Lilian Alvarez, was barely a teenager when I began kindergarten. According to María Izquierdo's biography of me, I would often accompany Señora Lilian on horseback to Salgar to collect her salary. I was proud when, some four decades later, she helped me with my first presidential campaign.

Lest I begin to sound like I was some kind of perfect country gentleman from the very moment I left the crib—I most certainly was not. I was, then as now, prone to regrettable explosions of temper. I yelled; I sometimes became unreasonable and had to be talked down by cooler heads. My parents attempted to channel my energy in a constructive fashion by making me swim fifteen hundred meters' worth of laps in our pool every day after school.

During the ensuing decades, I would also try yoga nidra, bicycling, and homeopathic drops, among other techniques, with decidedly mixed results.

There was also some fretting within the family about my size. While my appetite for physical labor was unmatched, I wasn't as big or as strong as some of my friends and relatives. "That boy will never grow," one of my aunts once said, according to María Izquierdo's book, "because he doesn't eat healthy things like *sopa de frijoles,* bean soup. He only likes sweets." I suppose she was right—to this day, my height often surprises people when they meet me. And, even as president, I always kept a secret stash of chocolates in my desk drawer.

It was around that time, also, that I became a passionate reader. And for this I could primarily thank my mother, Laura Vélez. She had graduated first in the class of 1950 at Madres de la Presentación High School. She chose not to go to university, opting instead to marry my father and begin having and rearing children; she and my father were both just twenty years old when I was born. This decision, typical of the era, could have stunted her intellectual growth—but Laura Vélez would not be so easily deterred. She found other ways to continue her education.

Over the years, my mother acquired an exceptionally deep and varied library of books of history, philosophy, and literature that reflected her modern, egalitarian worldview. She was deeply steeped in the philosophy that all people, no matter their class, race, or gender, had the right to choose their destiny—and, therefore, that democracy was the only virtuous form of government. She was willing to fight for her views: Laura Vélez actively campaigned in a national plebiscite in 1957 that, among other reforms, gave women equal political rights, including the right to vote. I was only five years old, but I remember hanging from her arm as she toured the town, convincing people of the need to vote "yes"—a struggle in which her side ultimately prevailed. "It's about time," she grumbled. And she was right—in Latin America, only Paraguay waited longer than Colombia to pass women's suffrage. With that battle won, my mother became part of the very first group of Colombian women to hold elected office: She was elected to the municipal council in Salgar as a member of the Liberal Party, and eventually became the council's president. Her oldest sister, Cecilia Vélez, was elected as a legislator from the Conservative Party.

This democratic spirit was passed down to the next generation like religion. We were taught by our family to treat all people the same. Few offenses were punished as harshly in our house as snobbery or elitism. By contrast, intellectual curiosity was rewarded as the highest of virtues; my paternal grandmother, whom we called Yeya, always encouraged me to ask people whatever I wanted, and she gently chided those who betrayed fatigue with my constant barrage of questions.

As the years passed, it was my mother who first identified—and nurtured— the flicker of ambition within her eldest son—and she watched over me like a general, pushing me to improve myself constantly and to read the works of great leaders: Rafael Uribe Uribe, Simón Bolívar, Abraham Lincoln, Winston Churchill, Alfonso López Pumarejo, and Alberto Lleras Camargo, among others. I spent long hours walking around the house, reciting their speeches by heart. Some people believe I have a naturally photographic memory; I don't, but I trained myself from a young age to memorize long speeches, as well as the works of poetry that my mother cherished above all.

Books were extraordinarily important back then, because, especially in rural Colombia, they were one of our precious few windows to the outside world. Another was the oversize Phillips radio that sat in the middle of our living room. The Colombian countryside was so isolated during those years that I remember my mother once climbed a tree outside our house to hang the antenna from the highest point possible, in a vain attempt to improve the quality of the signal.

Despite her best efforts, we could only pick up two stations: Voice of America, and Fidel Castro's Radio Havana. I wasn't yet fully aware of the competing visions that those two radio stations symbolized, and the trouble they would soon bring to Colombia—or the fact that, decades later, Fidel and I would develop a largely secret and somewhat surprising rapport.

3

The news traveled by word-of-mouth and was increasingly terrifying—houses set on fire, belongings stolen in roadside assaults, land confiscated by roving guerrilla armies. No one was immune: My maternal grandfather, Martín Vélez, was forced out of his home, along with several of his brothers. While I wish I could say that there was an innocent period during which I was oblivious to these events, there is a valuable lesson here: Children perceive everything, especially when it comes to violence. The very first image I am capable of remembering from my youth is one of my mother staring at the front door, wary of the demons that lurked outside.

It's very difficult, and maybe impossible, to say exactly how the killing began. Throughout Colombia's history, each spasm of bloodshed always seemed to be a continuation of the previous one. *La Violencia*, the civil war that I lived through as a child, was in many ways a product of political tensions left over from the War of a Thousand Days, which killed a hundred thousand Colombians from 1899 to 1902. That war was itself an echo of the numerous civil wars that my country endured in the nineteenth century.

Indeed, this vicious cycle of conflict, which brought terrible consequences for our society and our economy, was one of Colombia's defining characteristics from the very moment of independence. A well-known American traveler named Frank Vincent once visited Colombia and wrote: "The whole genius of the nation seems directed toward civil dissension and guerrilla warfare. Hence, while the people complain of poverty, they offer so little guarantee and security to foreign life and capital as to be quite unable to secure the presence and help of either." Vincent wrote this in 1890. A century later, it would still ring true.

Colombia wasn't alone in its problems—at least, not at first. During the 1800s, following independence from Spain and Portugal, many other Latin American nations also struggled with anarchy and civil war. Yet, as the twentieth century progressed, most of our peers, including Argentina, Brazil, and Mexico, were able to get a grip on the problem and establish a degree of law and order. Not Colombia. Why? In our case, we were held back by the same two intimately linked problems that have been our undoing time and again during the past two hundred years: 1) our difficult geography, and 2) the historic inability, or unwillingness, of Colombian governments to project sufficient federal authority.

Our capital sits on a cool, fertile plateau seventy-six hundred feet above sea level, separated from most of the rest of the country by altitude, jungle, and sheer distance. Colombia is a large country—1.15 million square kilometers, twice the size of Texas, or roughly the size of France, Spain, and Portugal put together. Our population has also historically been one of Latin America's most dispersed—not concentrated in one big city, like many of our regional peers, but spread evenly throughout a great many villages and cities, including Bogotá, Medellín, Cali, Cartagena, and Barranquilla. Each of these cities was like an island to itself, ringed by mountains, bodies of water, and other obstacles—even today, on a modern highway, Bogotá to Medellín is sometimes an eight-hour drive. Back in Frank Vincent's era, leaving Bogotá to travel virtually anywhere else in Colombia involved an arduous three-day trip down the mountain by mule, where extreme heat, ravenous insects, violence, and disorder generally awaited. Faced with these obstacles, many Colombian governments simply didn't bother making the journey at all. Well into the twentieth century, the effective reach of federal power often extended only a few miles in each direction.

Making matters worse: Colombia's ruling classes harbored a profound distaste for centralized power. This tradition dated back to the days of the Spanish crown, when colonial viceroys paid little more than lip service to orders from faraway Madrid. Following independence, powerful landowners were happy with the status quo—they did everything within their power to ensure that this tradition continued, so that their own authority would remain unchallenged. Our early constitutions made Colombia one of the most federalized systems in the world, granting the central government control over little more than foreign relations. In later years, the government's responsibilities were broadened, but the state never developed the resources necessary to exercise power over such a massive and problematic territory. Even as *La Violencia* raged in the 1950s, the army did not have enough of a budget to afford uniforms for all of its troops, and had ammunition for only two days' worth of combat. The air force possessed just five working, combat-ready warplanes; their newest munitions dated back to 1932, and only half of them were in working order.

With little to no central government presence to speak of, armed militias and factions inevitably stepped in to fill the void of power. For most of our history, practically anyone with a gun and a lack of conscience could declare themselves to be the law in Colombia—and face no consequences from Bogotá. Sometimes these gangs were ragtag armies put together by confederations of wealthy landowners; sometimes they were roving militias composed of rural peasants who had been oppressed for their political beliefs. Whatever their makeup, many of these groups committed all kinds of criminal and economic abuses. They went to war with one another whenever their power was threatened—which was to say constantly.

During the late 1940s, as my parents were finishing secondary school, this cycle of killings was revving up yet again. The country was bitterly divided into the same two factions that had fought the War of a Thousand Days: *liberales* and *conservadores*. Ostensibly, these were political parties with distinct ideologies; some historians describe the liberals as favoring a stronger federal government, while the conservatives supported the principle of order. There was an element of cold war tension between the two groups, and some religious sectarianism as well. Yet in Bogotá and throughout the entire country, most people joined a party not because of ideology, but out of the basic desire to protect themselves from enemies, or to exact revenge for past misdeeds. Party affiliation became a birthright, a matter of creed; hatred was passed down from one generation to another. As with many such episodes, the violence was made worse by low levels of education and economic development— the real-life consequences of a derelict state.

The mayhem escalated after the 1948 killing of a *liberal* presidential candidate, Jorge Eliécer Gaitán, unleashed murderous mobs that torched ministries, shops, and newspapers in the capital—an event known as the "Bogotazo," the ramifications of which spread quickly to the rest of the country. The violence was worst in isolated areas, especially where there was good farmland and other resources to fight over—such as rural Antioquia, where I was born in 1952. An estimated twenty-six thousand residents were killed by the time the decade was over. "We are riding a wildly spinning wheel where today's victims become tomorrow's executioners," the Medellín newspaper *El Colombiano* wrote in an editorial published two months after my birth. "Each victim feeds on the idea of retaliation, so that there will be enough hatred in Colombia for the next 150 years."

My parents did their very best to protect us. But, of course, there was never any shelter from Colombia's violence—it found you whether you were looking for it or not. One afternoon, when I was about five or six years old, a band of more than three hundred *liberal* guerrillas showed up at our family farm demanding food and shelter. I remember them vividly—hordes of unwashed, harried-looking men wearing sombreros and leather chaps, laughing and cackling as they roved our ranch on their *criollo* Colombian horses. They were led by the notorious Captain Franco, a charismatic man who had entered politics shortly after Gaitán's assassination, spent some time in prison, and then founded an armed resistance unit. Their base of operations was just outside Urrao—the same troubled area where, half a century later, Governor Gaviria Correa and Minister Echeverri would meet their end at the hands of the FARC.

Captain Franco's men were in a relatively peaceful mood—the *Frente Nacional*, the political deal that would temporarily end this chapter of Colombian violence, was very near. But I remember watching as my mother, the committed democrat with a budding political career of her own, cooked meals for this gang of men. I remember watching as my father, such a proud and democratic man, talked with these outlaws with guns. And I remember yearning, at the purest, most primal level, to live in a Colombia where armed men would never invade our farm, where my family would all be safe, and where no one would ever have to lock herself inside her house, staring at the door in terror.

4

Many people were surprised when, in 2005, upon receiving an honorary degree from the University of Beijing, I delivered a detailed, heartfelt speech about the father of Communist China.

Of course, Mao's record of mass murder and economic management violated every principle I've ever stood for. Yet I spoke that day in Beijing primarily of Mao's ideological flexibility and his willingness to evolve over time, which clearly contrasted with the rigid Marxist doctrines of Lenin and Stalin. I referred to Mao the writer in order to highlight the clarity and pragmatism of his theses—regardless of what we may think of them—and how he distanced himself from the Leninist ideal that proclaims the virtual absence of the state as well as the Stalinist vision in which the all-powerful state exists thanks to the total negation of the individual. I reiterated my interpretation of the Mao's Chinese model, one that provided his successors with sufficient latitude to adapt to events in the world—for Deng Xiaoping to declare that "To get rich is glorious" and undertake procapitalist reforms, which transformed China into the economic giant that we know today.

I understand why this scene raised so many eyebrows—here, after all, was the supposed "hard-line," "arch-conservative" "Yankee bulldog" discussing Chairman Mao and receiving a strong ovation from a group of Communist students in the heart of Red China. Yet anyone who attended university in Colombia in the 1960s or 1970s might have appreciated the reality a bit better. Yes, I had studied Marx, Lenin, and Mao in assiduous detail during my undergraduate years. I also studied other luminaries of the international left, such as Marta Harnecker and Louis Althusser, and I read most of the works of Nicos Poulantzas. I read them carefully when I was a law student at the Universidad de Antioquia in Medellín. During that period, the radical, Marxist-Leninist left had a near-monopoly on reason at Colombia's public universities.

It was certainly fertile ground: Many of my fellow students believed that the university was the venue from which the inevitable Communist insurrection would spring forth. Many were greatly seduced by the newly formed armed leftist groups, including the FARC. The early 1970s was a time of

near-daily strikes and occupations, as students agitated for the coming revolution; the university seemed to be closed almost as many days as it was open
because of the strikes. Classrooms, when they operated at all, were sometimes
little more than a forum for speeches inciting violence and class hatred.
Almost the entire student body believed that the world was moving inexora-
bly toward Communism; the only debate allowed was over which model was
better: the Soviet or the Chinese, the collectivism of Ho Chi Minh or the
permanent revolution of Fidel Castro.

I had dramatically different ideas. I believed fervently in democracy and
the rule of law. I also believed in the right of my fellow students to get an
education free of disruptions or the threat of violence. I yearned to study the
"subversive" works of "revolutionaries" such as Plato and Aristotle. This was
the Colombian equivalent of walking around the Berkeley campus of the
University of California with a NIXON '72 campaign button: My views were
unpopular and unglamorous, not to mention somewhat dangerous. And, for
a while, it seemed like I might be on the wrong side of history.

Indeed, the transition from *La Violencia* to the rise of the armed left was
nearly instant in Colombia. There was no real interlude of peace. In fact, many
of the participants were even the same: Pedro Antonio Marín Marín, who
later became the supreme FARC commander known as Manuel Marulanda,
alias Tirofijo or "Sureshot," started his life in the armed struggle as a member
of a *liberal* militia in the Colombian countryside in the 1950s before later
coming under the influence of the Communist Party. The FARC itself sprang
from rural self-defense forces created during this same era. This was no ac-
cident. The Cuban Revolution of 1959 excited many people in the radical
international left, and led many of them to believe that Castro's example
could be exported around the region: They chose Bolivia and Colombia as
their two preferred theaters for revolution in South America.

Our country was "attractive" for three principal reasons: 1) It had preex-
isting militias that could be rapidly co-opted or otherwise assimilated to the
Marxist cause, as Marulanda's example proved; 2) we had one of the region's
most enduring traditions of democratic government, which the left believed
would allow them to operate without fear of repression; and 3) Colombia
suffered from a large gap between rich and poor. The notion of "class struggle" was tremendously fertile ground in our country, and it allowed the left

to gain sympathizers among labor unions, student groups, farmers' movements, and other groups.

Few people remain unmoved by the living conditions produced by economic inequality. From my earliest days on the farm in Antioquia, I was fully aware that most Colombians did not enjoy the initial advantages that my family did. I remember when I first started traveling to Córdoba state, on our Caribbean coast, we saw people living in conditions that were heartbreakingly basic: People slept in ditches and pools of mud, sometimes with just a piece of cardboard or corrugated metal pulled over their heads. I watched as entire neighborhoods of ramshackle houses began climbing the mountains outside Medellín and Bogotá.

What I saw during those years was part of a regional trend. By 1950, Latin America already had a more skewed level of inequality than any other part of the world, according to the World Bank. The problem became more accentuated with each passing decade through the 1990s. In the specific case of Colombia, income distribution became more unequal throughout the 1960s. In 1970, as I began university, about two-thirds of Colombians in rural areas were suffering from "absolute poverty," as defined by the inability to properly feed and clothe themselves. This was appalling.

Yet it was equally apparent to me that this legacy of economic backwardness was, in large part, a consequence of the merciless chaos and bloodshed throughout Colombia's history. *La Violencia* and other spasms of anarchy had made private and public investment impossible, and rendered the government unable to extend basic services such as education and infrastructure, which could have boosted living standards. Many of the poorest Colombians, including those I saw in the precarious dwellings outside Medellín and Bogotá, were subsistence farmers who had been forced off their lands during the troubles of the 1950s. Thus, I concluded that violence was a primary *reason* for poverty and inequality. How could violence be the solution?

There was another point that was equally crucial in my mind: Colombia was a democracy. In Cuba, the Castros had taken up arms against another military dictatorship (and then established one of their own). Armed movements in Argentina, Peru, Bolivia, and elsewhere in Latin America were often fighting against undemocratic regimes. This was not the case in our country, where, with the exception of a four-year period of military rule during *La Vi-*

olencia, Colombian democracy was uninterrupted throughout the twentieth century. I never forgot how, in my house growing up, my mother and father euphorically embraced the return of democratic elections in 1958 as a sign that the worst of the bloodshed was coming to an end.

This strong democratic tradition made Colombia something of an exception in Latin America. It also explained why I generally refused, then as now, to describe the FARC, ELN, and other groups as "insurgents" or "guerrillas"— which, in the Latin American context, suggests a virtuous struggle against a repressive military regime. That was not the case with Colombia—in our country, these groups were trying to destroy democracy.

It was true, as some argued, that Colombian democracy had flaws—the political agreement that ended *La Violencia* guaranteed a sixteen-year period in which liberals and conservatives would share power and alternate in the presidency. Some said this justified the emergence of the FARC and other leftist groups because it left no electoral outlet for socialist reform. Still, no political movements or parties were banned during that period. Even Colombia's Communist Party was able to make alliances with mainstream groups such as the Movimiento Revolucionario Liberal, a wing of the Liberal Party headed by Alfonso López Michelsen, who later became president. And ultimately, I could not understand why my fellow university students did not try to fight for reform within the existing system. They certainly could have acquired political influence had they sought it. After all, whether my fellow students admitted it or not, they were unquestionably part of the nation's elite—in the 1970s, only about 5 percent of Colombians of university age were enrolled in higher education. They should have sought change in democratic ways. Surely this would have been better than subjecting our country to further armed struggle.

I remember riding my bicycle to campus early one September morning and seeing my fellow students gathered around a radio. As I drew closer, I discovered why: Salvador Allende, the democratically elected socialist president of Chile, was speaking.

"Surely this will be the last opportunity for me to address you," Allende said. He then detailed the military conspiracy against him. "I will pay for the loyalty of the people with my life. . . . Long live Chile! Long live the workers!"

Horrified, we kept listening to the reports as Chilean air force jets strafed the La Moneda Palace. News quickly came that Allende was dead, and that forces led by General Augusto Pinochet had taken control of the Chilean government.

By this point, many of the students were sobbing uncontrollably—Allende had been a hero to leftists all around Latin America. I shared their grief, too—not because I supported Allende or his politics, but because I hated to see any disruption to democracy and the popular will at the hands of an armed minority.

"Ousting a democratic government by force is always a tragedy," I said softly, trying to console them. "Dictatorships never last."

Some of my classmates embraced me, tears streaming down their cheeks, welcoming my condolences. Yet out of the corner of my eye, I could see that some others were glaring at me, furious—a sign of the trouble soon to come.

5

If growing up in the heart of *La Violencia* had given me a different perspective from many of my classmates, then the experiences of my university years would take me even farther away from the beaten path. For it was in that period that I experienced one of my first tastes (so to speak) of entrepreneurial capitalism: a diner that we opened in Medellín called El Gran Banano—literally, "The Big Banana."

With my partners, Eduardo Navarro and José Roberto Arango, the latter of whom was later a trusted adviser during my presidency, we opened our first location on Seventieth Street in Medellín while I was still a student at the University of Antioquia. I would often attend to the clients myself. The signature dish was a frozen banana that we topped with chocolate and peanuts, hence the name of the establishment. We also sold excellent ice cream. We had a cream cheese business that was a huge success in its own right, because nothing of similar quality was available anywhere else in Medellín—we bought the cheese wholesale from the agriculture department at the Universidad Nacional. I would often close down the Gran Banano myself at one a.m., go home, and then wake up at four a.m. to go buy milk, *arepas,* and fresh plantains. I would leave the day's supplies at the restaurant—and be at class by the time it started at seven a.m.

The idea of my slathering cream cheese onto plantains or waiting tables after midnight is probably amusing to most Colombians today. Yet the work came naturally to me, and the diner was a very successful endeavor. It was also a small window into a larger truth that, at the time, was considered heresy among many in Colombia: Capitalism works. For seven years, we generated jobs, and the business turned a nice profit.

Later in the 1970s, I also witnessed firsthand how Marxist-Leninist agitation could spoil profitable, job-creating enterprises. With my father as my partner, we owned an operation in northeastern Antioquia that produced panela, a kind of solid brown sugar. The operation was a model of good working conditions: There were houses, a school, and other amenities for the workers. I labored there myself with great frequency. Yet by the late 1970s, productivity had cratered compared to my father's other panela operations, and we were losing money and the laborers there were making unreasonable wage demands, well out of proportion with anything else in the country. The problem was that the FARC was active in the area, and they had infiltrated the union.

Finally, in June 1979, exhausted by the constant trouble and the mounting financial damages, my father and I decided to simply give the operation to the workers. We instructed them to go to the Ministry of Labor and see how much we owed them in future pensions and wages; the amount was six million pesos, and the company was worth twenty million pesos. We signed it over, transparently and with all the proper documentation; essentially, it was a fourteen-million-peso gift. Despite our good intentions, that would not be the last we would hear of the matter.

I have never been one to hide my opinion. It's a character trait that has become more evident over the years. When I was still a student, I became convinced that students should be allowed to attend their classes without the constant interruption of strikes; I helped organize a solution that moved law school classes off-campus, so that those of us who wished to continue our education could do so in relative peace. I believed that the university needed to be a place where various points of view were tolerated, not just the Leninist dogma of the times. I believed in democracy, individual liberties, and the rule of law. And I was willing to stand up for these beliefs—in speeches, at rallies, and elsewhere.

At first, the other students reacted by whistling or trying to shout me down. When that didn't silence me, soon the little crumpled notes started coming, in the law school's cafeteria, at my home, and elsewhere:

You will die, traitor!

You've been judged.

The execution is near.

The situation became unsettling. But I had developed strong beliefs that, because of my growing body of life experience, I was willing to defend. So when the death threats began, I refused to yield. I've been living with them ever since.

6

One morning in Medellín, I saw a striking young woman leaving the university, accompanied by a friend. I followed her for a few blocks, dazzled, and decided to approach her and introduce myself. She was surprised and very reserved at first, but she eventually seemed to warm up just a bit, so I decided to be bold and ask her name.

"María Teresa," she replied.

"María Teresa, you have a beautiful name," I said. "Where do you live?"

"In Sonsón."

I became worried. Sonsón was a small village in Antioquia, more than five hours away. It might be impossible to see this beautiful woman again.

"How is it possible for you to attend classes in Medellín, living so far away?" I asked.

She hesitated for just a moment. "I travel here every day," she replied.

I wondered whether she might be trying to avoid me, but I would not be so easily deterred. I managed to get the name of María Teresa's father from one of her friends. I tracked his name down in the phone book, so that I might call her to continue our conversation. I was surprised to learn that María Teresa's father lived not in Sonsón, but right there in the city. I soon discovered that "María Teresa from Sonsón" was in fact Lina Moreno from Medellín, a philosophy student and daughter of a well-respected family with deep roots in the city. Eight months after our first chance meeting on the street, we were married.

The day after our wedding, we traveled to the cattle market in La Ceja. I plunged into the crowd, as usual, and I started making the rounds: shaking people's hands, asking about their families and businesses, calling everyone by their first name. Lina lingered toward the back, watching the scene with mounting surprise—and no small amount of dismay.

"I was horrified," she told our friends afterward with a wry smile. "I thought I was marrying a farmer, and that was the day I realized I had married a politician."

She was exaggerating a bit—after all, I *did* buy a mare that day at La Ceja!

I jokingly told Lina that it was a "tip" to celebrate our wedding. But the politics shouldn't have come as *that* big of a surprise. Politics came naturally to me; I had grown up steeped in my parents' democratic philosophy and my mother's activism. The scene at the market that day was simply a case of my acting as I always had: making friends, building alliances, taking an interest in other people's affairs and well-being.

There is a story, possibly apocryphal, that when I was very young, someone asked my brother Jaime and me what we wanted to be when we grew up. I supposedly answered "president," while Jaime said, "The brother of the president." Whether true or not, the essence of this story is essentially correct—my childhood dream was to rise in politics, for the purpose of fixing my country's problems.

I've had an intense career in politics: during my childhood and teen years I participated in political campaigns; I was elected to the Salgar municipal council in 1974; after working at the Empresas Públicas de Medellín, I was appointed to a senior job at the labor ministry, then at the aeronautical agency and then I became mayor of Medellín. I was elected to the Medellín city council in 1984 and was then elected to the national Senate when I was thirty-three years old. I became governor of Antioquia in 1995 and before I turned fifty, my fellow Colombians elected me as president. I believe I have won all the elections in which I have been a candidate.

With talent, dignity, class and her own unique style, Lina has greatly contributed to my political career. She insisted on having as normal and private a life as possible, and dedicated herself to raising our two boys. Even when security became necessary for the entire family in the mid-1990s, she would find ways to escape the house and go shopping alone. This made me sick with worry, but I understood why she did it: This was Lina kneeling in front of the bull. She was always ready with a joke, knew how to enliven the mood when necessary, and she didn't mind tweaking people's sensibilities. When I was president and some friends gave us a pug as a gift, she decided to name him "Mao Referendo." Back then, there was talk about having a referendum on a possible presidential reelection, which Lina was against. The press asked her why; she would just giggle.

Fortunately, she knew how to laugh at me, too. In 1991, we spent a year living in Cambridge, Massachusetts, while I took classes at Harvard University for a postgraduate degree in administration and management. I was supposed to study at Harvard many years earlier, but postponed the opportunity when my father was murdered, so I could attend properly to family affairs. I was in the Senate at the time, and because of a late change to the electoral calendar, I had to campaign for reelection while still in the United States. This posed a dilemma; campaigning in Colombia is about speeches and, especially, interacting with the people. But this was the era before cell phones and the Internet, much less Skype and videoconferencing. So I settled on the only solution possible: I arranged for my colleagues in Antioquia to set up loudspeakers in town squares and hook them up to a phone. At a pre-arranged time, I would ride my bicycle down to a phone booth in the middle of Harvard Square with a grocery bag full of quarters, and I would dial a number in Colombia. That way I could give my speech live, and field questions from the audience.

I have always tried to address the public with the same degree of respect and enthusiasm, whether it's an audience of twenty or twenty thousand. For those speeches from Cambridge in particular, I imagined an entire arena packed with people. I'm not always the world's most self-aware person, and in retrospect I suppose this made for quite a spectacle—a man carrying a grocery bag full of coins, bellowing excitedly in Spanish into a public phone in the middle of campus at a hallowed Ivy League institution. One day, a policeman followed me back to our little apartment, apparently just to make sure I wasn't insane. Lina laughed and laughed; she still hasn't let me live that one down.

Things got harder over the years, due to the explicit and implicit threats against all of us—her, too—and the other, more traditional demands of higher office, which foisted many burdens upon all of my family. Lina insists to this day that she had no idea I would seek a career in politics, much less the presidency. I've always been grateful for her love, patience, strength, and intellectual and political support. Ours has been a true partnership; our journey would have been impossible without her.

One day early in our marriage, my father gently took Lina aside and asked whether she was comfortable with the pace and demands of a life by my side.

Lina threw her head back and laughed. "This?" she exclaimed. "It's like a new adventure every day!"

7

Around the time that Lina and I were married, we acquired a working cattle ranch, a place called El Ubérrimo. Tucked into the flat, lush tropical lowlands near the Caribbean coast in Córdoba state, El Ubérrimo was an opportunity for me to indulge my lifelong love for ranching—and to periodically escape the fast political life of Bogotá or Medellín for something slower.

For the first twenty-five years after we purchased the ranch, our only house there was a little concrete dwelling that had only the basic comforts, a matter of pride for me. The kids and I worked all day and we'd take quick naps by lying under a tree or on the cool concrete floor when temperatures hovered around a hundred degrees. At night, I slept in a hammock. Visitors always complained about the many mosquitoes that buzzed around in prodigious numbers; Lina endured them without uttering a single word and the kids and I didn't even feel them. Nevertheless, we all enjoyed the symphony of frogs and constellation of lightning bugs that announced the beautiful and dangerous tropical storms rumbling on the horizon.

I took great delight in the austerity of the place, and in the work, which I undertook with no small degree of nostalgia. By day, I was up at four thirty a.m. to go milk the cows, and then off to the pastures on a horse to check on the cattle. In the evenings, I would go swim laps in the pool, as my mom had once mandated. Over the years, the ranching operation there became quite productive, thanks to a sustainable pasture rotation system that we developed. Indeed, ranching subordinated all else at El Ubérrimo. Only toward the end of my first term as president did I keep my long-standing promise to build a larger, somewhat more comfortable house with high ceilings and a second floor that would ease the high temperatures. Made entirely out of local materials, the house was built in an open style, integrating the trees and the pastures; you can almost chat with the cows, mares, and colts that peeked into the hallway. There were electrical fans instead of air-conditioning and no hot water. I still sleep outside on the balcony, in my hammock, as do Tomás and Jerónimo.

When we bought El Ubérrimo, we knew that being in Córdoba posed a certain risk. This was, after all, near the same area where the armed group EPL had invaded my father's ranch and set the house on fire when I was an adolescent. Upon my father's death, my brothers decided to leave Córdoba entirely. For years I slept with a shotgun and a revolver next to me on the floor. Still, we never had any major problems. Until one morning in August 1988.

I was driving into town around eight or nine a.m., accompanied by a few political friends from the Senate, where I was serving at the time. Lina was in Medellín. My friends and I saw the foreman waiting for us by the side of the road on his tractor. He began waving frantically for us to stop. Surprised, we pulled over. He informed us that there was a group from the EPL waiting at a small building near the ranch to kidnap me. This was a new experience for me, and for a moment I hesitated, unsure how to react. After some discussion with my colleagues, I decided to avoid El Ubérrimo for the moment—and proceed directly to the nearby coastal region of Antioquia, where we had some political events later that day.

Following a long day of speeches and driving over dirt roads, I returned to El Ubérrimo at around one a.m. I trudged into the house, exhausted, and found two of my most trusted workers—Silvia and Robin—waiting for me there, in tears.

"They were here until eleven," Robin said. He was a strong man, one of our best farmhands—and he was sobbing, he was so deeply shaken.

"They said they're coming back," Silvia said. "They said: 'Uribe will arrive home tired, and we know he sleeps in a hammock, so we'll come back at five in the morning and Uribe won't have time to react.' They're going to take you away from us!"

The EPL militants had threatened to kill Silvia and Robin if they related any of this to me—I'll forever be grateful for their loyalty. Both of them still work with me to this day.

I left the ranch and went to the nearby town, Montería, to sleep at a hotel. The following morning I went to see the police and the DAS—the *Departamento Administrativo de Seguridad,* the official intelligence agency—to see whether they could help. The officers and I returned to El Ubérrimo just before noon. Robin told us the EPL had been back already, brandishing weapons, saying they would kill me if I resisted. They had also left a message: I was supposed to meet them later that day on the shores of the Sinú River with a large amount of cash—if I paid, they would supposedly leave me alone, at least for a while.

The DAS agent had an idea: They would choose one of their agents to pose as me, and drive up to the meeting site at the arranged time. That way, the EPL kidnappers would be lulled into the false belief that I had consented to their deal—and then the police could surprise them with an overwhelming show of numbers and arrest them all. "All we need is one of your hats," the agent offered, "and I'm certain we can apprehend these men."

The idea was reasonable. But I have always believed that it is irresponsible to ask other people to take unnecessary physical risks on my behalf—no person's life is worth any less, or any more, than my own. "I agree with your plan," I replied. "But I have to be the one who goes."

After some back-and-forth, the police consented. They went to the designated site and studied it, plotting out the tactics for our operation. And then that evening I drove up to the river in my car, as planned.

A band of eight EPL kidnappers was there waiting for me in a little roadside restaurant. They seemed oddly relaxed.

I turned off the car, opened the door, and slowly got out, carrying a briefcase. I had placed a pistol inside the briefcase in case things went awry. I wore a stern look on my face, but my senses were on full alert, and my heart was racing; the memory of the circumstances of my father's death was barely five years distant.

"Hey, you," one of them called. "Did you bring the money?"

"Yes, I have it," I replied.

"How much?"

And then, as is typical in these situations, the thugs immediately demanded more.

I snorted in anger—the emotion was genuine, even if the situation was a ruse. "I don't have that much," I replied.

"You'll have to bring it to us later then," their leader said, "or else you surely know what will happen!"

I nodded gravely. At that moment, the criminals turned to walk away. Finally:

"We have you surrounded! Put down your weapons!"

A group of heavily armed agents came out of the boat where they were waiting. The kidnappers did not have their weapons drawn at the moment of the surprise, and they were easily subdued. The security forces' professionalism was remarkable; there had been no trace of them until the moment of capture, and they quickly and efficiently took the EPL members into custody.

From there, I accompanied them to the courthouse. I asked the judge to verify, and note for the record, that the kidnappers had been remanded into state custody in perfect physical condition. I would not tolerate any risk of allegations that the men had somehow been hurt or subjected to an abuse of their human rights while in my presence, or anyone else's.

Since that day in 1988, the Colombian security forces have known where I spend my nights. They have provided me with more than one bodyguard at all times; they have a record of every meeting, every meal, every visitor. Starting in my second year as governor, similar protection was extended to the rest of my family.

Over the years, the threats to me and to my family would only escalate further. Córdoba continued to be an especially volatile area of Colombia. The armed groups there grew ever more powerful, ever richer, and ever more willing to use violence to accomplish their goals. Indeed, the night of the EPL "kidnapping," I remember returning home to El Ubérrimo and contemplating how violence in Colombia—which had been so bad for so long—seemed to be getting even worse.

This seemed almost implausible. After all, elsewhere around the world, armed leftist groups similar to the EPL, the ELN, and the FARC were disappearing at a rapid pace. All of the wars in Central America had either ended already or were drawing to a close. The Berlin Wall would fall just a year later, followed quickly by the collapse of the Soviet Union. Democracy was on the march around Latin America. Guerrilla forces were becoming a thing of the past. Yet in Colombia, these groups were becoming more powerful, more numerous, and better armed—and were beginning to pose an existential threat to the state for the first time.

We were going against history and there had to be an explanation.

8

On weekends when I was growing up, my father, my brothers, and I often attended horse shows around Antioquia. These were opportunities to indulge our passion for horses and also socialize with many of our neighbors in a unique setting. We came into contact with a great many people from around the state, including one family who shared our love for horses, and which had ties with our family that went back several generations. This family's last name was Ochoa Vásquez, and by the early 1980s three of the brothers would achieve global notoriety—as the leading kingpins of the feared Medellín drug cartel.

Watching my hometown transform into the global epicenter of the cocaine trade was a surreal, heartbreaking experience; at first, I failed to comprehend the sheer scale of what was transpiring. Seemingly overnight I noticed that some acquaintances who were my age—mostly in their twenties and thirties—were acquiring fast cars, large houses, and other displays of sudden, extreme wealth—including new show horses. This initial flash of exuberance was followed by the appearance of bodyguards; new friends; and then, inevitably, the shadier associates from the criminal underworld. Many of these young men came from very good families, and their actions brought great suffering upon their kin. I remember thinking, *Is there no end to the plagues that strike Colombia?*

The answer was no—because my country was exposed yet again by the same two chronic weaknesses: geography and the absence of the state. At first, almost all of the world's cocaine was being produced in other Latin American countries, mainly Peru and Bolivia. Yet by the late 1970s, international smugglers realized they needed a relatively risk-free, strategically located place where they could take coca leaf or its semiprocessed form, known as coca paste, convert it into cocaine, and then engage in the riskiest and most profitable part of the production chain—distribution. Given the requisites, Colombia was almost too good to be true: It was positioned at the very top of South America (between the coca-growing areas and the two big consumer markets, Europe and the United States), it was accessible via two different oceans (a perfect departure point for speedboats and submarines), and it had vast stretches of geographically impenetrable and sparsely populated territory (perfect for hiding drug labs). Most relevantly, Colombia had a weak federal government that did not control its territory and was already focusing its meager resources on a struggle against other armed groups. In other words, it was gangster heaven.

By the early 1980s, more than 80 percent of the world's cocaine was flowing through Colombia's borders, most of it through the two cities of Medellín and Cali and their cartels. This extraordinary growth in the drug trade was driven by a number of factors beyond Colombia's control. These included chemical "advances" that made cocaine cheaper to produce, socioeconomic trends such as the baby boomers moving into adulthood in the developed world, and the growing concentration of wealth in the United States and other countries. Virtually overnight, cocaine became a status symbol among the jet set in Los Angeles, New York, London, Madrid, and beyond: a symbol of wealth during an era in which wealth suddenly meant everything.

"The biggest moneymaker in Hollywood last year was Colombia," quipped the American comedian Johnny Carson during the 1981 Oscar awards ceremony. "Not the studio—the country." Carson was right: The numbers were simply staggering. At its peak, the revenue generated by the cocaine trade was the equivalent of 6.4 percent of Colombia's gross domestic product, overtaking coffee during several years as our country's primary export earner. The inflows of foreign exchange from narcotics were so colossal that they caused Colombia's peso to become significantly overvalued compared to other Latin American countries throughout much of the 1980s. The possibilities for profit were enormous—one study showed that the price of a kilo of cocaine rose by a factor of two hundred by the time it was sold in the United States. Anybody with a boat, an airplane—or a lot of guns—wanted a piece of the pie.

Illicit money on this kind of a scale was enough to make even the strongest country tremble. From Manuel Noriega's Panama, to Peru and Bolivia, to the shores of south Florida, cocaine tore at the very fabric of civilization. But in Colombia, especially, it was an epic disaster. The kingpins of Medellín and Cali spread their cash around everywhere, invading many sectors of our economy and our society. At first, some Colombians laughed or at least winked at the problem, much as Johnny Carson had, either in the shortsighted belief that cocaine was a "rich country" problem, or because they benefited in some way from the largesse of the *capos*. One of the Medellín cartel's leaders, a former car thief named Pablo Escobar, became a kind of Robin Hood figure among some of the city's poor—and a fixture among some in Medellín's high society as well—by building houses, taking an interest in politics, and acquiring a massive fleet of cars, Jet Skis, and other "toys."

In 1983, when my brother was wounded in the FARC assault at Guacharacas and we enlisted the Red Cross to try to bring him back to Medellín, they could find only one nearby helicopter equipped with the modern technology needed to fly after dark in bad weather, at that high altitude. Although that helicopter was registered with a serious entity, the real owner was reportedly Pablo Escobar, according to some media reports at the time. Despite its superior instruments, the helicopter was unable to land in Yolombó and it had to turn back, empty. Years later, the incident would be cited by some of my critics as "proof" that I was friends with Escobar. I was not, and I never was, not even when it was considered fashionable in some quarters of Colombian society.

The lesson was clear enough: With all the drug money floating around, there was only one way to rise above the fray: to embrace a policy of absolute, uncompromising purity in one's conduct. Whether during campaigns or in office, I instructed my staff to follow Saint Teresa's example: "When in doubt, abstain." We implemented a number of strict rules and followed them to the letter—even when they upset or offended people. During my political campaigns, I refused to accept any money personally. My campaign managers, whom I selected primarily on the basis of their integrity, handled all incoming donations. I told them that if we had any suspicions whatsoever about a donation, we should conduct a thorough investigation into its source. If our probe suggested even the remotest possibility of a link to narcotics or any other kind of illicit income, we would politely return the check. There were no exceptions.

Once, during the late stages of a very tight race for governor, we received an extremely large check from a donor—some thirty million pesos, enough to make a substantial difference in the campaign. My campaign managers told me they had doubts about the origin of the funds; they couldn't be certain, but they thought drug money might be involved. I told them that I would rather lose an election than win it with illicit funds. They returned the check. We ended up winning that election by fewer than five thousand votes.

Of course, my teetotaling stance carried substantial risks of its own. Escobar arrogantly claimed in those days that everyone in Colombia had to choose between "*plata o plomo*"—silver or lead, money or an assassin's bullet. Meanwhile, the Colombian government was about to start a much more intense crackdown. The years of true lunacy were about to begin.

9

It was a match made in hell: The cartels, seeking to protect their empires from the growing government offensive, needed muscle and organizational strength. Meanwhile, the "guerrillas" needed money to ensure their continued existence as the Cold War drew to a close. The cartels' leaders personally oversaw many of the initial contacts; others took root organically as the cartels planted coca in territory controlled by the armed groups. Before long, virtually every armed faction in Colombia had a hand in the drug trade. According to *Guerras Inútiles,* a definitive history of the FARC written by the Corporación Observatorio para la Paz, a Colombian nonprofit group, many within the armed left came to see cocaine trafficking and smuggling as "the fundamental factor" that would ultimately provide them with the resources to topple the government in Bogotá.

All this was going on around the time of my "kidnapping" at El Ubérrimo—at exactly the moment in history that Colombia's "guerrillas" should have been fading into irrelevance, they received an infusion of billions of dollars in cocaine money that allowed them to build up their forces, acquire new arms, expand their kidnappings and bombings, and otherwise continue pretending it was still 1968.

The Colombian state, with its meager army and insufficient tools, was simply no match for this unholy alliance. Every time the government authorities tried to clamp down, the criminals would up the ante with an even more brutal counterattack. In 1984, when the Colombian police staged their first major raid of a cocaine-producing facility, and dumped $2.6 billion worth of cocaine in today's dollars into a river, making the waters turn white with foam, the *narcos* retaliated by executing the justice minister. When the authorities threatened to start extraditing drug barons to the United States, cartel leaders, including Escobar, paid millions of dollars to the M-19 to stage an invasion of the Palace of Justice, according to the findings of a 2006 truth commission. The confrontation at the palace left more than a hundred people dead, including many members of the Supreme Court.

From 1980 to 1988, more than 178 Colombian judges were assassinated, along with an attorney general, the police chief of Medellín, and countless others. The following year, 1989, would see the bombing of an Avianca jet that was supposedly carrying five police informants. All 108 people aboard died. In the lead-up to the presidential elections of 1990, four presidential candidates were assassinated, including Luis Carlos Galán, an honorable man and a Senate colleague of mine who had bravely taken a hard line against corruption and drug trafficking. Galán had asked me to be his campaign chief in Antioquia. I declined because I had already committed my support to another candidate, but I did create conditions so that those within my political organizations could support him if they chose to do so. Galán's death shattered all of us, another sad milestone that showed us just how far Colombia had fallen.

As this chaos raged even further out of control, yet another category of killers began to emerge on the Colombian scene. By the mid-1980s, some rural landowners banded together and created "paramilitary" groups, ostensibly to protect themselves from the armed left in areas where the Colombian state deployed insufficient resources or was absent altogether. At first, some of the paramilitaries were almost like private security organizations, equipped with light arms and intended for self-defense purposes. Some of the groups worked in coordination with segments of the Colombian military, who mistakenly believed that the added manpower could aid their fight against the "guerrillas." Yet, as has happened time and again in Colombian history, the proliferation of armed groups without the proper regulation or supervision of the state resulted in tragedy. Put another way: A monster was created.

Many of the paramilitaries realized that they were accountable to no one, and became intoxicated by their own power. They began to commit atrocities. These crimes were often committed in the name of "cleansing" the country of armed leftists, but they resulted more often than not in the massacre of innocent Colombians. The paramilitaries' list of targets grew to include anyone they believed to have Communist sympathies, including labor union leaders, journalists, teachers, and members of the *Unión Patriótica*, the political wing of the FARC. And inevitably, the paramilitaries also became deeply involved in the drug trade, which they, just like the armed left, saw as the economic motor by which to enrich themselves and grow their ranks. In other cases, the reverse metamorphosis took place—ordinary drug dealers declared themselves to be paramilitaries in order to give their activities a false veneer of political legitimacy.

All told, the paramilitaries would grow from around two thousand people in 1987 to well more than seventeen thousand in 2001, according to some estimates, rivaling the FARC in both manpower and ruthlessness. Just like the armed left, they were responsible for the murders of many people close to me. One of my most beloved advisers in the Senate, Leonardo Betancur, who came from the democratic left, was murdered by the paramilitaries in 1987. Héctor Abad, a renowned doctor and human rights advocate, was killed that same day. I made an emotional speech in the Senate that day explicitly denouncing both crimes, and the gangsters responsible for them. In ensuing years, the paramilitaries would ally themselves with the cartels—and eventually supersede them, joining the ranks of the world's worst and most ruthless drug traffickers. They ultimately became just as bad as the original sin they were intended to combat.

Trying to keep track of all the different armed groups in Colombia, and their ever-shifting alliances, could be bewildering—even for Colombians. But that was because the killings knew no ideology; they knew no logic. Neither of those things really mattered anymore. It was clear to me that from the late 1980s onward, the primary motivating force among Colombia's criminals was not Marxism, or social justice, or a supposedly virtuous vigilantism. No, the only cause that really mattered anymore was cocaine. Everything else was just an excuse. Thus it became clear to me that for all practical purposes, Colombia was no longer divided into right and left. It was divided between the criminals and the law-abiding majority. The *narcoterroristas* and everyone else.

10

Lina opened the letter.

We've judged you, it began, using the same "revolutionary" language as the scrawled notes I'd received during my university days. *We've found you to be an enemy of the revolution. We have declared you a military target and we are going to exact justice.*

My alleged sin: From my seat in the Senate, I was sponsoring a labor reform bill. The existing labor code had numerous flaws, including a provision that linked benefits retroactively to inflation. Taken in their entirety, these requirements were bankrupting companies as well as workers, because many firms simply went under due to the weight of their debts and couldn't meet payroll. This bill, called the "Law 50," maintained some labor protections while modifying unrealistic obligations that could never be kept, especially for smaller and medium-size companies.

I was convinced that, without the reforms, unemployment in Colombia would never fall from its double-digit levels. To the *narcoterroristas,* though, I was trampling on workers' rights—so, according to their calculus, I deserved to be killed.

For nearly two decades now, I had been ignoring such threats. But given the extraordinary mayhem sweeping the country from both "left" and "right," none of us had that luxury anymore. I approached an old classmate from my university days, who I knew had once had connections with the leftist groups. The group that sent me the letter was a small faction named Jorge Eliécer Gaitán (named after the presidential candidate whose 1948 assassination caused the Bogotazo), which in turn had close ties to the ELN. I asked this acquaintance to try to figure out whether the threat was authentic.

The response came back quickly.

"Senator, I have made the inquiry and I have found out it is true: These people are trying to kill you," he said. "You have to be careful."

He informed me that the group had extended an alternative proposal, one that would allow me to escape assassination: I would allow myself to be kidnapped, and then be put on "trial" by their leadership. I would be found "guilty." Then I would agree to drop my sponsorship of the reform bill. If I complied, I would be released from captivity and not harmed any further—provided I steered clear of future such reforms.

My former classmate didn't need to wait for my official response. He knew me better than that.

This same former classmate served as a go-between in a separate incident, personally delivering ransom money in return for the liberation of Manuel Santiago Mejía, a friend of my family's who was kidnapped in a joint action by Escobar's thugs and members of the ELN. It was yet another example of the often bewildering mix of criminal mafias that prevailed in Colombia during that era. Yet my colleagues and I refused to let blackmail deter us; we knew that what we were doing was for the good of the country. There were a great many brave patriots in Congress, such as Guillermo Alberto González, Fernando Botero Zea, Fabio Valencia, and others, who were committed to reforming Colombia, and laying the groundwork for a world in which our economy and society could one day prosper. Congress passed the Law 50 in 1990.

In the end, I wasn't the one who suffered the most immediate consequences. Just a few weeks later, on a particularly hot January afternoon, I was with my family at a friend's ranch in Córdoba. Lina and the boys were watching the news on TV when the anchor related that Iván de Jesús Gómez Osorio, one of my closest colleagues in the Senate and a cosponsor of the Law 50, had just been kidnapped.

Lina and the boys swiveled their heads around; I could feel their eyes upon me. But I didn't move, except for a laconic, dismissive wave of my hand. "This news cannot stop us from enjoying our time at this ranch," I declared.

There was a small river nearby where I liked to swim, and our host, a man who sold me cattle for El Ubérrimo, was a kind farmer who made a delicious *sancocho de gallina*.

Analysts later stated that Senator Gómez Osorio's kidnapping had been a mistake and that the outlaws' true intention was to kidnap Álvaro Uribe.

This was an old tactic, performed for my family's benefit; on this occasion it fell flat. After a few moments I opened my eyes and saw Tomás. He was eight years old—slightly older than I had been when Captain Franco came to my parents' farm. Tomás was no longer watching the TV. He was staring down at the floor, his eyes wide open, like he had just seen a ghost.

I knew that expression. I knew it all too well.

11

During those years, I did the only thing I knew: I kept working. I tried to make a positive contribution to the country's future from my perch in the Senate. Two years after we passed the Law 50, I took up sponsorship of another piece of legislation known as the Law 100. This bill sought to reform the social security system, which invited the rage of the armed left once again. I knew what was coming; it was just a matter of time.

On the night of December 9, 1992, after a day of difficult debate, I returned at around nine p.m. to my Bogotá residence: a room on the thirty-sixth floor of the Hotel Orquidea Real. I opened up a computer that I had brought back with me from Harvard, a laptop, and sat down to write a congressional brief. I recall that I had just started to type when my hands felt greasy, so I rolled up my sleeves and went to the bathroom to wash my hands.

As I left the bathroom, a bomb went off. It sent me staggering. The second blast, in rapid succession, felt like it detonated inside of my left ear: The shock wave almost knocked me to the ground. It felt as if the side of my head were on fire.

I stood there for a moment, doubled over in pain and shell-shocked. I turned back to the bathroom and saw that the walls had collapsed; three seconds earlier and the bomb would have killed me. On the other side of the room, the explosions had blown out part of the hotel's exterior wall: Through the ochre-colored smoke and the wreckage of wires and busted furniture, I could see downtown Bogotá beyond the gaping hole in the building. For a moment I felt as if I were hypnotized by the twinkling city lights and the pouring rain, which mingled with the water from the busted pipes, flooding what was left of the floor. Sparks flew everywhere: yellow, white, gold. I stared at them, momentarily stupefied.

I took a tentative step forward, my left ear still ringing as if it had been struck by a sledgehammer. The main hotel lights had gone out, and as I felt my way through the dark, illuminated only by the sparks and the ambient light of the city, my neck slipped into a loop of cables that had been left exposed in the ceiling. I stumbled, and the noose tightened abruptly around my neck. I thrashed about, trying to free myself, gasping for air. Finally the wires slipped off and I lurched forward.

It was then that I heard whimpering coming from above.

"Help," the voice said softly. "Help, please."

The voice belonged to a seventeen-year-old Colombian high school student named Julián Sosa, who had the life-altering misfortune of staying in the room directly above mine. He had been invited to the hotel for an award ceremony by Ecopetrol to celebrate his athletic and academic achievements; an ace swimmer, he had expressed dreams of becoming the national swimming champion. But the force of the explosions that night threw young Julián against the wall of his room on the thirty-seventh floor, instantly shattering his legs and his vertebrae, permanently paralyzing him from the waist down.

I found a stairwell, went upstairs, and located Julián. A small group of people was helping him, and had picked him up to carry him away from danger. I joined them, and we started making our way together down the stairs to the lobby. On our way down, we saw that the hotel had been ravaged all the way to the twenty-eighth floor. A few floors below that, we finally ran into the rescue workers as they made their way up to look for survivors.

"There were two car bombs!" one of them said. "Are you both okay?"

The rescue workers were wrong—police later verified that the bombs had been planted in the bathroom adjacent to mine, on the thirty-sixth floor. But the sheer force of the explosions had caused such an enormous amount of debris to rain down on the street below that it destroyed two cars, causing the workers to believe that they were the source of the bombs.

The rescue workers assumed responsibility for Julián. I made my way down to the lobby. I was furious, probably shell-shocked, and most of all, determined not to let this stop me or our cause. Without so much as breaking my stride, I walked straight out of the lobby and immediately departed the grounds. Then I simply checked into another hotel across town. I didn't seek medical attention. I didn't talk to journalists or the police that night either.

The next day, with no fanfare, I went to the Senate as planned and we continued our debate. Law 100, too, would eventually pass, despite continued threats from the ELN, which claimed responsibility for the hotel bombing and other attacks in the city that night. They failed in their objective—they succeeded only in wounding innocent people, and galvanizing Congress and the nation to pass the reform. Julián, it must be noted, has gone on to lead a productive, inspiring life as an engineer, just as he had dreamed.

As for me, in the end, there were two lasting consequences from that night: 1) that ringing in my left ear has, frankly, never stopped, and 2) a curiosity related to that old laptop. Almost inexplicably, the machine was still in perfect working order. The force of the explosions was enough to tear a hole in the wall and the pipes, and cause mass devastation to the hotel. Yet, whether by dumb luck or design, something about the computer made it resistant to the force of the bombs.

I held it in my hands, turned it on, and just stared at the screen in wonder. My files—all the data—were still intact. Somewhere in the back of my mind, I made a mental note. It wouldn't cross my mind again until exactly fifteen years later.

12

The attacks would never stop, not ever.

The hardest thing to cope with was the threats against my family. I left El Ubérrimo one morning to run an errand, and came back to find our house surrounded by a squadron of men with guns. My heart nearly exploded inside my chest. I jumped out of the car before it even fully stopped, and started running toward the house. To my utter relief, the men were from the Colombian security forces—they had received intelligence that I was to be kidnapped that night, and they told us to depart El Ubérrimo immediately. We threw our belongings into the car and drove for hours, and then stopped for the night in a small hotel by the side of the road. I remember looking around the room at my sleeping wife and kids and feeling so very small— humiliated by having to flee the ranch for the second time in my life, and guilty for having subjected my family to the danger.

During my second year as governor, in 1996, we discovered a plot to kidnap our children from their school bus; from that moment on, Lina and the boys have been under the official twenty-four-hour protection of our security forces. We narrowly averted a separate FARC plot to kidnap Lina in 1991. Not even my mother was exempt: On my first Mother's Day as governor, I went to her house to pay her a visit. Apparently I was followed. From that day forward, our intelligence services detected multiple plots to abduct her. She never accepted a bodyguard or an official car; eventually she agreed to sell the house and moved to another location, which we kept secret.

I knew how hard all of this was on the people I loved. When Jerónimo was about twelve, he told me he didn't want to sleep in rooms facing the street because of his fear of bombs. My brother had to stop visiting a small property he owned because of threats against both of us. A house on his farm was incinerated by the "guerrillas." Meanwhile, my family couldn't do the normal things, like eating at restaurants or driving our own cars, that families usually do. And, above all, I was haunted by the constant fear that history might repeat itself—that, God forbid, my boys would have to prematurely bury their own father, just as I had my own.

So why did I do it? I think the forlorn look on Tomás's face at the ranch said it all. I saw how Colombia's legacy of violence was being passed down to my own children—and I wanted to make it stop. My generation has not known a single day of peace: from *La Violencia,* to the emergence of the armed left and the paramilitaries, to the growth of the cartels and the rise of the *narcoterroristas,* our lives had lurched from one violent tragedy to another. I was determined that Tomás and Jerónimo's generation would one day be able to experience marvelous Colombia, in all its glory, with none of the squalor. That they would be able to raise their own kids one day in a Colombia where men with guns did not threaten their homes.

I believed in God; I trusted in His plan. I believed that one person, surrounded by the right people and guided by the right values, was capable of making an enormous difference in a country's destiny. Those beliefs, in the end, were enough to sustain me through the darkest times. They were what kept me moving relentlessly forward.

After so many years, my body is like a register of all the trauma: My hair has gone gray, my joints get stiff, and my ear still rings from that night at the Orquidea Real. But I also recognize that I have been extremely, perhaps bizarrely fortunate. The very worst scars, bruises, and knots on my body are not from the bullets and bombs—but from the work on my farm, from the indiscriminate wrath of horses, cattle, and mules. Somewhere in the distance I can still hear my dad yelling at me to stay down on my knees, laughing heartily at the following fact: Through all these years, through all this struggle, animals have done me more physical harm than people have.

SECTION THREE

Perseverance

"God concedes victory to those who persevere."
—SIMÓN BOLÍVAR

1

"Come meet me on Saturday at the Hotel Intercontinental in Panama City," the voice on the telephone said. "I have a message for you from a friend."

The caller was Gabriel García Márquez—and the "friend" turned out to be Fidel Castro.

It was early 1997, and I was the governor of Antioquia, struggling to hold on to some of the progress we had made in my state. The call from García Márquez was not entirely unexpected—I had known "Gabo" since we were introduced by common friends at a dinner party a few years before. I have always had enormous admiration for the man, not just because of his literary prowess, which won him the Nobel Prize in 1982, or for the way that he has enhanced Colombia's profile in the world. Despite having lived in Mexico for many years, he had a strong, consuming passion for trying to achieve peace in his home country. That, in conjunction with his natural intelligence and charisma, explained why García Márquez was also a unique and highly useful emissary, able to talk to people from all ideological perspectives and backgrounds.

A few months prior, García Márquez had asked me if I had any interest in establishing a dialogue with the FARC. I replied yes, absolutely I would be interested in any conversations that might lead to peace, and, if conditions allowed, I'd be happy to talk to the FARC in coordination with the national government. García Márquez then told me that he would be spending Christmas and the New Year with Castro in Havana, and he would report back. A few months passed with no news, and then, just as suddenly, the phone call came with the mysterious invitation to Panama.

On the agreed day, I flew to Panama City, accompanied by Pedro Juan Moreno and Jaime Jaramillo Panesso—one of my top advisers and my peace commissioner, respectively. We spent many hours with Gabo in a hotel suite—talking, asking questions, trying to get a fuller picture. The crux of the message was this: Castro had been in regular contact with the FARC's senior leadership, and he reported that they were extremely eager to enter into a new peace process with the Colombian government. However, Castro also reported that the FARC's only interest in negotiating was to create conditions for a cease-fire—so they could secretly build up their military strength.

"I thought you should know," García Márquez said. He was very matter-of-fact; he wasn't judging my position or theirs. He was astute, as usual, in his verdict on what it all meant: "Tough years are coming," he said, a sad glint in his eye.

I suppose that we—and here I speak for myself, as well as many other Colombians—were all hoping at that stage for some kind of breakthrough. Some of the smaller armed groups had indeed reached an amnesty deal in the early 1990s. There had been speculation that, with the collapse of the Berlin Wall and the clear-cut twin triumphs of democracy and capitalism, the FARC might soon follow suit. Yet Castro, who later confirmed his thinking in his book *La Paz en Colombia*, was able to see what few others did: The FARC, high from a steadily increasing torrent of drug money, had no intention of making peace. It was building up its positions, not tearing them down.

The idealistic leftist movement that had once attracted my university classmates had essentially disappeared, replaced by something different—and, ironically, profit-driven. The transformation that had begun in the 1980s was now nearly complete. "By the 1990s, the FARC's actions had much more to do with plunder and a self-sustaining militarism than with any residual social grievances," Michael Reid, the Latin America editor for the magazine *The Economist*, wrote in his book *Forgotten Continent*. Colombian and U.S. intelligence agencies both believed that as many as two-thirds of FARC units were dedicated almost exclusively to drug trafficking. The FARC had gotten into the narcotics business at first by imposing a "tax" on producers of coca in areas where they operated, but by the end of the 1990s they were moving into all aspects of the supply chain. When Colombian forces captured and arrested the infamous Brazilian drug trafficker Luis Fernando da Costa, a.k.a. "Fernandinho," for trading arms for cocaine with the FARC near the Colombia-Venezuela border, they asked him what it was like to do business with the FARC's leadership. Fernandinho replied, "They have no ideology. They're there for the money. They've become capitalist, and they only want the money, the money, the money."

The "ideology" had faded—in part because of reality. Many of the Colombian injustices that the FARC and others once claimed to fight against were showing tentative signs of improvement. Between 1970 and 1995, extreme poverty in Colombia—as defined by the inability to meet basic needs—fell from 70 percent to 27 percent, thanks to prudent macroeconomic management and modernizing reforms like the ones we had fought for in the Senate. Inequality fell. Our democracy became more open, with more developed institutions. Colombia was still a country with terrible deficiencies in education, health care, and unemployment, among other areas—but these elements surely would have improved had there been a greater degree of peace and security.

Unfortunately, all the money that Fernandinho spoke of was enough to buy the FARC a lot of guns—as well as a steadily expanding rank and file, which grew to more than eighteen thousand operatives by the end of the decade, plus an estimated twelve thousand urban militia. The FARC was also deepening its alliances with foreign terrorist groups, like the Basque separatist group ETA and the Irish Republican Army, which sent people to Colombia to give training in creating car bombs and other forms of urban warfare. Meanwhile, the FARC weren't the only ones on a rampage: The ELN's ranks also grew, while the paramilitaries relentlessly expanded their murdering sprees and drug-running activity as well.

Given Colombia's historic lack of political will to confront the armed groups, it didn't take much for them to overwhelm us. The gusher of cash coming into Colombia from drugs in the late 1990s was estimated at between $2.5 billion and $3 billion a year, equivalent to roughly 3 percent of our gross domestic product. By contrast, our entire defense budget was only $2.8 billion—and that included pension outlays. All told, our military had about a hundred and forty thousand troops—only half of what we needed, according to some estimates. Among these, only twenty thousand or so were considered combat ready, according to some estimates.

General Manuel José Bonnet, the commander of the Colombian military, took the extraordinary step of stating in 1998 that our forces were in "a position of inferiority" compared to the FARC. His was such a widely accepted view by that point that it didn't even cause much of a stir. The chief of the U.S. military's Southern Command, which includes South America, also stated in a public letter that Colombia's armed forces were "not up to the task of confronting and defeating" the FARC. He called Colombia "the most threatened" country in the western hemisphere. Our territory was so fragmented that the

UN human rights commissioner described Colombia as "Latin America's Bosnia." Perhaps most disturbing of all: A 1997 report by the U.S. Defense Intelligence Agency concluded that the FARC could potentially defeat the Colombian military within five years unless our armed forces received a dramatic infusion of resources. In other words, for the first time, the seat of government in Bogotá was in real danger.

Gabo was right: tough years indeed.

2

It was an unusual scene for rural Colombia—some two hundred people crammed into a small pavilion, getting ready to listen to a bona fide Ivy League university seminar. But then again, the circumstances of that era were unusual, too. And I feared that we were running out of time to address them.

I had invited my old Harvard professor Roger Fisher, the author of the world-famous negotiating book *Getting to Yes*, to give a seminar on how to resolve conflicts peacefully. The site was Urabá, a troubled region on the Caribbean coast of Antioquia, which was in the grips of a turf battle that was horrible even by Colombia's depraved standards. Urabá was a prime agricultural region, home to almost 62 percent of the country's banana crop. The paramilitaries and the armed left were willing to go to any length, and commit any atrocity, in order to wrest control over such prized territory. At least seven hundred people died in Urabá during the first nine months of 1995 alone, including many banana workers. In just one weekend shortly before the seminar, thirty-four people lost their lives. Citing the events in Urabá as a main cause, the president declared a state of emergency, and ruefully described Colombia in a televised speech as "the most violent country in the world."

"You think a market in Sarajevo is dangerous? Or a bus in Jerusalem?" wrote *The Economist*. "Try Colombia's Urabá region."

To some people, it might have seemed useless, or even frivolous, to invite a distinguished Harvard professor to talk about "positional bargaining" and "compatible interests" in the middle of a gang war. Yet I always believed that, if our goal was peace, we could never accomplish it with soldiers alone.

When I was the governor of Antioquia, and in the years that followed during my presidency, many people would associate my name most closely with my security policies. But the truth is that my commitment to social issues—to addressing the factors underlying the violence in Colombia—was just as strong and enduring. I did not believe that inequality *caused* violence, per se; after all, there were many countries in the world with worse poverty and inequality than Colombia's, but very little bloodshed by comparison.

However, I did believe that any lasting solution for our security necessarily involved addressing these ills, by healing the rifts in our society, creating more opportunities for people, and beginning to change the culture of violence that had permeated most of our history.

Sadly, the violence had become a part of our social fabric, an "easy" way for people from all levels of society to solve their problems. Decades of thuggery by the armed groups had contributed to the desensitization of many Colombians, teaching them to kill and diminishing their respect for human life. To address this problem properly, our society needed civic education from top to bottom: We had to improve the relationships between kids and parents, husbands and wives, teachers and students, employers and workers. We thought that if we could give people better tools to solve their problems, whether at home or in the street, we could make a significant difference. Perhaps most critically, we could also reduce the likelihood that young people would be recruited by the armed groups.

Urgently seeking to reach as many people as possible, we trained schoolteachers and other leaders throughout Antioquia so that they could teach Dr. Fisher's conflict management course themselves and spread the word. My former Harvard classmate the late Sandra Ceballos gave many of the seminars herself. By the end of my three-year governorship, more than ninety thousand people were certified in the principles of Dr. Fisher's program. In addition, we handed out thousands of little business cards with the basic tenets of conflict resolution; I kept them stuffed in the pockets of my suits and briefcases, and gave them to practically everyone I met. Meanwhile, we tried to do everything else we could to provide not just short-term fixes, but long-term solutions to the violence.

In order to succeed, we had to be creative. I've often joked that God gave me an enormous attention span, but a small checkbook. Antioquia's finances were very precarious at the moment I took office, so we were obliged to seek solutions that didn't involve large amounts of money. For example, we expanded a program of music schools that put youth orchestras in every municipality of Antioquia; the belief was that once a child embraces an instrument, he never picks up a gun. Faced with a chronic shortage of space in our schools, we implemented a program in which the state paid the Catholic Church and other private, nonprofit operators to create new seats for students. This program allowed us to create one hundred thousand new openings for students in three years, twice as many spots as had been created in the previous ten years combined.

Meanwhile, we took a deep breath and committed ourselves to freeing up as much money as possible for real programs—even if that meant angering entrenched interests in the public sector. During my governorship, we massively reduced Antioquia's state payroll by more than 60 percent. This cost cutting earned me many enemies, but it was absolutely essential so the state government could afford infrastructure projects and social programs that principally favored the lower and middle classes. We introduced competition into the social security system for state employees, cutting costs by two-thirds and improving the quality of coverage despite the protests of those who screamed "privatization." Thanks to the social security reform passed in Congress in 1993 following the Orquidea Real bombing, we were able to provide subsidized health care to more than a million needy residents of our state—out of a total population of five million. We set up cooperative banks so that we could increase microlending and other sources of credit for lower-income people. We tripled the amount of paved highways in the state, and we finished and put into service the *Tren Metropolitano* in Medellín—a project I had helped start many years before as mayor.

All told, our efforts won recognition at home and abroad: A 1997 *Wall Street Journal* profile proclaimed that my governorship was "a tale of a society being reconstructed, complete with the risks that must be taken, and a lesson for the rest of the country."

Yet . . . even in our finest moments, the core, inescapable truth of Colombia always had a way of making itself present.

One morning during Dr. Fisher's weeklong visit to Urabá, I woke up as usual at four thirty a.m. to do some exercise. Minutes later, I received a call: Another two dozen banana workers had been removed from a bus, made to kneel on the ground outside, and then the murderers slit their throats one by one.

As dawn broke, I sped away from the conference site in a caravan so I could visit the scene of the crime and oversee the beginning of the investigation. I looked out the window, beholding this lush land of plenty, so rich in minerals, oil, and other resources—but so troubled. In my heart, I felt great sorrow, as well as a reaffirmed conviction: In order to solve our problems, we would need more than just good social policies. We would have to stand up to the criminals.

3

"*¡Hombre, Gobernador!* Please help us! The guerrillas are destroying the town!"

It was one a.m., just two weeks into my governorship. The phone call was from my friend Jesús Arcesio Botero Botero, the former mayor of El Peñol, a city just northeast of Medellín. I knew El Peñol very well from my time as an official at Empresas Publicas de Medellín, when I directed the very difficult job of moving the whole town so that a dam could be built. Screaming with panic, Jesús Arcesio told us that his town was being overrun.

Unfortunately, there were no good options to save El Peñol. We had no military helicopters available to us in Antioquia—inexplicable, given the size and terrain of our state. So I phoned the defense minister in Bogotá, Fernando Botero (no relation to the mayor), to ask him for reinforcements. Fernando Botero was a serious and responsive minister—but, just like us, he was chronically short of resources. He apologized and said the only rapid-response tool he had available was a single helicopter in Santa Marta—two or three hours' flying time from Medellín. I told him that wasn't soon enough. He offered to send the army by ground—risky, given the danger of roadblocks and other obstacles, but we had no better choices.

I had to get to the scene myself; I didn't know exactly how I could help, but I always believed I had to be there, in the middle of any crisis, to do whatever I could. I grabbed my coat, ran outside, and boarded the civilian helicopter belonging to the governor's office, and we set a course for El Peñol. As we landed, the terrorists and our army were still exchanging gunfire in the streets. In short order, our forces prevailed—as they usually did when they were actually able to make it to the scene in time. We convened an impromptu town meeting right there at the city hall, and I assured the residents of El Peñol that the state would protect them.

Later that same day, I found Jesús Arcesio. I thanked him, and gave him a big hug.

"We've regained control of El Peñol," I declared. "We're here to support you now. The city is secure."

To my eternal regret, I was unable to keep my commitment. The terrorists discovered that Jesús Arcesio's call to me had triggered the military response. Just two weeks later, as he was leaving his house with his bodyguard, *sicarios* opened up on them with a burst of gunfire. Both men died.

I made every possible effort to protect all 125 of Antioquia's mayors, and to ensure that they could perform their jobs properly. But the truth was that we had more willpower than resources. We gave them full police protection, and we equipped special armored trucks to escort them back into towns where the terrorists had taken control. These were crude vehicles, put together on the cheap, but they could absorb plenty of bullets, and they sent a powerful message of strength. Yet the FARC and the ELN, especially, were hell-bent on keeping out the mayors, as well as any other representatives of the legitimately elected Colombian state, so that they could run drugs, set up roadblocks, and conduct their other criminal activities in "peace." One by one, to my utter horror, we continued losing mayors to bullets and to kidnappers.

There was a distinct hypocrisy to the FARC's actions. Until 1988, mayors throughout Colombia had been appointed by state governors. The FARC decried this as proof that Colombia was not a true democracy, and the group listed the direct election of mayors as a primary condition for their eventual disarmament. Yet, by the time of the attack on El Peñol, the law had been changed to allow for popular election. Did the FARC decide to lay down its arms? Just the opposite: They began systematically assassinating and abducting these symbols of the democracy they claimed to support.

Heartbroken and frustrated, and lacking the resources to address the problem properly, we decided to try a nontraditional solution. We instituted a new policy whereby, if the terrorists kidnapped or killed a mayor, we would appoint an army officer to take his or her place. As we had hoped, this ended up being a powerful deterrent for two main reasons: 1) A military mayor was almost always accompanied by an increased military presence in the area, which placed greater pressure on the terrorists and made their drug-smuggling operations more difficult, and 2) the appointment generally angered the townspeople, who rightly valued the right to elect their own civilian representatives, so my policy had the net effect of making the terrorists tremendously unpopular.

The killing of mayors stopped, but this solution, too, was not viable; our politics were poisoned with misguided ideology, drug money, and a new philosophy that was becoming increasingly en vogue: the mistaken idea that, by appeasing the terrorists, we could convince them to leave us alone. One morning, several mayors came to Medellín to stage a noisy protest and present me with a letter demanding that I stop the practice of appointing military mayors.

Immediately before they gave me the letter, some of those same mayors requested a private meeting in my office.

"Governor, please don't stop!" one of them blurted out, as the others in the room nodded emphatically.

"Your policy is the only thing that's saving us," another said. "Please understand that we have to deliver you this letter, because otherwise the guerrillas will kill us!"

This happened to me over the years with maddening frequency: People telling me in private that I was right, but saying something entirely different in public. Such double-talk always carried a tangible cost. Before long, the courts ruled that the policy regarding the mayors was unconstitutional. The killing began anew.

Despite the threats, despite the lack of resources, despite the shortage of political will, I refused to cloister myself in my office. I spent my entire governorship traveling from one town to another, challenging the terrorists with my very presence. My motivation was not *machismo* or narcissism, but the belief that, given our chronic lack of other resources, leading by example was one of the most powerful tools I had. I had to demonstrate to the people of Antioquia that we would not be intimidated by the violent ones, that we would defeat them, that life would go on.

In one village after another, we were subjected to a merciless stream of attacks. When we dispatched our generals to visit troubled areas, their helicopters often came back pockmarked with bullet holes. Bombs exploded; police chiefs died; many good people lost their lives. One of the most painful episodes came in Salgar—the little village near the family farm where I grew up, the very place where I used to ride with my schoolteacher, Lilian Alvarez. Immediately after I attended a ceremony in Salgar, my police escort passed through town—and they were ambushed by the terrorists. Many members of the unit died.

On a separate trip to Vegachí, a town in the northeastern part of Antioquia, I arrived a few hours earlier than scheduled. I held some meetings in the city hall, waiting for the rest of my staff to arrive by helicopter around six a.m. As the helicopter touched down, it came under a torrent of gunfire from ELN forces on a nearby mountain.

Bullets flew everywhere. My aides scampered out of the helicopter and into City Hall, which was also raked with gunfire. The terrorists, dozens of them, then swept into the village, shooting up buildings and throwing grenades at City Hall. I called Medellín, urgently seeking reinforcements, but was told none could make it to Vegachí on time.

What saved us? Sheer providence. The captain of the small army unit that was with us did not abandon us. We pressed our bodies against the floor while the two sides traded fire. The terrorists' plan was for the soldiers to run out of City Hall in pursuit, and they had a separate unit ready to enter the building and kill me. The army anticipated this, so they stayed in City Hall and, showing great discipline and tactical skill, fended off the assault until the terrorists finally retreated back to their mountain hideout on the edge of town.

The moment the shooting stopped, I grabbed a megaphone and stormed over to Vegachí's main plaza and delivered a speech against terrorism.

4

Colombians *hungered* for security. Their clamor for peace permeated everything; it was just as palpable during those years as the fear sown by the terrorists. Everywhere we went, people encouraged us and told us we were doing the right thing. Moments like the one in Vegachí did not go unnoticed—the entire population of Antioquia began to acquire a certain resilience, a swagger in the face of all the threats. They saw that there was hope in strength; that by confronting the terrorists, rather than running away, we could indeed prevail. It was everyone's fight.

"For anyone who visits Antioquia, perhaps the most notable aspect is not so much the attitude of the governor, but the fact that the people there seem to be on exactly the same page," wrote a somewhat skeptical-sounding journalist for the national magazine *Semana*. "It's unclear whether Álvaro Uribe Vélez is interpreting the collective will, or whether his leadership has imposed it. But the fact is that the people of Antioquia, known for their drive and efficiency, are channeling these virtues toward a solution to their problem of security."

Every morning at seven a.m., we gathered Antioquia's top military leaders for a meeting to discuss the security issues of the day. This group was chaired at first by the very capable General Mora Rangel, and attended by representatives of the army, the police, the DAS, the prosecutor, the peace commissioner, and my aide Pedro Juan Moreno. As a governor, I had no direct operational control over any of the security forces—the federal government formally controlled both the military and police. Yet the simple act of having a leader present who was constantly monitoring, encouraging, and following up on matters of security was enough to make a big difference.

We also threw open our doors to the public, placing a huge emphasis on transparency and citizen participation. Prosecutors, attorneys general, and ombudsmen attended—people who were independent of the governor's authority and who had a grassroots view of our most pressing security issues. We sought constant feedback from the public at large, so that we could respond more quickly to their needs. For example, if there was a wave of car thefts, we would meet with the insurers and the car dealers, take their suggestions, and then establish a direct nexus with police. I was constantly doing interviews on talk radio, answering people's questions and hearing their complaints. By focusing on good administration and constant involvement in details, we began gaining traction on crime.

However, it wasn't enough. We searched for other options that would allow us to tamp down the raging violence in our state. In 1994, the year before I became governor, the Colombian president approved the creation of new private groups that could aid the military in some activities under the close supervision of the state. Shortly thereafter, a new president took office, put the groups into action, and created a name for them: the "Convivir," Spanish for "getting along." Some of the Convivir were essentially networks of informants, not unlike "neighborhood watch" groups in richer countries; they were provided with sophisticated walkie-talkies, and reported criminal activities so the military could then act to stop them. Other groups were allowed to have weapons, but their activities would be closely monitored by the relevant authorities. The interior minister of that era said the government established the Convivir "so that citizens can cooperate with the armed forces, with the goal of offering Colombians greater margins of security, especially in rural areas."

The Convivir initiative enjoyed broad support from two successive presidential administrations and a wide variety of Colombian politicians, and its charter was approved by Colombia's constitutional court. Yet some people looked at the proposal through the prism of recent Colombian history and feared that it might give rise to a new generation of paramilitaries. As we considered whether to deploy the Convivir in Antioquia, we weighed this risk carefully.

In the final balance, I decided that we urgently needed the extra help to fight back. To my regret and constant frustration, the Colombian military and police did not have sufficient firepower on their own to counteract the ever-greater cocaine-fueled resources of the *narcoterroristas*. Throughout my governorship, I would vividly witness evidence of this shortfall in the attacks on Vegachí, Urabá, and elsewhere; the signs were irrefutable and all too numerous. As a governor, the resources of the military were beyond my control. But the Convivir groups offered a framework for civilians to provide intelligence and tips—essentially growing the number of people who were taking an active role in our security. I always believed that, in a country with Colombia's geographical and social challenges, security would not be possible if it was solely the responsibility of the police and the armed forces; I also thought citizens had an obligation to help guarantee the fundamental right of rule of law.

Another deciding factor was the program's mandate of strict oversight. If abuses were detected in a Convivir group, it would be shut down. That was the fundamental difference compared to the paramilitaries—the Convivir would be placed under the supervision of the state. The point was not to aid the paramilitaries or create new ones, but precisely the opposite: to regulate and control auxiliary security groups, and thus make the illegal ones unnecessary and obsolete.

During the years that I was governor, more than six hundred Convivir groups operated throughout Colombia. The number of Convivir in Antioquia was roughly in proportion to Antioquia's percentage of the national population—our state had between sixty and seventy such groups. The relevant authorities detected abuses by two of them, and they were shut down.

Antioquia was not the only state that deployed the Convivir; a relatively low percentage of groups experienced problems, and we immediately took action to address those issues. I made the mistake of proposing that some of the Convivir be allowed to carry long arms such as rifles in order to protect them from the growing firepower of the terrorists. This was bad judgment on my part, and I withdrew the idea.

Many of my political detractors have accused me of being an ally of the paramilitaries based on the decisions I've made regarding security. This is not true. While it is true that some of these criminal organizations were founded to carry out personal vendettas—such is the case, for example, of Castaño Gil, whose father was killed by the FARC—this is not my case. I have always believed that the best way to honor the memory of my father is to work so that future generations of Colombians don't have to suffer through the same violence we have been through.

During the 1990s, most mainstream Colombian politicians favored "dialogue" with the armed groups as a solution to our country's violence. Many of them falsely equated appeasement with civility, as if the state's only function were to act as a mediator rather than the guarantor of security and territorial control. Thus, almost everyone who advocated a strong security policy was tarred as an uncivilized extremist, and many were automatically assumed to be in league with the paramilitaries. Sensing fertile ground on this issue, the FARC's and ELN's kingpins began referring to me as "the paramilitary governor" in their propaganda and in other public statements as a way to discredit our overall security policies—especially as we began to accrue successes in our fight against them. In those years, and afterward, I patiently, clearly, and thoroughly responded to all accusations, both vague and specific. But I never let this propaganda deter me from doing what I believed was right.

In fact, thanks to the hard work and sacrifices of Colombia's armed forces and police and to the support of the Convivir, we were able to make tangible improvements in Antioquia's security. We reestablished a degree of control over the highway from Medellín to Bogotá, chasing away many of the kidnappers and their roadblocks. Overall, kidnapping in Antioquia fell by about 30 percent. Just as critically, people began to believe that, by actively standing up to the violent ones, we could in fact improve our lives. "If the belief among people in Bogotá is that their city is a hell with little chance of changing, the people of Antioquia think the opposite," *Semana* magazine wrote. "Their state has become a kind of pilot program, and the rest of Colombia is watching their experiment with great interest."

Yet, to my despair, our so-called "experiment" would not last.

It broke my heart, but I knew exactly what was coming. In security, at least, much of what we accomplished would unravel with disturbing speed. Within just two weeks of the end of my governorship, the terrorists would take back control of the road to Bogotá. The illegal armed groups would resume their expansion of territory and drug-smuggling activities. Kidnappings would spike again to their previous level.

Why? There were a variety of reasons—some of them logical, some of them simply bizarre. Some of them had to do with the Colombian reality of the 1990s, and others could be traced to events and trends abroad. One sordid episode, in particular, captured the extraordinary challenges of those times.

5

Maybe it's the tropical sun; maybe it's a romanticism that some people associate with guerrillas and jungle warfare, having never really experienced either. Whatever the reason, Colombia's woes have been compounded over the years by a certain kind of person who suddenly finds himself in the jungle and starts engaging in behavior that he would never, ever consider back home. Sometimes well-intentioned, other times not, these people often believe they can treat Colombia like a playground for all their deepest fantasies, with no consequences for anyone, much less themselves. I have come into contact with my share of these people over the years, but few examples were more disturbing—or illustrative of a bigger problem—than the case of the German named Werner Mauss.

The first time I ever heard of Mauss was when I received a call from a manager of a cement company called Río Claro. A few days previously, a group of European consultants had been kidnapped by the ELN, and after having paid a $2 million ransom in Europe through a German man, almost all the hostages had been released.

By this time, the FARC, ELN, and the paramilitaries were making colossal fortunes off of kidnapping and extortion, often involving multinational corporations. One estimate held that Colombians were paying $350 million a year in ransoms by the mid-1990s—at the time, the equivalent of Colombia's annual exports of bananas, our third-biggest cash crop. In many cases, international companies made regular cash payments to the illegal groups in return for "protection." Others paid ransoms on a case-by-case basis. The sums became so large that I believed kidnapping had transformed into a self-perpetuating industry, with rogue middlemen turning a profit for themselves—and, in some cases, acting in complicity with the criminals at various steps of the "supply chain."

How right I was! A short time after the Río Claro incident, the ELN kidnapped a German woman named Brigitte Schröder. Her husband had been a manager for a German company. We started working with the police to secure her release, and before long the police had managed to lower the terrorists' ransom request down to twenty million pesos. Everything seemed to be going according to plan until I received a call from two top police leaders, Colonel Mauricio Santoyo and Brigadier General Alfredo Salgado Mendez.

"The deal's off," Salgado spat, clearly furious. "The ELN is now demanding a hundred and fifty million pesos in ransom."

"Why?"

"Because that German man is now involved, and now the guerrillas are asking for more money."

We soon learned several new details, Werner Mauss's name among them. We also learned that he originally told Brigitte Schröder's husband that the kidnappers were paramilitaries. Mauss was in the jungle with the ELN when he made the call from a satellite phone. As the evidence mounted against him, the attorney general's office issued an order for his capture.

A couple of days later, I received another phone call from General Salgado: The police had captured Mauss as he tried to board a small plane in Medellín with the hostage, Brigitte Schröder, in *his* custody. Mauss had in his possession several passports with different aliases. The authorities also found documents on Mauss's person detailing amounts of money and names of Colombian officials, a discovery that caused authorities to suspect possible bribery.

No sooner had they arrested him than our police started receiving a deluge of phone calls from the Colombian foreign ministry in Bogotá, demanding Mauss's immediate liberation.

"We're under a tremendous amount of pressure here," Salgado said. "I think we might have to let him go."

"Do not set that man free," I said. "I'll be right there."

I threw on my clothes and rushed out the door. On my way out, I grabbed a weapon to protect myself. I had already looked more deeply into Mauss's story, and I knew who his friends were. I wasn't about to take any chances.

6

"Ian Fleming might have been proud to have created Werner Mauss," wrote the *Los Angeles Times* in a 1997 front-page profile. The story compared Mauss to a "German James Bond." Whether foreign media would have glorified a terrorist anywhere else in the world in such a manner is impossible to know. But they were not the only ones to be dazzled by Mauss and his unusual history; as the *Times* story and other accounts plainly illustrated, he had been deceiving people for decades.

According to the foreign press, Mauss began his career in Germany as a vacuum salesman and a failed horse trainer before turning to private detective work in the early 1960s. Mauss quickly demonstrated an unusual talent for helping high-dollar clients and insurance companies recover stolen luxury property, such as Porsches, and stolen jewelry. Mauss's special skill was his ability to cultivate high-level contacts with both law enforcement officials and criminal networks, the *Times* said. Business boomed for Mauss's little detective agency and, before long, he had reportedly acquired a Porsche of his own—as well as a Cessna and even his own medieval castle.

Things went swimmingly for Mauss until 1983, when his photo was published in a German newspaper—blowing his cover, and thus making it impossible for him to continue his work in Europe. Mauss looked around the globe for a new place to practice his craft. Given the circumstances of the mid-1980s, Colombia probably seemed to him like heaven on Earth.

Mauss arrived in Bogotá and quickly discovered that, unlike Germany, Colombia was a place where he could not only infiltrate government, but transcend it. He found a new niche—helping European companies negotiate ransom payments and protection money with armed groups. He seemed to be in luck. Mauss's top client was a German company that was building an oil pipeline through territory where the ELN operated. According to the *Times*, the ELN was "an obscure little (group) led by a renegade Spanish priest." Once Mauss became involved, the ELN experienced a dramatic upturn in its financial ability to recruit members and sow terror throughout

Colombia. Within a few years, the ELN became the second-biggest armed group in all of Colombia, behind only the FARC.

Mauss's role in the ELN's abrupt rise was a totally open secret. As the British newspaper *The Guardian* noted in its November 1996 profile of Mauss: "No one in Colombia would dispute that the revival in the ELN's fortunes [in the mid-1980s] was closely linked to German money."

Along the way, as had been his *modus operandi* for decades, Mauss acquired a long, varied, and extremely powerful roster of friends. Another media article, by *Dow Jones*, described Mauss as "a German private detective with links to German intelligence, high-ranking members of the Colombian government, and leftist guerrillas." From the moment that Mauss was arrested, virtually all of these parties brought their resources to bear on his behalf. The German consulate in Bogotá declared that Mauss had been carrying out a "humanitarian" mission at the time of his arrest, and called for him to be freed immediately. Our commanders in Antioquia also received several calls from senior officials in Bogotá, urging them to liberate Mauss as soon as possible.

I was determined not to allow that to happen. Our judicial system was pleading for an opportunity to try Mauss on the merits of the case. An official for the attorney general's office said, "In that Mauss has attempted to smuggle a kidnapped person out of the country, he is a threat to our national security." My beloved friend Gilberto Echeverri, the former governor of Antioquia who would perish tragically near Urrao years later, called me and told me that he recognized Mauss' face from a separate scandal years earlier involving the Metro system in Medellín. When I rushed to the police station on the morning following his arrest in November 1996, my goal was to give our legal system the political support it needed to resist the pressure from the Colombian and German federal governments, and to perform its job properly.

While I am thankful for the many individuals from Europe and the United States who have made valuable contributions to Colombia over the years, I watched in horror as others undercut our efforts to implement security and the rule of law. The Mauss case was symbolic of a much larger issue: the corrosive involvement of some outsiders in Colombia's affairs. Some of these were individuals—the kind of globe-trotting mercenaries who, since the beginning of time, have been drawn to weak or failing states where they can turn a quick profit. But in truth, the problem was much broader than just a few isolated cases. During those years and later on, many nongovernmental organizations openly allied themselves with the armed leftist groups, providing them with funds and other forms of logistical support. In turn, these organizations systematically denounced legitimate operations by the Colombian state, often under the guise of human rights. Some politicians in Europe, in particular, insisted on treating the FARC and the ELN as equal to our democratically elected government.

I could never understand this hypocrisy: These same politicians would *never* have tolerated these groups' atrocities had they occurred on their own countries' soil. Perhaps they indulged Colombia's armed left out of a misplaced nostalgia for the socialist philosophies that many had espoused in their youths; perhaps they did not fully understand that these groups had evolved many years before into little more than glorified, murderous drug cartels. Whatever their rationale, I was determined to put an end to the all-too-real negative consequences of their actions. I declared that Mauss's arrest was "an opportunity to work toward the dismantling of the international network" of those who supported the illegal armed groups.

By explicitly denouncing Mauss's actions we were able to successfully deflect the political pressure to release him—at least for a while. He was held in jail in Colombia for a few months until he was then released. To my astonishment, a court in Antioquia ruled that his arrest had been illegal and acquitted him. Mauss returned to Europe, but he did not disappear entirely from Colombian politics. In ensuing years, high-ranking Colombian officials traveled to Germany to see him. The ostensible purpose: so that Mauss could negotiate a peace deal on behalf of the ELN! Unsurprisingly, this "mediation" never yielded any significant results.

My final contact with Mauss came shortly after his release from jail, when I was at Oxford. I received by mail an envelope that appeared to be from Mauss's lawyers. I had heard that he was considering a lawsuit against me for slander. I didn't even open the envelope—I just marked, "Return to sender," and dropped it back in the mail. That was the last I ever heard of the matter.

7

As my governorship drew to a close, Colombia's terrorist groups faced a dilemma: Our experience in Antioquia had demonstrated to Colombians across the nation that, through the strength of our security forces and effective administration, the criminals' reign of terror could be effectively challenged. We exploded the long-standing myth that standing up to the *narcoterroristas* would only produce more bloodshed and suffering. The armed groups thus felt compelled to strike back, to make a public show of power before I left office. They did so by displaying, once again, their utter contempt for Colombian democracy—by attempting to sabotage the 1997 elections for my successor as governor.

The FARC issued a statement ordering Colombians to boycott the vote in Antioquia, denouncing the so-called "paramilitary governor" and saying the election would be "manipulated and distorted by the oligarchies and their political lackeys." The ELN declared an "armed strike" to paralyze road transport on the day of the voting. All groups made death threats against the candidates, which included not only the aspiring governors but also people running for mayor and city council spots throughout the country. The campaign of intimidation was nationwide—but Antioquia was clearly ground zero.

In the run-up to the vote, fifty-three candidates were killed nationwide. More than two hundred others were kidnapped. Nationwide, more than nineteen hundred candidates officially dropped out of the running prior to election day because of the threats—sixteen hundred candidates withdrew in Antioquia alone. The crest of violence was so severe that the head of the Senate ordered the purchase of 102 bulletproof vests—one for each senator. The Associated Press described the campaign to disrupt the elections as "the most serious challenge to Colombian democracy in more than 30 years."

As the violence and threats escalated, the federal government considered suspending elections in Antioquia. As governor, I opposed this idea with great vigor, and vowed that we would not allow the terrorists to intimidate us. I spent some of the final days of my governorship touring the communities of Antioquia's interior, encouraging people to defy the threats and exercise their democratic rights. We walked the streets with a megaphone and told people not to be afraid; we assured them that together we would overcome the threats.

On a Saturday morning just before the election, I gathered my team early at the airport so we could board our helicopters and take our message to two municipalities east of Medellín. I was accompanied by several of my closest aides, including Andrés Uriel Gallego, Pedro Juan Moreno, and Any Vasquez, plus the top military official in the region, General Carlos Alberto Ospina Ovalle, the commander of the army's 4th Brigade. In the first town we visited, Argelia, we found people who were terrified of the violence but came out to greet us nonetheless. The mayor came out to greet us when our two helicopters touched down, as per the usual protocol.

But not in San Francisco. Our final stop was a village that had been troubled for years, exactly the kind of place that needed our support. The military had arrived the previous Wednesday to secure San Francisco for the elections, and had come under heavy fire from the terrorists. Now, as we landed on a hillside just outside the village, I was surprised and disturbed to see that there was no greeting party waiting for us. This couldn't be a good sign.

I climbed out of the helicopter, looked around, and then motioned for my staff to accompany me down the hill toward the town. As we descended, we finally saw the mayor, puffing his way up the slope to meet us. I was pleased to see that he was accompanied by Father Antonio Bedoya, a priest and a great friend and colleague, who was the local coordinator of one of our best initiatives in Antioquia—the *Sistema de Aprendizaje Tutorial,* a learning program for rural communities. They both greeted me in a relaxed fashion, and we continued down the path together, toward San Francisco's town square.

Acting on sheer intuition, I decided not to go to the town square, where they had prepared a tribune for me to address the town. Instead, I stopped at a random street corner and gave the same speech I had been giving all over Antioquia—why voting was important, how previous generations had fought for the right to elect local officials in Colombia, and how I didn't really care whom they voted for, as long as they showed the courage to come out on election day.

"We can't vote, because they'll kill us!" one of the villagers yelled.

I nodded. "These are difficult times," I said, "and that makes it especially important that we all show strength by voting."

The meeting ended with glum silence. This was clearly a very troubled place.

The mayor turned to me and smiled, somewhat awkwardly. "Governor, would you like to have a drink before you leave?"

It seemed like the mayor had something he wanted to tell me, so I consented. We made our way up to the second floor of the city hall. Waiting there, I was surprised to see a fellow alumnus from the University of Antioquia, who was now serving as San Francisco's *personero,* the local attorney general.

He looked me up and down, apparently just as surprised at our meeting as I was. Then his eyes narrowed.

"Governor," he said, "you're very *berraco* coming here today."

Three things immediately disturbed me: First, the nervous tone in which he said this—using a word that roughly means "brave" in Colombian Spanish, but carries a somewhat crude connotation. Second, I realized that he had not attended my town meeting, which was odd, since this was the local attorney general, the local official charged with protecting the democratic rights that we were there to defend. And finally, I remembered that when he was a university student, this man's loyalties had never been entirely clear— he hadn't openly embraced the FARC, but he hadn't rejected it either. I sat there for another moment, feeling a prickly, slowly intensifying heat on the back of my neck. And then—acting again on pure intuition—I abruptly said good-bye and gathered my staff, and we made our way back up the hill, where the two helicopters were waiting for us, starting to fire up their engines.

I bade farewell to the mayor and to Father Antonio. As I turned to board our helicopter, gunfire erupted. Using my elbows, I crawled into a nearby ditch, my face dragging through the dirt. The bullets came in sheets now. Our soldiers returned fire. The rotor blades were churning fast.

Staying as low to the ground as possible, I ran toward the helicopter and jumped in through the side door. General Ospina helped pull me inside and slammed the door shut. Our helicopter began to lift off the ground.

We still had a problem: the second helicopter, which had still not taken off. I saw how its passengers remained down on the ground, totally exposed, as the terrorists continued firing from their hideout. I reached into the side panel of our helicopter and grabbed the first weapon I could find—a machine gun—and tried to provide covering fire so my colleagues could escape. Finally the second copter was able to take flight.

Once we were out of range, we radioed the other aircraft. Miraculously, no one had been hurt. But our relief was short-lived: Before we landed in Medellín, we learned that the terrorists had shot Father Antonio in the head, killing him. What sadness!

The tragedy did not end there—by no means. That same day, the terrorists also kidnapped four election officials. They blew up a power station in Buenaventura, wiping out power to a third of the city. On election day, nationwide turnout was just under 50 percent—and it was much lower in Antioquia. In San Francisco, only twenty-nine out of the sixty-five hundred eligible voters cast ballots. In dozens of other towns, nobody voted at all.

The ELN had blood on their hands yet again—having murdered a priest who had dedicated his life to God and educating the Antioquian public. But ridiculous rumors soon began circulating that it was the Colombian army that had executed Father Antonio. Shortly thereafter, I was on an airplane talking with Carlos Gaviria Díaz, a former law professor of mine from the University of Antioquia who was now the head of Colombia's Constitutional Court.

"I heard that the army killed Father Antonio," Gaviria said.

I was stunned. "How can you say that? I was there! It was the ELN that killed him!"

"You always defend the army," Gaviria replied.

"*Profesor,* my God, I was there! I saw it!"

Gaviria insisted on his interpretation of events. But God always rewards the truth. Weeks later, several members of the Colombian government and the international community descended on Antioquia, including the United Nations' high commissioner for human rights for Colombia. They were there to seek the liberation of two election officials from the Organization of American States who had come to Antioquia at my request to supervise the elections—and who had been kidnapped by the ELN a few days prior to the vote. At a public event, that took place during their visit, the ELN's leadership confirmed that it was responsible for the assault on San Francisco. The ELN leaders also swore they would continue trying to assassinate me until they succeeded. The audience was totally silent in response.

A few days later, Lina quietly requested a private meeting with the UN high commissioner.

"The guerrillas threatened to kill the governor," Lina told her. "You were there; you were all sitting there listening, and you didn't say a single word in protest. Doesn't my husband also have human rights?"

8

On New Year's Day, 1998, the last full day of my governorship, I made a trip to the Antioquian countryside to bid farewell to my mother. I was about to depart for a year of postgraduate study in England, as a senior associate member at Oxford University. I refused to ever use the governor's helicopter for personal reasons, no matter the circumstances, so I set out by car that day with Tomás and Jerónimo and my cousin Jorge Vélez to go see her at her house on the Río Cauca.

My mother had recently been diagnosed with cancer. The doctors told me it was beatable, though, and she was only sixty-five. She greeted me at the door that day, smiling as if nothing in the world were wrong. We spoke for a long while about the situation in Antioquia. She said she was worried about the number of threats against me, and she expressed great relief that I would be leaving Colombia as soon as possible. As we left, she gave me a blessing, the same blessing she had given me since I was a young boy, and wished me the best of luck in England.

I left for Oxford the very next day, a Friday. A week later, my mother passed away.

I desperately wanted to come back to Colombia for her burial, but my family would have none of it. "Absolutely not," my brother said. "She was so relieved, knowing that you were safe in England. Please don't come back to Colombia for her funeral. It would be too dangerous."

Everyone in public life makes sacrifices. We spend extraordinary amounts of time away from our families. These moments are irreplaceable, but we tell ourselves that we are working for a higher good, and that makes the sacrifice worth it. On many occasions in my life, this has been the case. Not this one. No one should have to be absent from his mother's bedside at the moment of her death, or miss her funeral because he fears bringing harm to his loved ones. I recall being in Oxford on the day of my mother's memorial service, sitting in a cold, barren house five thousand miles away from home, determined to turn Colombia into the kind of place where people would not have to make such sacrifices any longer. My soul cried for not being able to be by my mother's side at the time of her death and as she made her way to her last resting place.

9

Lina would later describe those twelve months as the only "traditional" time the Uribes had as a family. We resided in a comfortable two-story house generously lent to us by a professor on leave from the university. I rode a bike to and from campus. On weekends we often rented a car and drove for hours around the countryside, admiring the intelligent way the British set up their pastures. We occasionally visited restaurants. Tomás even worked for a time at a Burger King, washing dishes on the night shift in order to earn some spending money.

Still, everything made me think of home. Literally everything. There was a sign on the door of our borrowed house that said, NEIGHBORHOOD WATCH. I wrote some of my friends back in Antioquia and said: *You see? Here, too, they understand that the only way to be safe is if ordinary people cooperate with the security forces.*

The truth of our situation ate away at me, picking at my insides like a vulture: I was effectively in exile for the second time in just seven years. Much as when I left for Harvard in 1991, multiple threats had forced us to depart Colombia under extreme pressure—the armed left had vowed not to let me leave the country alive. The moment my successor as governor was sworn in, I left the office and headed for the airport with my family in an armored car belonging to the Medellín businessman Fabio Rico Calle—I declined the use of a state vehicle, since I was no longer a public official. We arrived in Bogotá, where I was received by Arthur Leycester Scott Coltman, the British ambassador to Colombia, who took us immediately to his house for safety purposes. A few hours later, he escorted us back to the airport, where we departed for London.

I realized that my family, in many ways, was extremely fortunate. During those years, hundreds of thousands of Colombians were being uprooted from their homes every year by the violence. Many of them did not have anywhere at all to go, much less the relative luxury of an academic appointment at one of the world's finest universities. Ambassador Coltman had generously provided me with the Simón Bolívar scholarship from the British Council,

which enabled me to study. Malcolm Deas, the renowned professor of Colombian history, was a marvelous mentor and sponsor. I also knew that there
was never any shame in a well-considered tactical retreat—to live to fight
another day. But for the experience to be worth the trouble, I would need to
return to Colombia fortified, stronger than ever.

I immersed myself in the academic material, studying topics such as
twentieth-century Latin American history. I read or reread books that
inspired me, such as *Lincoln on Leadership* by Donald T. Phillips; other works
on leadership by John Kotter and Rosabeth Moss Kanter; Indalecio Liévano
Aguirre's books on Bolívar and Rafael Nuñez; works by Jean-Jacques Rous-
seau, Thomas Hobbes and John Locke; and *Democracy in America*, by Alexis
de Tocqueville. I gravitated toward smart Colombians who were also studying at Oxford, such as Jaime Bermúdez, an extremely bright and articulate
student who would later become one of my top aides and, eventually, my
foreign minister. The rigorous study and the stimulating social environment
were like therapy for me.

I worked hard; I met new people; I healed. And before long, I began to
set my sights on the next step in our journey.

10

One of the more unusual and illuminating friendships I made at Oxford was with Joaquin Villalobos, a former guerrilla commander from El Salvador. Villalobos had joined the People's Revolutionary Army, or ERP for its initials in Spanish, in 1971 when he was still a teenager. Villalobos acquired a reputation as a feared rebel commander, but he evolved over time, and by the early 1990s he was in the surprising role of peacemaker. He admitted that the ERP had employed brutal tactics that he now regretted. He played a role in the 1992 peace agreement that ended El Salvador's civil war. Like me, Villalobos was now in Oxford on a scholarship from the British Council; we were almost exactly the same age. We regarded each other somewhat warily at first, but I soon sensed that this was a man with a democratic spirit, who shared my passion for peace and security.

One day, I turned to him with what, for Colombians in 1998, was the critical question of the moment.

"Give me two reasons that you guerrillas in El Salvador ended up agreeing to peace talks," I said.

He thought for a moment. "First, we were in a military stalemate," Villalobos said. "Also, our money dried up. The end of the Cold War meant the end of funds from Eastern Europe. Many Western European NGOs stopped sending us money as well."

"Really?" I asked. "Western European NGOs?"

"Yes," he replied. And it was true—just as in Colombia, the Salvadoran guerrillas had enjoyed a support network in Europe.

Villalobos then turned the question back on me: "Okay, now you give me two good reasons why Colombian guerrilla groups should want to negotiate."

I shrugged. "Frankly, I don't believe the guerrillas have any interest in genuine negotiations."

Villalobos smiled. "That's the problem, you see," he said. "Colombian guerrillas don't need money from NGOs. They are very rich because of drug trafficking. And, unlike in El Salvador, your guerrillas actually do think they can win militarily—because of the lack of determination of the Colombian state."

Back home, events were bearing this out. President Andrés Pastrana won election in 1998 after promising to start peace talks with the "guerrilla" groups. Within weeks of winning the vote, before he was even inaugurated, Pastrana traveled deep into the jungle and met with the FARC's leader, alias Manuel Marulanda, and its military chief, Jorge Briceño, a.k.a. Mono Jojoy. Pastrana agreed to one of the FARC's most contentious demands: that Colombia remove its troops from a large area of our territory approximately the size of Switzerland, some forty-two thousand square kilometers, supposedly so the FARC could gather for peace talks without the fear of being attacked. Pastrana also dispatched several officials to meet with the ELN in Germany.

President Pastrana made these moves in good faith, and his philosophy was consistent with the popular thinking in Colombia at that time. Totally exhausted by the violence of the 1980s and 1990s, many Colombians were certain that dialogue and compromise offered the only path to peace. Through displays of power such as the election-day attacks that accompanied my departure from the governorship, the violent groups had successfully convinced the Colombian population that armed confrontation would only bring more suffering to the masses. Many people believed we were now at a historic juncture. "This peace process is the only opportunity that today's Colombia has to leave behind its tragic history," wrote one prominent Colombian essayist. "If it fails, the only outcome is a brutal war that in just a few decades could devastate any possibility of prosperity or of civilization, and whose next phase will be the eruption of political violence in the cities." This kind of thinking—that Colombians had to choose between either peace negotiations or the apocalypse—was extremely common.

It was also totally wrong. I remembered the message that had been communicated to me from President Castro, via Gabriel García Márquez, the year before, regarding the FARC's real intentions with any negotiations. I was also reminded of one of the Marxist tenets that I'd learned during my university days—the "guerrillas" believed that when the so-called class enemy extends you a hand, you must exploit his weakness.

I certainly did not rule out the concept of negotiations as a possible path to peace in Colombia. During the late 1980s and early 1990s, the Colombian government had brokered cease-fires and demobilizations with members of smaller groups, including the EPL and the M-19, both of which had been debilitated for various reasons. Some of the initial results were mixed: For example, a few of the EPL members who participated in the plans for my "kidnapping" at El Ubérrimo in 1988, and who were released from jail under the amnesty and pardon of 1991, promptly returned to my ranch and stole several dozen cattle, apparently out of sheer spite. Others slipped seamlessly into the drug trade or other criminal activities. Yet a great many others transitioned successfully into civilian life; one group started a new political party that was also named the EPL, except instead of the *Ejército Popular de Liberación* (Popular Liberation Army), the acronym now stood for *Esperanza, Paz, y Libertad* (Hope, Peace, and Liberty). Throughout my career, I enthusiastically worked alongside several individuals who had left the armed struggle behind, people such as Dario Mejía, Mario Agudelo, Rosemberg Pabón, Everth Bustamante, and others.

However, the situation in 1998 with the FARC and ELN was radically different—these groups had never been stronger than they were at that moment. I feared that if Colombia entered peace talks out of weakness—which was clearly the case—then the violent groups would only exploit the government's offer to their tactical and economic advantage, just as Castro had warned. They would use the negotiations as an excuse to build up their numbers and their drug-smuggling operations, and sow even greater terror.

To my regret, this was precisely what happened. As they entered negotiations, both armed groups made almost comically bland concessions—the ELN promised to stop kidnapping "old people, pregnant women, and children," for example—while they continued to terrorize the Colombian population and systematically destroy our infrastructure. Kidnappings would rise geometrically, from 1,038 in 1996 to 3,572 in 2000. Colombia's main oil pipeline was blown up or otherwise attacked on 170 different occasions just in 2001. Meanwhile, the FARC started trying to run the "demilitarized zone" as their own little quasi-state—"Farclandia," some called it—raising their own "taxes" and illegally appointing their own mayors.

Two years after talks started with the FARC, the two sides hadn't even agreed on what the agenda would be. Time and again, the groups would seemingly walk right up to the precipice of a peace deal and then, at the very last moment, change their conditions—or launch a new wave of brutal attacks on Colombian soldiers and civilians. Both sides were paralyzed by unrealistic expectations: Alfonso Cano, one of the FARC's top leaders, declared that the FARC would not demobilize in return for "houses, cars, and scholarships"—or even seats in Congress. "This country will be saved when we have the chance to run the state," he said.

At the very first meeting, Marulanda failed to show up at all—leaving the indelible image of an empty chair as the TV cameras rolled and President Pastrana stood nearby. The FARC's apologists said that it was the government's fault—that the state had still not made enough concessions, and that Marulanda's security was at risk. Unfortunately, Colombia would endure one last cycle of hope and disappointment before a definitive change would come.

11

As my year at Oxford drew to an end, the university's Latin American Centre hosted a seminar with a special guest speaker—a forty-four-year-old former army paratrooper who had just been elected the president of Venezuela.

At that juncture, Hugo Chávez was still an enigma. Nobody quite knew what to expect from him. He had been briefly jailed in 1992 for leading an attempted military coup, but was now, six years later, promising the Venezuelan people that he had moderated his views and believed in democracy. Chávez won the election by heavily criticizing Venezuela's existing political class for having spent the last century squandering the country's immense oil wealth, and for using the royalties to line their own pockets instead of for the good of the people. I found myself agreeing with some of his analysis—I, too, believed that Venezuela needed to find a more equitable way to distribute its natural wealth, for example. But there were two red flags regarding Chávez that had me worried.

As the twentieth century drew to an end, a backlash was taking hold throughout much of Latin America against the policy mistakes of the previous decade. Following the end of the Cold War, many governments around the world had begun overhauling their economies to reflect a new global order in which capitalism was supreme. This transformation—which usually involved the privatization of state industries, the deregulation of business, and the slashing of public-sector payrolls, among other steps—was encouraged by the International Monetary Fund and World Bank, among others. The overarching goal of these changes was to reduce the role of the state and empower private initiative, which had decisively established itself during the previous half century as the best tool available for propelling economic growth and raising living standards around the world.

Some good came out of this long-overdue period of modernization: Some of the reforms of the 1990s would make Latin American economies stronger. But in many cases, the reforms were performed sloppily or with dogmatic zeal, dismantling too much of the social safety net and leaving countries overexposed to abrupt shifts in capital flows. The state ended up abdicating its essential functions out of the mistaken, overly simplistic belief that government is always bad, and the "market" always knows best.

My studies had led me to believe in a middle path—I thought, for example, that we needed to open our economies to trade, but through carefully negotiated bilateral or multilateral agreements that ensured fair rules and benefits for all sides. I believed we should try to attract foreign investment of all kinds while simultaneously strengthening financial regulation; that way we could ensure that the rules were followed, and punish those who violated them. We clearly needed to eliminate excesses in state payrolls and in bureaucratic expenses. But the state also needed to be robust so that we could implement smart measures to take care of the environment, to protect workers' rights, and to ensure a degree of social equality via sound health, education, and other policies. These were functions that the private sector simply could not fulfill. The state needed to actively cultivate a more inclusive kind of capitalism in which all people would benefit: what we called a "Communitarian State." In sum, I believed that, to fully harness the benefits of capitalism, we should not eliminate the fundamental functions of the state, but reaffirm and strengthen them.

This was the first element that concerned me about Chávez—many people suspected that he had a different, more radical agenda in mind. While he had not yet divulged full details of the economic policies he would pursue, Chávez seemed to be compelled by a nostalgia for the failed Marxist revolutions of Latin America's past. For him, the backlash against the "neoliberal" excesses of the 1990s would consist of lashing out at the private sector and undermining investment, as well as institutions. One sign of this was Chávez's early and ardent alliance with Fidel Castro—who, despite the crumbling buildings and crippling poverty in Cuba, had never quite abandoned his dream of spreading his revolution to the rest of Latin America. Castro had been saying publicly for decades that Latin America needed a socialist country with oil— Venezuela fit the bill perfectly. The two leaders, together, seemed set on laying the groundwork for a new, activist bloc of leftist leaders in the region: a "twenty-first century socialism."

Another reason had led me to attend Chávez's talk that day: I wanted to know what would become of the unique brotherly bonds between our two nations, which shared a common liberator in Simón Bolívar and had once formed part of the same country. Venezuela was also Colombia's second-biggest trading partner behind the United States—meaning that an extended period of economic dysfunction next door would have direct implications for our house, also. After listening to what he had to say, I felt that he had been ambiguous regarding the support he would offer Colombia in its struggle against illegal armed groups.

When the right moment came, I raised my hand, and Chávez called on me.

"Mr. President-elect," I said, "what is your vision with respect to the armed groups in Colombia?"

Chávez smiled and said that he was compelled to remain "neutral" in matters regarding Colombia and the FARC.

His answer surprised me. This was not like, say, Yugoslavia deciding to remain neutral between the two great powers of the Cold War. No—this was the leader of a neighboring democracy with which Colombia had a long tradition of peaceful and positive relations. He seemed to be saying that as the president of Venezuela he would not make a distinction between Colombia's democratically elected government and rogue terrorists who massacred our citizens and profited from the trade of illegal narcotics. I simply could not understand this stance.

I raised my hand to speak again. "I hope you'll reconsider," I said, "because Venezuela is our brother nation, and in Colombia we are trying to fight these drug-trafficking terrorists. Venezuela cannot remain neutral—I hope you'll help the democratic Colombian state."

Chávez politely nodded, smiled, and quickly changed the subject. This conversation would simply have to be continued at another time. A few weeks later, I boarded a plane back to Colombia.

12

"You're going to lose this election. You'll be vindicated by history, just like Churchill eventually was. But you will not win."

I had recently returned to Colombia, and I was having lunch with one of the country's senior statesmen—Alfonso López Michelsen, who had been president from 1974 to 1978. Colombian presidents generally did not retire from public life once their time in office was up, per the American tradition; instead, they tended to remain very active in our nation's affairs, serving as ambassadors or as leaders of their parties. President López Michelsen remained a critical figure in Colombian politics, respected by me and many others for his intelligence and academic knowledge. I had been invited to his house by him and his wife, Cecilia Caballero, and we were discussing the upcoming 2002 presidential campaign.

In some respects, President López Michelsen was right—I faced long odds. At that juncture, in late 1999, polls showed that my name recognition nationwide was about 50 percent, compared to 97 percent for my two principal opponents, both of whom had been candidates in the previous election. Even those who knew me weren't particularly interested in voting for me; I was polling around 10 percent. Complicating matters further, I was running as an independent candidate. The Liberal Party had already decided to nominate the same man who had lost in 1998. I believed Colombia needed a fresh start in every sense, so I decided to run outside of the party structure. This was risky: No candidate had won Colombia's presidency outside the traditional two-party system for decades. In fact, the last two prominent candidates to run outside their political parties' establishments were Luis Carlos Galán and Jorge Eliécer Gaitán—both of whom died at the hands of assassins.

"Wait just a moment, Alfonso," Doña Cecilia said. She smiled regally and turned to me. "What is it exactly that you will propose?"

"*Seguridad democrática*," I said. "Democratic security." And then I offered them a brief summary of what this entailed.

Doña Cecilia listened with great interest. She then turned to her husband. "Alfonso," she said, "with that proposal, Álvaro will win this election."

Indeed, the idea was relatively basic: I proposed to extend security and the rule of law throughout Colombia, while simultaneously strengthening our democracy. The concept was easy enough to understand. But to Colombian ears, especially, it was something very new—and even radical.

In fact, since the 1960s, people in Latin America had generally equated security with fascism. The word—indeed, the very concept of enforcing the law—conjured up images of storm troopers in riot gear, clouds of tear gas, presidents announcing states of siege, and various abuses by the right-wing dictatorships of countries such as Chile and Argentina. I, too, was horrified by the atrocities that were committed over the years in the name of fighting communism or other causes. I believed that governments that tried to improve security while trampling on human rights might very well achieve short-term pacification, but they would never achieve long-term reconciliation. That just wasn't good enough for us; we wanted a lasting peace.

So what I proposed was totally different. I believed that we could regain control over 100 percent of Colombia's territory while respecting human rights and *extending* the reach of democracy. We would send the military, the police, and other agents of the state such as teachers and doctors into areas where they hadn't been for years—if ever. This was not "war"—this was enforcement. It was the legitimate and necessary exercise of power by an elected government. We would extend the writ of the state to everyone, regardless of their ideology or socioeconomic status; workers, union leaders, businesspeople, and journalists would all enjoy the benefits of living in a strong, secure Colombia. For the millions of Colombians who suffered from the tyrannical authoritarianism of the FARC and other violent groups, our policies would therefore mean more democracy, not less. They would finally get to enjoy security and the other full benefits of the democratic government they elected. Hence: democratic security.

In practice, this meant, among other things, a dramatic expansion of our security forces. If the common thread in Colombia's decades of bloodshed was a lack of resolve and resources by the central government, as our country's history and my own personal experience had led me to believe, then any solution had to start by putting more and better tools in the hands of the state. Several disturbing statistics reinforced just how woefully insufficient our resources were. At that moment, Colombia had seventy-five thousand active police in its entire national territory; the New York City Police Department had forty-two thousand. Put another way: We had about 1.73 police per one thousand people, while the Inter-American Development Bank recommended that a country with moderately high criminality should have at least 4.2 per thousand. Obviously we needed far more than that.

Our message was simple enough—but it certainly did not catch on right away. With all apologies to Doña Cecilia's political acumen, most Colombians initially had misgivings about democratic security. Some people still clung to hope for the peace talks; others believed that while my plan might sound good in theory, in practice it would prove impossible—or lead to even more bloodshed. Meanwhile, most within the Colombian media refused to take my candidacy seriously. The national newspapers treated me like an exotic species of snake: interesting to look at, but hazardous to touch. Many within Colombia's business establishment didn't have much interest in me, either: A group of prominent industrialists visited Lina and me at our house in Rionegro and said I would simply have to wait my "turn," until at least 2006, because they saw zero chance for me in 2002.

Our campaign moved forward with the usual austerity and dedication. The truth is, I never stop campaigning; it's not something I only do during election season. Someone once asked Lina whether I had already started my campaign. "Alvaro never stops campaigning," she responded. For the first several months, while traveling around the country, I occasionally slept in my friends' houses. The campaign apparatus in those early days itself consisted of only me and Any Vasquez, my trusted and loyal adviser from the governorship. We didn't even have a proper headquarters—my friend Juan Rodrigo Hurtado owned a call center, where he loaned us a cubicle equipped with a telephone, a fax machine, and a computer. Any helped arrange my schedule, while I traveled from town to town. We went months without actually seeing each other. But that was the path available to us: We would simply have to establish our credibility and earn Colombians' confidence, one vote at a time.

13

I didn't fully realize it at the time, but starting from near the bottom of the polls was the best thing that could have ever happened to me.

I listened to *everyone*. When campaigns start big, sometimes candidates think only of what they're saying, and fail to fully absorb what they're told. We experienced the total opposite. I traveled the entire country, from Pasto to the coastal plains of Santa Marta. I spent innumerable hours on radio call-in shows, some with a listening area of just a few miles of isolated area—the smaller the better, since the most isolated areas of Colombia were usually the areas most in need of help. Some programs lasted all night, from ten p.m. to six a.m. I took all kinds of questions, totally unfiltered and with no prior screening; sometimes people called only to insult or criticize me. But the vast majority were earnest, real people with real problems, expectations, and dreams. I often ended up asking them more questions than they did of me.

This concept was also somewhat new in Colombia—for years, our politicians had made a big spectacle of dialoguing with the country's criminals, but no one was listening to the actual community. For me, direct dialogue with the people was critical—as senator, as governor, and later as president, I made it my mission to talk to as many people on the "street" as possible. This allowed me to get information directly from the source, eliminating the middleman—aides, journalists, or anyone else who might have a vested interest in altering reality to suit their needs. Talking to people in the community was almost always more instructive than taking questions from journalists—who usually came into interviews with a bias, or were focused on the latest parochial political gossip or intrigue in big cities. In contrast, "real" people tended to focus on their real-life needs—on the big, substantive issues of the day. I would listen to stories of how their lives had been affected by Colombia's violence, how their businesses had suffered, but how they still had hope for their children's generation. I heard their concerns about education, health care, roads, and housing. I learned volumes.

Taking the concept a step further, we held frequent town hall meetings—what we called *talleres democráticos*, or "democratic workshops." This was

another concept that dated back to my governorship, and it essentially consisted of gathering people in a room or auditorium to exchange ideas about
solutions to Colombia's problems. For example, I would say, "Let's take ten
minutes and write down our five principal aspirations for Colombia in coming years." Everyone would jot down their ideas, and then I would randomly
select someone from the audience to start. We invited people from different
political parties, from different backgrounds. We invited university professors
who were specialists in certain areas. Their ideas informed and complemented
the "*Manifesto Democrático*," the 100-point government platform that was
composed so Colombians would know exactly what we stood for, and hold us
accountable later. We held hundreds of such meetings over the course of the
campaign, about seventy of which lasted all day—upward of twelve hours.
They were an invaluable tool for interacting directly with the community,
gathering innovative policy ideas, and building my credibility as a candidate.
It was one of these sessions that also produced the official slogan of our
campaign: *Mano firme, corazón grande:* "Firm hand, big heart."

Whenever possible, we held our rallies and conversations in broad daylight. We defied the terrorists who sought to intimidate us and deprive us of
our democratic rights. In those days, the simple act of holding a campaign
rally felt like a celebration of normalcy; we took great joy in it. But even then
we had to make allowances. I remember one rally in a small town, where
people began taking photos of me with their digital cameras—which were
still a relatively new phenomenon in Colombia in that era. I posed happily,
taking great pride in the bright-eyed young families who had come out to
speak with us. But then, like an epiphany, I realized the gravity of our actions.
Many of those present would have to return home via highways where the
terrorists frequently set up roadblocks. Anyone with an image of me on their
cameras would surely run the risk of severe retribution. Saddened, I urged
those present to erase the pictures, and they complied. It was a rare concession, but it was a necessary one. That was the country that we all lived in.

Even when I traveled abroad, I saw signs of the urgency of our task. I made
two campaign trips to Miami, where I spoke with many members of Colombia's expatriate community—which was, sadly, growing exponentially larger
by the day. As many as one million Colombians moved abroad between 1996
and 2001 in search of greater security and economic opportunity, according
to a study at the time by ANIF, a think tank. After one speech at a Miami

university, I was approached by a man who expressed his gratitude for our honoring our debts to his family following the death of my father.

I also made a point of talking directly to the individuals and groups who were most skeptical of my campaign. I spoke to labor unions, human rights groups, and others and assured them that democratic security would protect *everyone*—not just people of a certain socioeconomic group or political ideology. I answered every question about my past, about my years as governor, until there weren't any left. Some of the most intense criticism of me could be found at our public universities, including my alma mater—so I went to campuses constantly, and dialogued with many people from the extreme left. I told them that I would support a university system that enjoyed full liberties, that was scientific, pluralistic, and critical—though never violent.

I often concluded my speeches to young people by saying, "I know that some of you are for me, and others are against me. But please allow me to ask one question: How many of you have, at one point or another, contemplated the possibility of buying a one-way ticket out of Colombia—of leaving our country?"

Inevitably, the vast majority of them would raise their hands.

"So you see," I continued, "that whether you agree with my ideas or not, we are united in our belief that Colombia must change. All I ask is that you give me a chance to do my best, so our country becomes a place where you want to stay."

After two years spent mostly on the road, visiting far-flung corners of the country, I had a fuller vision of Colombia's reality than virtually anyone among the political establishment in big cities. I was also aware of one other hidden truth—I knew, long before anyone else did, that the momentum in the race was starting to turn.

14

As the election year of 2002 dawned, I was managing a consistent 27 percent in polls—about 7 percentage points behind the frontrunner—and trending upward. Our internal studies showed that the message of democratic security was resonating with much of the population, and that word-of-mouth was a critical factor in my support. The end-of-year holidays, when Colombians traditionally gather with their families to celebrate and chew over the big questions of the day, including politics, saw me move up in some polls. With this groundswell of support, our shoestring campaign was finally able to establish a real campaign headquarters—an apartment in Bogotá. Any Vasquez and I were now joined by a number of advisers who made invaluable contributions—people such as Jaime Bermúdez, Fabio Echeverri Correa, José Roberto Arango, Alicia Arango, Luis Guillermo Plata, Mario Pacheco, Alberto Velásquez, and others.

Meanwhile, the peace process was on life support. Three years of talks had failed to yield any concrete results, and the FARC and the ELN continued to mercilessly terrorize the population at large, while the paramilitaries expanded their murderous activities like never before. In 2001 alone, the violence resulted in about two thousand civilian deaths, there were more than three thousand kidnappings, and some three hundred thousand people were forced to flee their homes. Just as President Castro had warned years before, the FARC took full advantage of the demilitarized zone to build up their positions and become ever richer from drug trafficking. President Pastrana suspended negotiations on multiple occasions, only to restart them again after the FARC made new promises. In late January 2002, talks were halted and then resumed yet again—and the other leading presidential candidates agreed to visit the staging ground for the negotiations in San Vicente del Caguán. I refused, declaring again that the FARC had no real interest in talks at this time.

And then, with the suddenness of a mudslide, the whole thing came tumbling down.

On February 20, four FARC terrorists armed with handguns hijacked an

Aires airline flight bound for Bogotá, with some thirty people aboard. They forced the plane down on a narrow highway near the town of Hobo, very close to the demilitarized zone. There on the ground, several dozen terrorists were waiting to whisk away the flight's most illustrious passenger: Senator Jorge Géchem Turbay, the president of the Colombian Senate's peace commission.

The symbolism of the attack was evident to everyone—Senator Gechem was one of the most prominent voices of peace and reconciliation in Colombia. The FARC was essentially thumbing its nose at the Colombian people and the country's democratic leadership, demonstrating once and for all that they had no interest in negotiation. That the FARC had hijacked a commercial airliner only five months after the attacks of September 11, 2001, in the United States only served to accentuate the group's true identity as a terrorist group on a par with the world's worst. The FARC would hold Géchem captive in the jungle for the next six years.

Just hours after the kidnapping, President Pastrana went on national television and declared peace talks with the FARC to be definitively over. "It's not possible to sign agreements on one side while putting guns to the heads of innocent people on the other," he seethed, visibly furious. Midway through the speech, President Pastrana paused to exhibit vivid images of the destruction that the FARC had wrought while ostensibly negotiating peace: destroyed bridges, a child's lifeless body, buildings gutted by bombs. He showed aerial photographs of airstrips and other amenities that the FARC had built up inside the demilitarized zone. All told, the FARC's actions had proven their intentions once and for all, President Pastrana said. "Today, the guerrillas have been unmasked and have shown their true face, the face of senseless violence."

As he addressed the nation, people all over Bogotá honked their car horns in a resounding, emotional display of agreement with his decision to end the talks. I immediately telephoned President Pastrana and expressed my support for his decision. Resounding voices of approval also came from elsewhere. The United States, the European Commission, and the United Nations all issued statements of support. The secretary-general of the UN, Kofi Annan, condemned the FARC for "clear violations" of human rights and for undermining the peace process.

Hours after his address, President Pastrana dispatched warplanes and thirteen thousand troops into the former "demilitarized zone" and started bombing FARC positions in an effort to retake the area. Outraged by the loss of its prized staging ground, and perhaps sensing that an irrevocable tipping point in public opinion had been reached, the FARC responded by lashing out with a wave of unprecedented brutality. Their actions would set the stage for the coming eight years.

Three days after the peace talks collapsed, the FARC kidnapped Ingrid Betancourt, one of my fellow candidates for president. Betancourt had not been polling near the top of the field, but she had captured the imagination of many Colombians with her crusade against corruption and her unique personal story. I had met Betancourt in person only once as governor, but I was aware of her past as a citizen of both France and Colombia, and her work in our Senate. Despite warnings from the Colombian military, she had traveled to San Vicente del Caguán—the "capital" of the now-extinct FARC demilitarized zone—to show solidarity with the city's mayor, an ally. The FARC stopped her vehicle as she tried to drive to Caguán from the nearby city of Florencia, and took her hostage. Her abduction immediately became an international cause célèbre—drawing condemnations from the French government, the United Nations and others. The long, winding road to Betancourt's liberation would become one of the core focuses of my government.

Meanwhile, the mayhem intensified to a degree that shocked even the most hardened Colombians. In the city of Villavicencio, just south of Bogotá, the FARC exploded a dynamite stick in a crowded nightclub area, drawing bystanders to the scene—and then they set off a second, bigger explosion, killing twelve people and wounding seventy others. They stepped up their attacks on our infrastructure, blowing up pipelines, power pylons, and waterworks. Blackouts became ever more frequent in our cities. In March, two men shot dead Monseñor Isaías Duarte Cancino, the archbishop of Cali, as he left a wedding at a small church. Beloved by many Colombians as the "apostle of peace," the archbishop had been a vocal critic of the *narcoterroristas* and their crimes. Of the armed groups in general, he once asked God to help their members "understand that theirs is not a just war, but merely a repeating of savage acts of the saddest times in human history." I had personally worked with him when he was a bishop in Urabá during my governorship, and we developed partnerships in education that largely benefited the poor. Devastated by the death of such a brave, uncompromising, and inspirational man,

I attended the archbishop's funeral, along with twenty thousand other people from Colombia and around the world. Pope John Paul II issued a statement in which he lamented Archbishop Duarte's death, and called on all Colombians to embrace peace.

The violent ones paid no heed. A few weeks later, in April, the FARC disguised several of their operatives as members of a bomb squad and entered the state legislature in Cali. The FARC tricked twelve of the legislators into voluntarily boarding a bus—and then drove them away, taking them as their hostages. That same month, as the FARC and the paramilitaries fought a pitched battle over a major drug transit point near the town of Bojayá, the FARC fired a gas-cylinder bomb into a church where many people had taken refuge. That attack killed 117 civilians, including forty-eight children, and was denounced by human rights groups as a war crime.

The Colombian people had had enough. The FARC's role in the peace process had been exposed as a farce. The weakness of our institutions was painfully obvious. The hunger for security was insatiable. By the end of February, days after Senator Géchem's plane was hijacked, I began polling above 50 percent in voting intentions for the first time. The country clamored for a major transformative change—a total break with Colombia's past. Our proposal of democratic security offered a clear way forward.

The final hurdle to the presidency would be a straightforward one: to stay alive.

15

The FARC had already come for me at least three times in 2001. In one plot, a man pretending to be a theological student won the trust of my campaign aides, and then, in an apparent last-minute attack of conscience, he turned himself in to the police—the night before he planned to set off a bomb in my campaign office. Based on this man's confession, the police were able to capture other FARC militia members and a suitcase bomb that the police said used technology acquired from ETA and the IRA. In a separate attack, in the city of Barranquilla on the Caribbean coast, the FARC attached explosives to a carriage pulled by a donkey that was supposed to blow up as my caravan drove by. That bomb did explode—most of the damage was borne by a passing taxi and its passengers. The incident would become known as the *burro bomba*.

Those initial attacks were child's play compared to what happened as election day drew closer, and my status as the frontrunner became indisputable. We received a constant torrent of information regarding assassination plots hatched by the FARC, the ELN, and other groups—each faction now seemed to be competing with the others to see who could kill me first, as if it were a kind of blood sport. "Álvaro is not just a guerrilla military target," said my friend Andrés Uriel Gallego. "He is a war trophy."

The outlaws knew perfectly well what awaited them if I was elected president.

I decided not to pay too much attention to the threats I received and kept walking through the streets of Colombia unbowed. I put my faith in God and trusted the very capable people charged with my security. We also received critical support from the governments of Britain and Spain, which generously provided us with bomb-jamming devices and other technology aimed at keeping us safe.

My opponents also attacked me through blander, but equally predictable means. Constant rumors swirled that newspapers were about to publish a photo of me with Pablo Escobar. A new wave of false accusations surfaced alleging that my family members had made alliances over the years with the cartels or with paramilitary groups. In perhaps the strangest accusation of all, a book was published in Europe accusing me and my family of ordering murders at the troubled Antioquia *panela* sugar operation, which we had given to the workers in the 1970s. Why were the accusations so strange? Because the "murdered" workers named in the book were, in fact, very much alive.

We responded to all of these false charges with total honesty and transparency: I issued an exhaustive financial statement that included the name of the Colombian bank where I had kept my money since I was eighteen years old, and even the number of the account. I also gave reporters the names of the banks where I had temporarily opened accounts while at Oxford and Harvard—the only two foreign accounts I ever had. And I reiterated, yet again, that as president I would crack down on all of the *narcoterroristas* with equal vigor, with the goal of bringing peace to all Colombians.

As the campaign gained even more momentum, and a sense of inevitability began to take hold, the FARC made one last big roll of the dice. On April 15, six weeks before election day, a remote-detonated bomb exploded by the side of a busy street in Barranquilla as my caravan drove by. The force of the explosion was so massive that it blew out the tires and cracked a window on our heavily armored vehicle. Our driver was left momentarily shell-shocked. From the passenger seat, I grabbed control of the wheel and used my left foot to manipulate the accelerator and advance us a bit farther, in case there was a second bomb hidden somewhere.

I looked back and immediately checked on the other passengers in our vehicle: Alicia Arango with her three children, Julio Aldana, and Senator Dieb Maloof. By the grace of God, they were fine. In the background, though, I saw the twisted wreckage of motorcycles and broken bodies through a cloud of smoke. Once the vehicle was out of danger, I hit the brakes, jumped out, and ran to the scene to try to aid the survivors. Tragically, the bomb had exploded just as a city bus and many pedestrians were passing by. The final toll was three dead and twenty-two injured, including five police officers and a three-year-old girl who lost one of her legs.

By this point, such displays of barbarism and disregard for innocent people only intensified the Colombian people's desire for change. Following the bomb attack in Barranquilla, we decided to stop holding most outdoor events because the risk to civilians was too great. Much of my campaign staff was forced to live and work in a hotel with bulletproof windows in Bogotá. But our campaign would not be stopped. At one rally in Medellín, we gathered some eighteen thousand supporters in the city's bullring, and mounted television screens so I could address the crowd remotely from a TV studio in our headquarters in Bogotá. I was reminded of campaigning from the phone booth in Harvard Square in 1991—this time the invisible audience really *was* huge. The response was tremendous.

On May 26, 2002, despite a constellation of threats from every terrorist group imaginable, Colombians went to the polls. More than two hundred thousand soldiers and police fanned out across our territory and helped ensure a mostly peaceful election. When the votes were all tallied, I had won a resounding victory with 53 percent of the vote—enough to avoid a runoff, and 19 percentage points above the nearest challenger. We now had an overwhelming democratic mandate to pursue democratic security.

That night, I addressed the nation with my heart full of gratitude and hope. Holding back tears, I thanked my family, I thanked the country for their votes, and I promised to govern for all Colombians. I paid homage to my mother, and prayed for her to "accompany me from heaven with the love for my country that she always taught me." I honored the memory of my father, noting that he had been murdered when he was just a few months older than I was now. I also spoke of the fallen presidential candidates who had come before me: Jorge Eliécer Gaitán and Luis Carlos Galán; I had telephoned the latter's widow immediately prior to my speech.

I vowed to lead our economy to greater prosperity and provide opportunities for jobs and education through rigorous social policies. I asked our Latin American neighbors, and the rest of the world, for help resolving our problems. And I called on the violent groups to put down their arms, pledging "reconciliation" for those who obliged.

"We ask for God to illuminate us, to give us talent and energy, to help us leave a better Colombia," I concluded. "This is a moment of great responsibility."

Now the most trying part of our journey would begin.

SECTION FOUR

Confidence

"With public sentiment, nothing can fail; without it, nothing can succeed.
Consequently, he who molds public sentiment goes deeper than he who
enacts statutes or pronounces decisions."

—ABRAHAM LINCOLN

1

Minutes after I was sworn in as president, we heard the sounds.

Like distant firecrackers. Or faint metal drums. The truth is, I barely noticed them. At that moment, I was walking with Lina through the halls of Congress, having just taken the oath of office. I saw Lina's eyes widen with concern. I gave her hand a slight squeeze, trying to reassure her.

"Those were bombs," she whispered into my ear. "They were very close, Álvaro."

Her hands were trembling.

I nodded, projecting my best outward sense of calm. I was now the president, and I knew that eyes were upon me. As we rushed to descend the stairs outside Congress, Lina stumbled and nearly fell. I caught her by the arm at the last moment.

Captain Rodolfo Amaya, who would become one of my most trusted and valuable aides, was waiting for us at the bottom of the stairs.

"Mr. President, there have been some dangerous explosions," he said. "We're very worried."

I thanked Captain Amaya, and then looked across the plaza toward the Casa de Nariño, the presidential palace. President Pastrana, his team, and members of the high military command were standing outside the palace's front door, waiting for me. I briskly crossed the plaza, feeling my focus build with each step. I shook President Pastrana's hand, and sincerely thanked him for his four years of service to our nation. Then I turned to address the military commanders.

Right there, standing outside the presidential palace's front doors, as smoke billowed in the near distance and sirens echoed throughout the capital—this was the first Security Council meeting of my presidency.

"Strength," I urged them. "This is what we came for. This is why we're here."

2

For weeks, we had suspected trouble. We knew that the FARC, unnerved by my election and the dramatic shift of public opinion that enabled it, would attempt to flex their muscles. They would try to intimidate all Colombians and show us they would not go down without a fight. As inauguration day drew closer, we received persistent but vague reports that the terrorists were planning an attack. It became clearer than ever to me that our intelligence capabilities were not yet what they needed to be. Even in our capital, even for an event such as this, we had no real clue what the FARC was planning.

The FARC appeared to be gunning for the symbolism of an attack as much as any strategic result. The roster of planned visitors to the inaugural ceremonies was extensive: Dozens of foreign dignitaries from around the region and the world, ranging from President Hugo Chávez of Venezuela to Robert Zoellick, the U.S. trade representative and future president of the World Bank. This group had executed a symbolic attack in order to obtain strategic results. By attacking the heart of government power as the world watched, and perhaps even disrupting the ceremonies themselves, the FARC believed they could send a message that no one was safe—that they could reach anyone, anywhere, at any time. An attack would reinforce the tired old theory that a posture of confrontation by the Colombian government would only lead to even greater violence. They may have also believed that a dramatic disruption on day one would give them a stronger position in future negotiations with my government.

As the day grew closer, the outgoing government took numerous preventive steps. Commercial airspace above Bogotá would be closed during the ceremonies. Helicopter gunships and a P-3 surveillance aircraft—belonging to the U.S. Customs Service—circled overhead. All told, more than twenty thousand soldiers and police were posted throughout the capital. The visiting foreign delegations would have been forgiven for thinking they'd arrived in Kabul rather than Bogotá.

On the morning of the inauguration, while I was engaged with protocolary meetings, representatives from the U.S. Central Intelligence Agency requested an urgent meeting with Lina and some of my top aides at the Hotel Tequendama in downtown Bogotá, where we were staying. The CIA told them, point-blank, that the FARC was not going to "allow" me to take office. They said they had intelligence that the road between the hotel and the foreign ministry was mined with explosives. While they did not explicitly recommend canceling or modifying the inaugural ceremonies, they did say the threat level made our plans for that day "extremely dangerous."

I was determined that we would proceed as normally as possible, without bowing to the terrorist threat. So Colonel Mauricio Santoyo, the National Police official charged with my security, opted for an unorthodox solution. He dispatched a large caravan of SUVs and motorcycles from the hotel to the palace. There were no attacks. So then Santoyo did it again. And again. Three separate caravans, all of which appeared to be carrying me, passed without incident. Finally, all of us quietly boarded into a separate vehicle: Lina and the boys; Vice President Francisco Santos Calderón, his wife, and his children; my chief of staff, Alicia Arango; Sandra Suarez; my top communications aide, Ricardo Galán; and me. With just two motorcycles flanking our vehicle, we sped through oncoming traffic on the wrong side of Carrera 10 in downtown Bogotá, headed for the palace.

For decades, Colombian presidents have traditionally walked from the Palacio de San Carlos—the seat of the foreign ministry—to Congress in a celebration of our democracy and division of powers. Yet shortly before the big day, I was approached by the Colombian military and informed that this walk—only two blocks!—would not be possible because of the security threat. My family and I would have to ride in an armored vehicle instead. Ultimately, we would rely upon the same vehicle I used during the campaign—an SUV owned by Dr. Carlos Ardila, equipped with a signal jammer lent to us by the government of the Spanish prime minister, José María Aznar.

This was Colombia on the day of my inauguration—our airspace closed, an American surveillance plane circling overhead, tens of thousands of troops patrolling the streets, untold numbers of terrorists lurking in our midst, and the president confined to a borrowed armored car equipped with borrowed foreign technology.

And still, it was not enough.

3

On August 7, 2002, terrorists from the FARC fired at least fourteen mortar shells upon downtown Bogotá in an attempt to disrupt or force the cancellation of my inaugural ceremonies. One of the projectiles hit within the grounds of the Casa de Nariño, injuring four policemen, but the others missed their mark. Tragically, some of the errant shells landed in Cartucho, a humble neighborhood just a few hundred meters from the palace. An empty elementary school and several nearby houses were also hit. The final toll: nineteen dead, among them three children, and more than sixty wounded.

None of the visiting dignitaries were hurt. But the trauma and mayhem sown by the attack were immense. "Panic reigned in the minutes after the explosions," read an account by the *Los Angeles Times*. "Bleeding soldiers ran through the streets and air force jets and military helicopters thundered overhead. Bodies lay twisted in rubble. . . . Some buildings were left with gaping holes."

The tragedy could have easily been even more severe. The police managed to quickly zero in on the house from which the mortars were fired, where they found an additional eighty or so 120-millimeter shells, plus several sacks of explosives and coils of detonator cords. Elsewhere in Bogotá, the police discovered a second battery of about ninety mortars that were aimed at a military academy in the northern part of the city. The scale of the attack marked yet another new low point in the FARC's methods. General Hector Dario Castro, Bogotá's chief of police, compared the attack to 9/11 because it disregarded innocent civilian lives in a way that Colombian law enforcement officials had never seen in our country before. "We knew an attack was possible," General Castro said, "but we never established the method the terrorists were going to use."

The reaction at home and abroad was resounding. President Bush denounced the attacks as an attempt to "kill the aspirations of the Colombian people for a free, prosperous and democratic state." The United Nations condemned the attacks as well. Yet there was also a new round of predictions that the attacks signaled the beginning of an even worse era of bloodshed and suffering for Colombia. One so-called expert predicted on CNN that my policies would lead to a hundred thousand deaths in Colombia during my first year in office, and unemployment would soar to 40 percent. Another foreign analyst said, "Uribe's embrace of militaristic solutions to stubborn social problems could contribute to an intensified stalemate for years to come."

I was not cowed, and I didn't think Colombia needed to be either. Even during those challenging initial moments of my presidency, I believed that the direction of our struggle had already begun to shift course once and for all. Years later, in defending Colombia and our government, President Clinton would wisely observe: "It's important to look at Colombia not as a photo, frozen in time, but as a film that's still in progress, and has to be observed from the very beginning." In other words, we could not allow individual moments in time to break our will, no matter how tragic—we had to look at where we had been, and above all where we were going. Our political will was strong. We had most of the country behind us. We had a clear plan for success. Deep in my heart, I knew that my government would not be defined by these abominable acts of terrorism by a desperate, marginalized minority. No, it could not be so. The attacks of that August day were merely a preamble: the first few seconds of the dramatic story that would follow.

4

Was it airpower? Was it intelligence work? Was it the aid we received from the United States? Over the years, I've often been asked, What was the first step that led to Colombia's breakthrough? How did we start our journey from the chaos of my inauguration, with corpses scattered across the streets of Bogotá, to the qualified successes that came later? What was the tipping point? Truth be told, I have always been hesitant to oversimplify what happened—it was eight years of hard labor, and there was no single, magical cure for what ailed Colombia. But when asked to pinpoint one element that got the virtuous cycle moving in our favor, I think back to a conversation I had in March 2002, when I invited my running mate, Francisco Santos Calderón, to join my ticket.

"Pacho," as his friends called him, was a shining example of Colombian integrity and bravery. A career journalist, he was kidnapped in 1990 on the orders of Pablo Escobar and the Medellín cartel, and then used as a pawn as the *narcos* coerced the government to drop their efforts to extradite their leaders to the United States. Following his release from eight long months in captivity, Santos became a passionate and uncompromising advocate against kidnapping, denouncing it as a tool of terrorism, and founding a nonprofit group that supported kidnap victims and their families. His was such a clear and righteous voice that, inevitably, the violent ones sought to silence him. At the moment that I invited him to be my running mate in March 2002, Santos was living in exile in Spain, where he had spent the previous two years following innumerable threats on his life. Accepting my offer would mean not only being constantly by my side—with all the risks that implied—but also returning to a country that had chased him away, as it had so many other millions of Colombians.

We had met in person eleven years before, as graduate students at Harvard, and we had only seen each other on a few occasions since. Despite our lack of personal familiarity, I never shied away from taking a chance on people who I determined could be effective as leaders. I had admired Pacho for years for his passion and conviction, and I was certain that he could offer our government many attributes, among them a clear moral voice on questions of human rights. Still, when I made the offer, he initially balked.

"I'm honored," Santos said. "But I have to tell you, I don't know anything about government."

"You'll be fine," I assured him. "At the beginning, we'll only have to worry about one thing."

"What's that?" he asked, surprised.

"Confidence."

An easy thing to say—a much more difficult thing to execute. But I had been elaborating a detailed plan in my mind for decades. And at four a.m. on my first full day as president, we got to work.

5

Before dawn on the morning of August 8, we were wheels-up on FAC-001 for Valledupar—one of the most violent cities in all of Colombia. Valledupar was a kind of crossroads: a leafy and well-planned city near but not quite on the Caribbean Sea, and also close to the confluence of two mountain ranges and the Venezuelan border. Its strategic location made it extremely sought-after territory by the drug traffickers—and the FARC, the ELN, and para-militaries had been battling for dominance over Valledupar for years, turning the city into an epicenter of kidnappings and massacres. Valledupar was also well-known nationally as a cultural capital, the home of the *parrandas val-lenatas*, a festive Caribbean music performed by beloved artists such as Rafael Escalona. When I campaigned there, many people complained that Colombia's politicians came to their city only for its festivals. "We're covered in blood," one man told me, "and they only come here to drink whiskey and listen to our music."

This was exactly the kind of place I was determined to turn around, and I promised the people of Valledupar that I would be in their city before sunrise on my first morning as president. This meant skipping the usual meetings with foreign dignitaries in Bogotá. But I was determined to spend as much of my presidency as possible outside of my office. I wanted to walk among the people and get a true, unaltered vision of the country's challenges, just as I had done during the presidential campaign. It would be so from the first day.

I'll never forget the experience of landing in Valledupar that first morning—hard and fast, like landing in a war zone—and then making the harried, white-knuckled drive by convoy into the city center. Military snipers lurked on seemingly every roof. Tense-looking soldiers with rifles stood guard every few meters. Some people on my staff stared out the windows wide-eyed, maybe even frightened. And when we arrived at City Hall, the towns-people and officials were eerily silent—too scared to talk, able to manage only a nervous hum of worried whispers and scattered applause when we entered the room.

These people needed something they could believe in. And it needed to happen quickly, before the violent groups could strike with more attacks like the one on my inauguration and erase the fragile hope that had accompanied my election.

Thus, one of the most important strategies at the beginning of my presidency was to focus on "early victories"—quick, tangible signs of progress that would demonstrate to Colombians that our government's policies were feasible. We considered this separate from our larger strategic initiatives, such as expanding the police force—these were important, but they would take months to show concrete, real-world results. We needed something that people could see and touch right away—preferably from the first day. We certainly didn't have much money, so any plan would have to be low in cost. But it had to be dramatic. Because without that short-term burst of confidence, in a crisis like ours, faith could quickly erode, and we would never have a chance to implement any of those long-term plans; in order for people to believe in our plans we needed to transform skepticism to hope.

So what would our "quick victory" be in Valledupar? We decided on a strategy that was deeply rooted in the Colombian psyche and the reality of recent years: We would steer our limited resources toward retaking control of the highways leading in and out of Valledupar.

Some of our military leaders respectfully told me that they thought this idea was, in a word, crazy. They wanted what few troops we had to be available for large-scale offensives in the southeast and elsewhere, where the FARC's numbers were greatest. They also warned us that trying to protect long stretches of road would risk spreading our troops and resources too thin, expose our rear guard, offer no enduring tactical advantage from a traditional military perspective, and might not even be feasible, given the reality that the armed groups were strongest in rural areas.

I always welcomed my commanders' feedback, and I respected and understood their point of view. But I had witnessed in the previous three years how the anarchy on Colombian highways had taken a massive toll on the nation's commerce, and on its morale as well. For several years now, most Colombians had avoided traveling by road between our major cities. The armed groups freely erected roadblocks on highways, which they referred to as *pescas milagrosas*—literally, "miraculous catches," a reference to a biblical story in which Christ's disciples cast their nets into the Sea of Galilee, and reaped their bounty. In this case, the bounty was innocent Colombians—people of all ages and income levels, whom the terrorists dragged from their cars and took hostage until their loved ones agreed to pay a ransom. For many Colombians in urban areas, where violence had always been lower than in the countryside, the fear of highway roadblocks was probably the manner in which terrorism most directly impacted their lives. In fact, one reason that Colombia's domestic aviation industry had historically been so strong was because there was usually no other viable option available for intercity travel. There was perhaps no greater symbol of the state's impotence.

We believed that by retaking the highways, we could accomplish several objectives at once. First and foremost was the issue of confidence: We believed that the simple act of being able to drive wherever they wanted, whenever they wanted, would have a dramatic effect on the morale of many millions of Colombians. It was freedom in the purest sense—the freedom to move about, without the worry of danger. Second, by putting cars and trucks back on the roads, we could stimulate the economy in areas all up and down the highway—hotels, gas stations, and restaurants, not to mention normal intercity commerce. This would have an immediate multiplier effect, too, by putting more money in the pockets of people in rural areas and companies in the cities. And finally, by stopping the practice of random highway kidnappings, we would deprive the terrorists of a major source of income worth untold millions of dollars a year to them, a development that would ultimately leave them weaker as we engaged in military operations later on.

Under the skilled leadership of our defense minister, Marta Lucía Ramírez, as well as our police and military commanders, we would implement this plan in numerous places around the nation. Valledupar would be a symbolic—and intentionally audacious—starting point. We started with three stretches of highway: Valledupar–Riohacha–Maicao, Valledupar–Pailitas, and Valledupar–Fundación–Santa Marta. This was more than five hundred miles of road in total, but we wouldn't have to control every last inch of territory—not at first, anyway. Instead, we would start by organizing convoys. People would gather in their cars and trucks at a certain prearranged time, and then our military would escort them down the highway with sufficient firepower to repel any attacks.

Just as important, we would also create networks of ordinary citizens up and down the road—at gas stations and little shops, for example—who would be equipped with radios or phones to report any roadblocks or other threats as they materialized. This concept of citizen cooperation was an old strategy of mine, dating back to the governorship—and, predictably, it prompted another round of hand-wringing and accusations that I was trying to create "new" paramilitary groups.

I made many of the same arguments I had as governor—that security could not be solely the responsibility of the security forces, and that the intelligence and other tips provided by civilians would be instrumental to our success. Some human rights groups protested that ordinary citizens would lose their "neutrality"—to which I replied: "What neutrality?" Ordinary citizens had been the biggest victims of terrorism over the years. There was no shame in asking them to support the government they had just elected; no one was forced to participate, and these people would be equipped with walkie-talkies rather than guns. In the end, the response from the civilian population was overwhelmingly positive: Over the course of my government, four million civilians collaborated with our security in some capacity. Their contributions were critical.

So there we stood in Valledupar, outside City Hall, next to a small collection of the military vehicles that would be deployed in the convoys. People looked on, some of them obviously skeptical.

"We have to overcome fear," I said in a brief speech. "We do that by getting everybody involved. . . . We are going to act with strength and determination to reestablish peace, and we call on all Colombians to cooperate with the armed forces with the aim of defeating the violent minority."

Everywhere I looked, there were raised eyebrows and expressions of cynicism. The townspeople's lack of faith was understandable; it was human, given the last half century of our history, to expect that violence would continue. It was all some Colombians had ever known. But the results would soon speak for themselves.

6

By eleven a.m. on that first day, we departed Valledupar and we were en route to Florencia, a city deep in the south—on the very edge of the former demilitarized zone that the previous government had ceded to the FARC. "Straight into the wolf's mouth," as Ricardo Galán put it. Here, too, we wanted to send a symbolic message with our visit: The Colombian state had returned to stay, even in the areas that were most associated with the *narcoterroristas*. But instead of outlining another new security initiative, we came to Florencia to talk about schools.

Just as when I was governor, I believed that we could not win the peace with guns alone. During the campaign, and then as president, I spoke often of what I called the "triangle of confidence," with three equally important elements: democratic security, investor confidence, and social cohesion. All three of these mutually reinforcing components had to be strengthened in order for Colombia to undergo the transformation we all yearned for. To achieve social cohesion, we wanted to improve the well-being among the poorest members of our society, and help ease the class differences that had plagued Colombia for so long.

During my government, we would launch a wide range of programs, including health care, microlending through the participation of private and public banks as well as a number of specialized foundations: childhood nutrition, risk capital for small businesses "forest guard" families, and social programs with great coverage, such as a subsidy for poor families that would guarantee that their children attend school. Through these programs, we would create a healthier, more equal, more educated society. We would show people that, by embracing the Colombian state, they could improve their lives. And we would reduce the appeal of violence as a solution to society's problems. Much of the foundation for our success was attributed to the hard work and dedication of Juan Luis Londoño, our gifted minister of social protection, who died in a tragic plane crash in 2003. Juan Luis's death was a terrible loss to me and to Colombia, but his legacy would survive through our policies.

Thus we went to Florencia to talk about education. We considered it to be

the best way to improve income distribution, increase productivity, and enhance Colombia's competitiveness over time. In Florencia we wanted to talk
about a program we called the *Revolución Educativa,* the "Education Revolution." The initiative, one of the main pillars of my campaign platform, sought
to modernize our education system by focusing more on science and other
areas of study, while also extending coverage of the system as a whole—
another set of "quick victories." Our idea that day was to have a meeting with
mayors from the province to discuss how to implement the plan as quickly as
possible.

As in Antioquia four years earlier, though, we quickly discovered that,
without security, it was very difficult to focus on other subjects. When I arrived, I found that *all* of the mayors from the surrounding province were
marooned in Florencia, because so many threats had been made against them
in their hometowns. Their situation was sadly typical nationwide: roughly
four hundred of Colombia's eleven hundred mayors were unable to exercise
their duties because the *narcoterroristas* had run them out of town. That afternoon, as many Colombians watched on television, I sat and listened as the
mayors described the violence they faced and demanded more effective protection from the government.

"Could you help me get a little bulletproof vest," one of the mayors said,
his face reddening, "so that if they want to kill me, at least they have to aim
for my head?"

Another mayor asked for an armored car. Still another demanded a
helicopter. And another asked for "at least a radio," he said, so that he could
call for reinforcements when the FARC came to kill him, too. With each new
demand, the other mayors murmured or applauded. Some of my aides started
to nervously look about the room.

Yet I quickly realized what was actually happening here: These people
weren't angry. They were *afraid.* And to a large extent, they were right to be
making demands—the Colombian state had not done enough to protect
them over the years. My government would need to do a better job of shield-
ing not only them, but all others who were threatened because of their pro-
fession or identity. Over the course of my government, we would double the
number of Colombians under the protection of the state to more than eleven
thousand people, including mayors, judges, journalists, human rights activ-
ists, and others. Nearly a fifth of those under state protection, or roughly two

thousand, were labor union leaders, who had been killed in alarming numbers in preceding years. Throughout my presidency, we would make it our mission to protect the human rights of all members of society, especially the most vulnerable.

In those difficult early days, though, we could make no guarantees. I told the mayors that day that they would have our best effort—that we would even put them in tanks, if necessary, so they could return to their towns and exercise their functions. But I did not make empty promises. I knew our resources were still meager, and that the armed groups would only intensify their efforts to terrorize and intimidate the Colombian population, hoping to destroy our willpower before we—inevitably—gained the upper hand. During the first five days of my government, 125 people would die in attacks around the country.

When I saw the first intelligence briefings after I took office, it became clear to me that the coming weeks and months would bring even more bombings, massacres, and raids around the nation. Some of them we would simply be unable to stop. We also received word of several new and imminent threats against me. Their obvious goal was to intimidate. They should have known me better than that.

7

Two aspects characterized my behavior during the presidency: 1) All my decisions—which initiative to favor, which minister to appoint, which terrorist stronghold to target next—were based on a previously designed strategy. 2) At all times, practically every single move I made was conceived to send a signal about our government's values and priorities. The symbolic aspect of this endeavor—that was just as important as the first point—led me to personally look after every detail: I wanted my every word, movement, and office meeting to convey to Colombians that it was ok to believe in their country again.

When visitors came to my office in the Casa de Nariño, one of the first things they saw was a painting that had been a special gift from Débora Arango. Débora was one of my dearest friends, a revolutionary in the world of Colombian art, a pioneer in the quest for women's equality in our country, and a tireless advocate for peace. For years she had sent me paintings and sketches of doves—which I appreciated, although I joked with her that nobody would believe they were actually intended for me. Shortly before she died, at the age of ninety-eight, I asked Débora if she would be so kind as to make me a painting of a rifle. This made her a bit uneasy, but she complied. Before I hung it in my office, I installed a plaque on the frame: THE ONLY UNOFFICIAL RIFLE THAT'S ALLOWED IN COLOMBIA IS THIS ONE, BELONGING TO DÉBORA ARANGO. My point was that we wanted security and authority in Colombia, but an unarmed and peaceful society. Sun Tzu wrote in *The Art of War* that the state must have a monopoly on life and death—and that was precisely what we were trying to recover.

On my desk I kept a toolbox filled with a hammer, screwdrivers, and other tools. The message was that, in order to fulfill our larger vision for Colombia, we had to be willing to roll up our sleeves and work hard on the smallest details. In Colombia there was a long tradition of people with smart ideas and grand agendas, but who did not properly use the tools of state that would allow for their implementation. I constantly spoke to my ministers and others within my government about the importance of executing their plan and then following up to ensure it had taken hold.

I've always believed in combining a macro vision with the involvement in the small details of execution; this allows one to motivate others through example and to make sure every objective is made a reality. In retrospect, when I look at our government, I would say that whenever anything went wrong, it was because we weren't looking after the details.

Each of the office's four walls had a painting of a famous general from Colombian history, each representing a virtue or a set of values. General Nariño represented human rights in the service of virtue; General Santander was emblematic of the rule of law in the service of virtue; General Uribe Uribe symbolized the importance of equality and personal integrity; and General Bolívar embodied authority in the service of virtue. In later years, I proudly displayed a copy of Abraham Lincoln's Gettysburg Address, which was a gift from the U.S. Secretary of State Condoleezza Rice. I had memorized Lincoln's speech as an adolescent because of its message of perseverance in difficult times, and could still recite it by heart. I also hung frames of several papers with sayings and short poems, including "*Autorretrato*," "Self-portrait," in which the renowned Chilean poet Pablo Neruda described himself as an imperfect, multifaceted soul—"For my part I am or believe I am hard of nose . . . generous in love . . . melancholic in the mountains . . . impossible to figure out. . . ." It was a reminder to myself of the difficult and necessary humility that all persons require in order to deal with our weaknesses and shortcomings.

In my speeches and other appearances, I strove to be consistent, often repeating nearly verbatim the same messages several times a day. I returned constantly to the triangle of confidence and its three elements. Nearly every morning at seven a.m. during my government, I conducted an interview with a local radio station somewhere in Colombia, continuing my tradition of speaking directly to the people, and receiving their unfiltered input. In all my speeches and private conversations, I tried to be hopeful and focused on the future. I attempted to be generous with my critics, and patient with all my fellow Colombians. I did not always succeed—sometimes I fell victim to my temper, particularly with high-ranking politicians and officials, but never with the Colombian people.

Back during the presidential campaign, as I started to rise in the polls, reporters and other people often asked me what our next step would be. My usual reply: *"Trabajar, trabajar, y trabajar."* To keep working, working, and working. This turned into a kind of catchphrase, one that became even more applicable during the presidency. Given our country's dire problems, my team and I knew we had to work tirelessly, so we tried to make a virtue out of it. We spoke in public about how we needed to remove words like *vacation* and *holiday* from our vocabulary. Seven days a week around the clock, the work of the nation continued. My ministers and other aides would groggily show their friends and relatives text messages from me that were time-stamped from four-thirty a.m. on a Tuesday, or midnight on a Friday. This high level of dedication became a badge of honor, and before long it became contagious throughout Colombia. When I met Colombians in the street and asked them how they were doing, many of them smiled broadly and replied: *"Trabajar, trabajar, y trabajar."* And many people including business executives came to the Casa de Nariño and told us that they, too, had begun working on Saturdays, inspired by our collective example.

Could work also be fun? Yes, of course! I made a point of attending events and ceremonies that would showcase not only our country's opportunities for economic growth, but our resilience as well. It was important to demonstrate that, for all of our challenges, life in Colombia would go on. When entrepreneurs opened up a new water park in Caldas state, I made a point of going down one of the water slides myself. When I visited the Chicamocha Canyon in Santander state, I strapped myself into a small harness attached to cables and—still wearing a suit and tie—I rode across a deep valley, suspended several hundred feet in the air. (I enjoyed this so much, in fact, that I did it twice.) I played soccer with schoolchildren; rode horses in public; and donned almost any hat or costume people asked me to wear. Once, I even served coffee to Juan Valdez, the famous fictional character who has promoted Colombian coffee abroad since 1959. For the sake of promoting our country, no act was too small.

Perhaps the most important symbolic gestures I made were with regard to those aides, ministers, generals, and other collaborators who worked so hard during those years. I knew that we would never be able to transform Colombia without the hard labor and dedication of a vast and diverse team of people. So, while I was often very demanding of them, I also worked to acknowledge their contributions publicly at every possible juncture. Our government was a true team—the sum of the contributions of many thousands of people in the Casa de Nariño, the ministries, the security forces, and beyond. I will always be thankful for their hard work.

Inevitably, some people thought all the symbolism was overdone—they rolled their eyes at the speeches, the visual cues, and my penchant for repetition. Especially among the traditional political and journalistic establishment, some found my behavior pedantic. "Critics say his style reigns over substance," noted *The New York Times*. But for many others, including those outside Colombia's cities, these small human gestures meant more than words ever could. They helped form a bond that many had never felt with their government before. Politicians, for so long, had been those faraway people up on the mountain. Now we were walking among the people, talking about their everyday problems, speaking a language they could understand.

8

The trip to Florencia on my first full day as president was freighted with additional meaning—the airport there was the last place where Ingrid Betancourt was seen before she was abducted by the FARC.

For the first three years of her captivity, the FARC kept Ingrid in chains twenty-four hours a day. On the occasions when she was allowed to bathe in rivers, she did so while fully dressed to shield herself from the guards, who leered at her constantly. When she walked, she had to wear a hat to protect herself from all the creatures that fell from the jungle canopy: biting ants, insects, ticks, and lice. "But the most dangerous of all was man," she later said, "those who were behind me with their big guns."

The daughter of a Colombian diplomat, Ingrid spent her youth and much of her adult life in Paris, living in places as varied and far-flung as the Seychelles and New York City. Yet she gave up the international life to come to Colombia on a self-described quest to wipe out corruption. She was renowned for her pluck and for her creativity in the Senate. Like all of us, she was under no illusions about the risks she faced as a presidential candidate; in an interview with NBC's *Today* show just three months before her abduction, she declared that she loved Colombia and was willing to risk her life for it. Yet she was human, just like the rest of us. And when the reality of her captivity settled over her, and she thought about her two kids back in Paris—who were only sixteen and thirteen at the time she was taken hostage—Ingrid felt enormous despair. She later wrote that depression, as well as insects and tropical disease, would be a constant enemy during the next six years.

During our government, we would make innumerable attempts to secure the release of Betancourt and the other hostages. The possibility of a prisoners-for-hostages deal—the so-called "humanitarian exchange," as it became commonly known in Colombia—dominated much of my time in office. In my inauguration speech, I extended an olive branch to the FARC and revealed that Kofi Annan, the head of the United Nations, had accepted my request to mediate efforts to get us back to the negotiating table. Not only did the FARC spurn my offer and belittle the UN as a potential mediator, but they reiterated their demand for a new demilitarized zone as a precondition for any talks. Given the way the FARC had used Caguán for their military buildup in the previous government, that demand was an obvious nonstarter—I would not agree to cede one millimeter of Colombian territory, and it's likely that the FARC knew that. Nevertheless, I was widely criticized in many quarters of Congress and the Colombian and international media for being a "hard-liner" who was supposedly interested only in "war."

From the moment I was elected, the FARC appeared to be betting on either defeating us militarily, somehow regaining its lost credibility with the Colombian public, or simply waiting out my presidency. They never ceased their attacks on our military patrols, our infrastructure, or on civilian targets. In May 2003, the FARC proposed on its Web site the creation of a new "clandestine government" of twelve "well-known people" who would then "suggest a new Colombian president." In June of that year, they suggested using the Rio Group—a collection of Latin American nations—as a mediator in our talks, an obvious stall tactic. A few months later, the FARC leader Raúl Reyes made perhaps the most revealing comments of all in an interview with a Brazilian newspaper:

"Uribe's serious problem is that he only has three years left, and the FARC has all the time in the world after 39 years of struggle," Reyes said. "We will take all the time necessary to achieve our objectives."

Faced with an apparently unwilling partner in negotiations, but determined to save the hostages as quickly as possible, we tried more creative options. We instituted a new policy: If a member of the FARC or any other armed group brought a hostage safely with them out of the jungle, turned themselves in, and agreed to desert the FARC, then we would give them a reward, and propose that judges give them a reduced judicial sentence with some kind of parole. Then the Colombian state would pay for them to live abroad. In ensuing years, many people told me that this initiative caused enormous turmoil among the FARC's leadership, some of whom then banned the use of radios in their camps for a while because of fear that the FARC rank and file would learn about the proposal and vanish during the night with the most prized captives. That was exactly what happened in 2008, when the former Colombian congressman Óscar Tulio Lizcano managed to escape after eight years of captivity with the help of a FARC member—whom we promptly resettled under a new name in France.

My father, Alberto Uribe Sierra. / Mi padre, Alberto Uribe Sierra.

My mother, who knew how to nurture the energy and tenacity in her children. / Mi madre, quien sabía alimentar la energía y la tenacidad en sus hijos.

My beloved brother Jaime and me, always together. Here, I am about three years old. / Mi querido hermano Jaime y yo, siempre juntos. Aquí tengo más o menos tres años.

On mules with Jaime, maybe headed to school. / Montando en mula con Jaime, probablemente camino al colegio.

My mother, Laura Vélez Uribe, with her five children. From the left to right: Me, María Isabel, Santiago, María Teresa, and Jaime Alberto. / Mi madre, Laura Vélez Uribe, con sus cinco hijos. De izquierda a derecha: Yo, María Isabel, Santiago, María Teresa, Jamie Alberto.

All photos on this page are courtesy of the author.

From my school yearbook, age eighteen. /
De mi anuario del colegio,
a los dieciocho años.

Alvaro Uribe Vélez

Marrying Lina, a glorious day surrounded
by our loved ones. / El día en que me
casé con Lina, un día glorioso en el que
estuvimos rodeados de nuestros seres
queridos.

With Lina and Tomás. /
Con Lina y Tomás.

The community councils began while I was governor of Antioquia. / Los consejos comunitarios empezaron cuando era Gobernador de Antioquia.

From the earliest days, we protested kidnapping. / Siempre protestamos contra los secuestros.

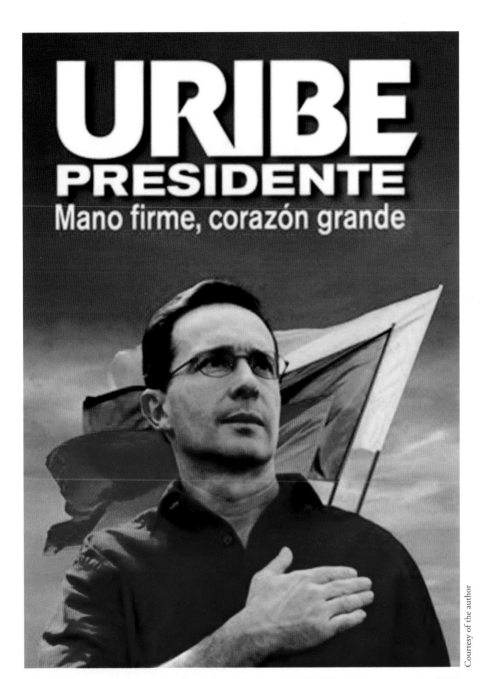

The campaign poster from 2002: "Firm hand, big heart." / El afiche de la campaña de 2002: "Mano firme, corazón grande".

With Lina, and our sons, Tomás and Jerónimo, during my inauguration as president. A tense and difficult day. / Con Lina y nuestros hijos Tomás y Jerónimo, en la posesión presidencial. Un día difícil y de mucha tensión.

Lina Moreno, without whose love and support our journey would have been impossible. / Lina Moreno: sin su amor y su apoyo, nuestra trayectoria habría sido imposible.

On inauguration day, with Bogotá under siege, we held our first security council meeting on the steps of the palace. / El día de la posesión, con Bogotá en estado de sitio, tuvimos nuestro primer consejo de seguridad en las escaleras de la Casa de Nariño.

All photos on this page are courtesy of the Press Secretary of the Presidency of the Republic of Colombia.

The funeral of my dear friend Gilberto Echeverri, whose memory would inspire us throughout the presidency. / El funeral de Gilberto Echeverri, mi amigo querido, cuyo recuerdo nos inspiró a lo largo de toda la presidencia.

Vice President Francisco Santos, a trusted friend and a clear moral voice. / El vicepresidente Francisco Santos, un amigo cercano, una persona moralmente intachable.

Gabriel García Márquez, a fine Colombian and a friend of peace. / Gabriel García Márquez, un gran colombiano y amigo de la paz.

The early years of the presidency were especially difficult, with many beloved ones lost. / Los primeros años de la presidencia fueron especialmente difíciles, con la muerte de muchos seres queridos.

The community councils were a powerful tool, enabling direct communication with the people on social and other issues. / Los consejos comunitarios fueron una herramienta poderosa, nos permitieron una comunicación directa con la gente acerca de temas sociales y demás.

I always sought to visit new investment projects, especially those that could showcase the marvelous side of Colombia. / Siempre busqué nuevos proyectos de inversión, sobre todo aquellos que mostraran el lado maravilloso de Colombia.

Yoga nidra and other techniques allowed me to center myself during difficult moments. / El yoga nidra y otras técnicas me ayudaron a mantenerme centrado durante los momentos más difíciles.

Ours was an active, vigorous government, always engaged with the people. / Nuestro gobierno fue un gobierno activo y vigoroso, siempre involucrado con la gente.

I was grateful for President Bill Clinton's support for Colombia and his remarkable perspective on the challenges we faced. / Agradecí el apoyo que el presidente Bill Clinton brindó a Colombia y su extraordinario punto de vista acerca de los retos a los que nos enfrentamos.

President George W. Bush was a great friend of Colombia. / El presidente George W. Bush fue un gran amigo de Colombia.

President Barack Obama supported our "steady strategy of making no concessions" to the terrorists. / El presidente Barack Obama apoyó nuestra "firme estrategia de no hacer concesiones" a los terroristas.

I drew the "triangle of confidence" for President Obama, who liked it so much he autographed it for me. / Dibujé el "Triángulo de la Confianza" para el Presidente Obama a quien gustó tanto que me lo autografió.

All photos on this page are courtesy of the Press Secretary of the Presidency of the Republic of Colombia.

With President Hugo Chávez. My love for our brother nation of Venezuela never diminished. / Con el presidente Hugo Chávez. Nunca se ha disminuido mi amor por nuestra nación hermana.

The moment of my friendly bet with President Chávez as to whether I could ride a horse without spilling a drop of coffee, at the recreational park Rionegro Tutucán. / Momento en el que hice una apuesta amistosa con el presidente Hugo Chávez, de si yo era capaz de montar a caballo sin derramar una sola gota de café, en el parque recreacional Rionegro Tutucán.

Ingrid Betancourt embracing her mother on the day of her rescue, after more than six years apart. / Ingrid Betancourt abrazando a su madre el día de su rescate, después de haber estado separadas durante casi seis años.

The rescue of Ingrid and the Colombian police and soldiers was one of the proudest days of my presidency. / Uno de los días más orgullosos de mi presidencia: el rescate de Ingrid, los policías y los soldados que estaban secuestrados por las FARC.

The "Concert for Peace," with the talented artist Shakira. President Luiz Inacio Lula da Silva of Brazil, President Alan García of Peru, and the singer Carlos Vives honored us with their presence that day. / El "Concierto por la Paz" con la talentosa artista colombiana Shakira. Aquel día el presidente Luiz Inacio Lula da Silva de Brasil, Alan García, el presidente del Perú, y el cantante Carlos Vives nos honraron con su presencia.

At my son Jerónimo's wedding in 2012, celebrating new additions to our family. / En el matrimonio de mi hijo Jerónimo en 2012, celebrando cómo crece nuestra familia.

With my brothers, Camilo and Santiago, my nephew Luis Martín, and my sons, Jerónimo and Tomás, at Jerónimo's wedding. / Con mis hermanos Camilo y Santiago, mi sobrino Luis Martín y mis hijos Jerónimo y Tomás en el matrimonio de Jerónimo.

In most cases, though, it wasn't so easy. As the impasse continued, the pressure for the hostages' release never dissipated, both inside and outside Colombia. Thanks in part to Ingrid's connections in the French political world, as well as the eloquent and moving activism of her children, her plight was a massive cause in France. A huge poster bearing her likeness hung outside City Hall in Paris, and European officials clamored constantly for her release in private meetings and public statements alike. We welcomed their compassion; it helped maintain pressure on the FARC, as well.

I had to place the interests of the nation above all other considerations— even when this wasn't popular. In July 2002, while I was still president-elect, I met in Paris with French president Jacques Chirac during a European tour to try to generate support for our policies. President Chirac received me at the Élysée Palace, where a group of protesters had gathered outside. They were criticizing me for my supposed unwillingness to negotiate with the FARC for the release of the hostages, including, of course, Ingrid Betancourt.

During a moment alone in the palace, President Chirac leaned into my ear. "I understand your position; I really do," he said quietly. "But this is a political problem," he said, gesturing toward the crowd outside, "and we need to put these people at ease."

"Mr. President," I replied, "if 'putting them at ease' means telling them what they want to hear, and changing my position, then I'm afraid I can't do that. Because maybe we could secure Ingrid's freedom by making concessions, but then the FARC would be emboldened and just kidnap more people. What we're trying to do is not just free the kidnap victims, but defeat kidnapping in Colombia altogether."

"I understand," President Chirac replied. "But perhaps you could just give them a few words upon your departure, to hearten them."

I shook my head. "I have to say the same things here as I say in Bogotá," I said. "I cannot change my speeches based on the audience. I have to be consistent in public and in private."

President Chirac nodded, obviously disappointed. He had not yet learned the hard lessons that we had spent the last two decades absorbing in Colombia. The FARC could be a seductive partner, walking all the way to the church doors—and then leaving you waiting at the altar. President Chirac's government found this out a year later, in July 2003, when a French army C-130 Hercules plane flew to the Brazilian city of Manaus, apparently as part of a secret mission to secure Ingrid's release without the knowledge of my government or the Brazilian authorities. Media reports from Agence France-Presse and others said that four French emissaries then chartered a private plane to a Brazilian town near the Colombian border, where they waited for the FARC to show up. They never did, of course. The French emissaries ended up walking away empty-handed and betrayed. They certainly weren't the first people to feel that way.

No, getting Ingrid back would not be as easy as flying into the jungle and negotiating some kind of shady deal. Achieving her liberation would require the full development of our military, intelligence, and diplomatic abilities. We never ceased in our efforts to save her. But in retrospect, it's clear that, in those early days, we weren't yet ready. We would have to invest more time, effort, and sacrifice before such a miracle would be possible.

9

When the FARC didn't get what they wanted, they would show their rage by lashing out. In a macabre way, you could set your watch by it: They would make a demand, wait for it to be rejected, and then launch a new and devastating attack within days to send a message to us, and to society, that they would not be denied. When the FARC's leadership issued a statement in February 2003 demanding, yet again, the creation of a demilitarized zone similar to the one they had enjoyed during the previous government, we knew what was coming. We alerted law enforcement officials around the country. And while we proceeded undaunted with the business of the nation, we also braced ourselves for the worst.

The list of heroes who gave their lives to break this vicious cycle, so that Colombians could one day enjoy peace, would fill a book of its own. It overwhelms me, even now, to think of their courage and perseverance. I wish I could somehow honor them all individually here, by name. It was much more than just the police and the armed forces—schoolteachers, nonprofit groups, religious organizations, and many, many others made their own contributions to Colombia's security. The performance of our prosecutors, judges, and our judicial system as a whole was particularly awe-inspiring. In many towns, for many years, there had simply been no justice. These brave souls, often unarmed and defenseless, moved into such places and put their lives on the line in the name of restoring the rule of law. They uncovered atrocities and criminal networks that we would have otherwise never known about. In too many cases, they paid the ultimate price for their work.

I will forever be personally grateful to Cecilia Giraldo Saavedra, a legendary prosecutor in the southern state of Huila whom newspapers called "the Colombian Margaret Thatcher." The FARC was very active in Huila during those early days, but Giraldo, a decorated former military prosecutor, refused to be intimidated. She took on the toughest cases—kidnappings, terrorism, extortions—and dedicated her life fully to the pursuit of the *narcoterroristas*. During the third month of my government, she coordinated an audacious sweep in which the authorities captured and jailed twenty-four terrorists—a major victory. Naturally, Giraldo's efforts made her a target. Just a month after the aforementioned sweep, the FARC sent her a bomb encased in a book. It exploded in the court building before it got to her. Giraldo accepted a contingent of bodyguards—but charged ahead with her work undaunted, often staying in the office past midnight. She also led the criminal investigation into the abduction of Jorge Eduardo Géchem, the senator whom the FARC abducted in the April 2002 hijacking that effectively ended the peace process of the previous government.

Days after the FARC made their newest demand, I was scheduled to travel to Huila's capital city, Neiva, for our weekly Saturday town hall meeting. When the authorities received tips that the terrorists were planning some kind of attack to coincide with my arrival, Giraldo did not hesitate—she took charge of the investigation, seeking to ensure the safety of my team, me, and the public in general. The tips pointed to suspicious activity at a cluster of houses very near Neiva's airport—just under the flight path that my plane would take. During the predawn hours on the day before my arrival, Giraldo personally accompanied the police as they began their raids of the residences.

As Giraldo and the police entered the fifth house that morning, the entire structure exploded in a giant mushroom cloud of fire and shattered mortars. The blast was so powerful that it left a thirty-foot-deep crater where the house had been, and heavily damaged or destroyed sixty other nearby residences. Giraldo and nine police officials were killed, along with a fourteen-year-old girl who had been waiting for a school bus outside, among others. The final toll: seventeen dead and thirty-seven wounded.

An investigation quickly confirmed the FARC's intentions: They planned to launch an attack on my plane, either by firing mortars with equipment we found at the scene, or by blowing up the house as my plane passed low overhead in an attempt to knock it from the sky. Cecilia Giraldo and the other brave authorities may have saved my life that day. For their sacrifices, and those of countless other Colombian soldiers, police, prosecutors, and others during my presidency, I am eternally thankful. We would honor their memory by following their example and pressing ahead, undaunted, with love and determination in our hearts.

10

Some people say the presidency is lonely. Yet I certainly never felt that way.

In moments of great national tragedy, such as the bombing at Neiva, my heart shattered, as if I myself had lost a loved one. Throughout the eight years of my government, I never distanced myself emotionally from the pain wrought by unnecessary death or suffering—each massacre, each murder, each kidnapping in Colombia struck profoundly within my own soul. I understood all too well what it meant for a family to lose a cherished relative. As president, I felt it was my responsibility to bring such atrocities to an end. It pained me greatly when we did not succeed.

During such moments, I always found the greatest solace by seeking out, and speaking with, the Colombian people. Showing my face, assuming full responsibility for our actions, searching for the facts and then disclosing them in public had a profound therapeutic effect for me. Transparency was like a bright, warm light; in our darkest moments, I ran to it as quickly I possibly could. I could see how people reacted, I could feel their support for our actions, and I was reminded of our profound, shared yearning for peace. Lonely? No. As president, I was never alone.

Lina has suffered in silence but her external calm and stoicism had a tremendous centering effect on me in moments of crisis. Colleagues including Jaime Bermúdez, Alicia Arango, Bernardo Moreno, Ricardo Galán, César Mauricio Velásquez, Jorge Mario Eastman, José Obdulio Gaviria, Alberto Velásquez and Paola Holguín insisted that our good faith transcended any failure.

During rare moments of solitude, I drew strength from my faith. I prayed. I was restored by exercise—on my bicycle, or the elliptical machine I used. Spiritual medical doctors such as Elsa Lucía Arango and Santiago Rojas offered valuable assistance. Yoga nidra, a type of mental yoga that I began practicing in 1986, produced a dreamlike effect that allowed me to disconnect without leaving the real world. It gave me the opportunity to reflect on our difficulties, to see the faults within myself, and to meditate upon the paths that lay before us—to try to determine what was right.

Often, all of this wasn't enough. There was no way to explain or rationalize the loss of people such as Cecilia Giraldo, and all of the other heroes who sacrificed for our cause. In those moments, the most difficult times of all, I knew that I simply could not succumb to my pain. It was me, and no one else, who had to lead the way forward. But even then, I could feel the vast majority of the Colombian people accompanying me, walking by my side.

11

It was no surprise that the FARC had targeted one of our *consejos comunitarios,* our weekly town hall meetings. They were one of the most powerful tools we had in those early days for building confidence, our signature method of engaging in two-way communication with the Colombian people. So when the attack on Neiva took place, we knew we had to send a signal to Colombians by proceeding as planned, and holding the *consejo* there anyway, despite our grief, in a public display of our perseverance. The only question was, How could we do so without incurring excessive risk? Our intelligence suggested the possible presence of yet another house filled with explosives somewhere in Neiva, or some other plan to attack us.

An attack on the *consejos* was almost like an attack on democracy itself—they were a celebration of participatory democracy. Almost every Saturday of my government, we packed as many officials as possible onto our plane and traveled to a different town or village—often to places where federal officials had not visited for years, if ever. Once we arrived, we held a public meeting wherever we could find space—in city halls, in plazas, sometimes in giant tents in sweltering hundred-degree heat and humidity.

The proceedings were attended by hundreds of people from all levels of society, and they were usually televised as well. Anyone present could ask questions; sometimes people called in. No issue was considered too small; we enthusiastically discussed everything from the state of local highways to sewage systems to job creation and agriculture policy and so on, usually for eight hours at a time or more. Security-related topics were treated separately, on Sundays and Mondays, in meetings that were also open to the public. Overall, the *consejos* were like a huge, marathon problem-solving session; I invited entire teams of ministers and government officials to participate, and state and local officials as well. Together we sought solutions to the problems that people raised. The meetings, which hadn't changed much since my time as governor, were a critical element of our concept of an *estado comunitario,* an austere but comprehensive "communitarian state" that sought to involve all Colombians in matters of public policy.

Naturally, the style of these meetings didn't sit well with everybody. Some critics accused me of micromanaging, and eroding the credibility of state institutions, by creating the impression that only the president or the executive branch could address even the most local issues. Some said that we were engaging in populism by promising too much. Still others voiced doubts that my officials and I would have the physical and mental endurance necessary to sustain the pace of the work over time.

In another country, under other circumstances, perhaps this intensive kind of approach would not have been as necessary. But in Colombia, where people had possessed so little faith in their government for so long, we believed it was necessary to demonstrate to people in an explicit, visible way that we were committed to solving the problems that affected them most dearly. We needed to look as many people as possible straight in the eye and show them how we operated. I believed that by shining light and transparency on how we worked, and bringing much of the government apparatus to towns and villages throughout Colombia once a week, we could win the confidence of the people—and improve the credibility of our institutions, not erode it. As for any questions over my endurance . . . well, those people didn't know me very well.

We took great care at the *consejos* never to promise anything we couldn't deliver. If the meetings devolved into a series of promises that we couldn't keep, then they would result in confidence lost, not gained. So, with the help of the Inter-American Development Bank, and the British and Finnish governments, we developed a proprietary database system that allowed us to track every single commitment we made, follow up on the results, and make them public. Meanwhile, we never hesitated to say no to requests that were unrealistic, or that were beyond our limited resources. Often this made members of the community frustrated, and they demanded that we seek other, creative options. This was useful, too.

Ultimately, as a listening tool, the *consejos* were simply without rival— they allowed us to hear a vision of reality that was often far more accurate than the anodyne briefings we received at the palace. As I often said, I couldn't depend on PowerPoint to get my information—I had to rely on PowerPeople as well.

After the attack on Neiva, I was absolutely determined that the terrorists would not deprive the citizens of that town of their democratic right to speak to their elected representatives. So, on the very same day as the *casa bomba*, a small group of us secretly set out by airplane from Medellín—twelve hours before my scheduled arrival. Night had already fallen. Because of the risks, we decided not to advise the airport in Neiva, or any of the local authorities, prior to our arrival. Instead, Ricardo Galán recalls that we arranged for a few cars to show up at a set time and illuminate the runway with their headlights. After landing, we climbed into those cars and drove to the local funeral home, where the relatives of the fallen were grieving. I spoke with the families and prayed with them. Then we visited the hospital and paid our respects to the wounded.

The following morning, under a driving rain, we held a minute of silence for the victims. And then I encouraged everyone to press ahead.

"This was total cowardice," I declared. "They're not capable of looking the state in the eye. So they proceed with their cowardly terrorism."

In the ensuing months and years, we would continue traveling to every corner of Colombia, rallying confidence in the country. During many weeks, we spent four to five days outside of the presidential palace. I was in the air so often that we made use of a tiny lounge at the Bogotá airport so that I could take quick naps, practice my yoga, and pray.

Meanwhile, we dealt with the threats as they came. We flew with our lights off, changed runways at the last minute, and tried every other trick possible. My security team, led by generals Mauricio Santoyo and Flavio Buitrago, Admiral Rodolfo Amaya, and Colonel Eduardo Ramírez, worked assiduously, monitoring and reacting to thousands of threats over the years, to ensure we all remained safe. Thanks to the grace of God, and the professionalism of my security team, we always managed to reach our destination safely.

Unfortunately, others would not be as lucky.

12

"Mr. President, we've lost an American plane."

That ominous message, delivered to me during the same awful week as the Neiva attack, signaled the beginning of one of the most serious and enduring challenges of my government. A small Cessna carrying four Americans and a Colombian soldier had disappeared south of Bogotá. The plane's pilot radioed in a mayday signal, and then their frequency went silent. We immediately dispatched helicopters on what we assumed would be a normal search-and-rescue mission. They located the plane in a tiny clearing of the jungle, and the aircraft was largely intact—but the passengers were gone. We never imagined the misfortune that had befallen them.

The Americans were contractors for the company Northrop Grumman, which had been hired to engage in drug interdiction flights throughout Colombia. This particular mission was designed to target drug labs controlled and operated by the FARC. Theirs had been a flight like any other—until the only engine on their plane suddenly went out. The pilot, a Vietnam veteran named Tommy Janis, managed with exceptional skill to crash-land the plane in a tiny clearing in the jungle. Janis was badly bloodied, and the other passengers sustained broken ribs and bruises. But everyone on board had survived, against all possible odds. They all believed it was a miracle.

It was. But the very instant the five survivors staggered out of the plane's broken fuselage, sheets of gunfire began cascading down on them from above. The source: a squadron of between fifty and sixty members of the FARC who had been patrolling in the exact same area when their plane skidded to a halt. "I couldn't believe it," one of the Americans later wrote. "We'd survived the crash, only to find ourselves in a situation that was arguably worse."

The passengers, seeing that they were outnumbered and outgunned, tossed aside the pistols that were packed on the plane and surrendered. As the FARC descended from the mountains, the Americans were surprised to see that most of their captors were mere teenagers, some of them as young as fourteen—"more like a bunch of kids dressed up for Halloween than soldiers," one of the Americans observed. The FARC promptly relieved the men of their watches and the cash from their wallets. Then they separated Janis and the Colombian soldier, Sergeant Luis Alcides Cruz, from the rest of the group. Their bullet-ridden bodies were discovered later; we'll never know exactly why the FARC decided to execute them.

In those crucial first hours, we would come tantalizingly close to rescuing the three remaining Americans. A helicopter arrived on the scene, spotted the captives, and began firing down upon the FARC's perimeter, hoping to pin them down until more reinforcements arrived. But the FARC knew this area like their own backyard. By shoving the hostages at gunpoint into a nearby hut, and then weaving through a field of coffee plants, they were able to evade the helicopter, and they soon disappeared into the jungle.

The Americans would spend the next twenty-four hours marching over mountains and wading through rivers, struggling to move despite their injuries—Keith Stansell had broken several ribs in the crash, Tom Howes suffered a concussion, and Marc Gonsalves struggled with back and hip pain. That first march was sheer torture for all of them. Meanwhile, I spent several sleepless days and nights in constant communication with my commanders, trying to coordinate an operation with more than twenty-five hundred Colombian soldiers. Our hope was to encircle the area and detect the Americans before they completely vanished. We did not succeed. Some of our commanders later said that a lack of transport helicopters and other equipment in the south prevented us from mounting a sufficiently nimble rescue operation. One of Colombia's most severe historical problems—a lack of resources for the state—had come back to haunt us yet again. If we wanted to continue on the road to progress and prevent future such disasters, the time had come for us to do something about it.

13

In late August 2002, just three weeks into my government, my finance minister, Roberto Junguito, asked to see me. He walked into my office with a stack of binders and a grave expression, looking more like a mortician than an economist. He sat down, folded his arms, and said, "We're broke, and we don't have any money to pay the soldiers beyond October."

His words took my breath away. Coming into office, I knew our finances were precarious. In 1999, the Colombian economy had experienced its worst recession in seven decades. Our recovery from that crisis had been anemic at best, and our fiscal accounts were severely out of balance. Our gross public debt had ballooned to $41 billion from just $10 billion six years before. I was shocked to hear that we were so short of cash that, in just six more weeks, we might not be able to meet payroll.

My entire presidency flashed before my eyes. What about the planned buildup of our troops and police? What would happen to the expansion of our social programs in health and education? All of these initiatives depended on our having *more* resources available, not fewer.

I realized right away that, unless we fixed our solvency issues quickly, we ran the risk of an even more catastrophic crisis. In late 2002, financial markets were closely watching countries all over Latin America for the first hint of trouble. Only eight months had passed since the total implosion of Argentina's economy, which saw that country default on more than $100 billion in sovereign debt and devalue its currency by some 80 percent. Brazil's economy was also under severe pressure as Luiz Inácio Lula da Silva, a leftist former labor union leader, was set to become president. With just the slightest hint of weakness, Colombia could be next in line for a speculative attack—and none of our dreams for the next four years would be possible.

Unlike many Latin American countries, Colombia had never defaulted on its debt or suffered hyperinflation. However, officials from multilateral institutions such as the World Bank told me that our situation was now dire. They warned that my government would need to make very tough decisions. They said that Colombia was on the brink of becoming a "failing state."

The same afternoon that Minister Junguito put our problems in such sharp relief, I spent several hours huddled with him and my top aides, scrambling to find a Band-Aid for our liquidity problem. It required some creative financial engineering, and I had to draw on every bit of my twenty-plus years of knowledge of the Colombian state. The Council of Ministers started by freezing a large percentage of our current expenditures. We also moved some funds around from other parts of the state's balance sheet. By mid-October, thanks to Minister Junguito's tireless efforts and the trust of our friends abroad, we had secured $9 billion in financing from multilateral organizations, including the Andean Development Fund (CAF), the World Bank, and the Inter-American Development Bank. But we knew these were all short-term fixes, not permanent solutions. We needed more than just a Band-Aid.

People knew we had problems, but I decided not to reveal the full extent of our financial difficulties to the Colombian public. As I said at my inaugural address, "We came here to work, not to complain." I had no interest in spending my presidency blaming our problems on the legacy I inherited from my predecessors. I wanted Colombians to be focused on the future, not the past—navel-gazing and recrimination would only delay our recovery. Optimism and hope were our biggest allies in healing our economy and our country. But those emotions also had to be rooted in reality—and I knew that we needed to come up quickly with bold, concrete solutions.

Within days of Minister Junguito's visit to my office, we decided on one big piece of the puzzle—a new, one-time-only "security tax." A 1.2 percent tax on liquid assets would be paid by high-income individuals only, and the revenues would be used exclusively for the expansion of our army and police forces. I had misgivings about the potential damage a new tax could cause to Colombia's business climate, but I decided the benefits far outweighed the costs. For one thing, we would gain specially earmarked revenues for our security buildup, without having to take money away from other valuable priorities like health and education. We could also show Colombians that the wealthiest members of our society, long criticized for being indifferent to

Colombia's ills, were willing to pay their fair share to make the country safer. This was an important message for the world, too: While traveling abroad, I sometimes heard leaders ask why they should provide Colombia with military or economic aid when Colombians themselves weren't making enough sacrifices. This initiative gave us an incomplete but still compelling answer.

At the same time, we took several steps to ensure the tax would be worth the risks. Defense Minister Ramírez, my finance minister, and I held frequent consultations with representatives from the Colombian business sector to explain our goals to them in minute detail. We offered them the opportunity to monitor, in near real time, exactly how we were spending our—their—money. Public perception was also important, so we were careful to cast the tax in a way that would avoid exacerbating the class divisions in our society: I described it as a levy on "people of means" who were eager to help Colombia, rather than a tax imposed on the "rich." Finally, and most important, we quickly followed up the tax with a much broader reform at the end of 2002 that sought to stimulate investment—by ceding tax breaks and other special treatment to companies that created jobs, purchased equipment, and made other long-term bets on Colombia's future. My trusted aide José Roberto Arango played an absolutely critical role in both the policy and the implementation.

These changes, by themselves, weren't enough to fix our economy; other, equally important reforms, such as our efforts to cut excessive costs from Colombia's budget, would come later. But the security tax was an important first step that set the tone for the next eight years by showing, yet again, that *all* sectors of Colombian society would be actively contributing to our well-being and security. Some people later told me how they took out loans to be able to pay the tax. Many of them did so with the full understanding that providing our government with the necessary funds was in their best long-term interest. Indeed, it was almost like an investment in itself—making the country safer led to faster economic growth, which in turn allowed these business leaders to expand their activities even further over the medium term. Indeed, just a few years later, in 2006, I received a phone call from one of Colombia's richest men, Carlos Ardila Lülle, who asked me whether we could implement the tax for a second time.

This didn't surprise me; in 2006 the results of our security policies had largely vindicated our efforts. But I have to commend the patriotism of my fellow Colombians—even in the dark, uncertain days of late 2002, I never received a single complaint about the tax. Their solidarity was fundamental. In all, the security tax raised some $800 million in revenues, a windfall that made possible many of the successes that followed.

14

I saw the images on television first: caravans of cars, a hundred or two hundred of them at a time, rolling down Colombian highways with all the pride and pomp of a holiday parade. Their occupants punched their fists joyously out the window, cheering and chanting, "Colombia! Colombia!" Others waved Colombian flags, singing the national anthem as they passed. We saw people get out of their cars to take pictures with the troops who were escorting them, throwing their arms around them and smiling broadly as they flashed peace signs. Others stopped to have picnics by the side of the road, practically overflowing with happiness and disbelief at what was actually happening.

It was real, all right—Colombia was getting its highways back.

During those early months, a group of us visited a stretch of road near San Jacinto, a particularly troubled village outside of Cartagena. A woman came running up, threw her arms around me, and exclaimed, "*Presidente*, thanks for giving me back my store!"

I looked around, but saw nothing. "Where is your store?" I asked, confused.

"The highway!" she replied, smiling.

This woman went on to explain that she sold hammocks and other artisanal goods along the side of the highway for a living. For years, the flow of vehicles had slowed to a trickle because of the violence. That had been an extremely lean period for her. But now that people were back on the roads again, she had her "store" back.

This same story repeated itself all over the country, at all levels of society. The owner of the car was happy because his or her family could visit parts of the country they hadn't seen in years. The owner of the gas station by the side of the road was happy because he had customers again. The owner of the hotel in the countryside was happy because now he could afford to invest in a new wing on the building. The workers at the hotel were happy because they had jobs again. And so on.

I was determined not to let this tentative progress go to our heads. No, we had to be more vigilant than ever. We knew that the armed groups often targeted these incipient symbols of hope in an effort to reverse our progress and demonstrate their might. So on long holiday weekends at the beginning of my presidency, I often stayed up all night, in constant contact with our military and police commanders to help monitor and coordinate the response to any threats on the roads. Some of these threats came in via my personal cell phone, which I gave out to the public at meetings or on the radio. People called me when they spotted FARC roadblocks, or for less dire matters— when the road had potholes, when there were long lines at tollbooths, and even when they had a flat tire. No matter the time of day, no matter how minor the complaint, I always tried to answer the phone. I always followed up—I'd call the transport minister and ask him to sell tollway tickets ahead of time, or open more tollbooths, for example. I suppose I did draw the line somewhere—I don't recall going out and changing any tires.

Taking back the highways was like a mass liberation from a collective kidnapping. It had a multiplier effect that surpassed even our wildest expectations. The caravan program was called *Vive Colombia, viaja por ella,* or "Experience Colombia; Travel Throughout Her." People bragged to their friends about where they'd traveled, and marveled at how much things were changing in Colombia. The economy started to turn around with the resumption of truck traffic and intercity commerce. Colombian soldiers and police, who had felt vilified for so long by some portions of society, began to feel more appreciated than they had in years. And Colombians from all walks of life simply started walking a little taller—daring to hope that maybe we could indeed turn our country around.

It was an "early success," just as we had hoped—fragile, easily reversible, but something people could see with their eyes and feel in their hearts. This, in turn, opened a door.

15

Maybe the most critical element of retaking our highways was that it made people feel closer to Colombia and the Colombian state. After so many years of feeling excluded or estranged from our country, people now felt like they had a personal stake in our affairs in general, and in our security in particular. Creating this kind of personal connection had been a special focus of mine dating back to my time as governor—security had to be a community-wide effort, not just a job for men in uniform. So, as we looked to extend the peace in other innovative ways that would not bust our limited budget, we kept this lesson firmly in mind.

One important low-cost program implemented with great skill by Defense Minister Ramírez and the high military command was called *Soldados de Mi Pueblo,* or "Soldiers from My Town." We recruited people across Colombia to serve in the military and be posted in their own towns and villages— rather than some distant corner of the country. There had long been a stigma within the military against this kind of service, because some commanders believed that the soldiers would not work as hard—or could be compromised by the armed groups—if they stayed too close to home. We believed the opposite—these soldiers could provide valuable intelligence through their social and family connections, and would also cause the townspeople to have a deeper emotional bond with our armed forces. "These men aren't just taking care of their country," one army sergeant in Pacho was quoted as saying in the international press. "They're taking care of their families." In the end, the program was enormously successful—by the middle of 2005, there were more than twenty-seven thousand Soldiers from My Town spread throughout twenty-eight of our thirty-two states, ensuring security in many areas where there had previously been none.

Still, we wanted to get even more civilians involved. So we started another key initiative named *Lunes de Recompensa,* or "Reward Mondays." The program was rather self-explanatory—every Monday, in villages and cities throughout Colombia, we paid out small cash rewards to citizens in return for critical information on the movements of terrorists, petty crimes, and other useful information. We had similar programs that offered rewards, and sometimes even a small monthly sum, to people who gave us information that allowed us to protect places or objects targeted by the terrorists, such as oil pipelines and electrical transmission towers. By the end of our presidency, we ended up with more than four million people nationwide, or about one in ten Colombians, who were providing information in some fashion to the state. Unfortunately, there were cases in which informants were discovered and then murdered by the outlaws. But overall, our record of protecting people was good. We took their safety extremely seriously—in each town, there was one trusted high-ranking security official who guaranteed the system's efficiency and also controlled access to the list of informants, so that it wouldn't fall into the wrong hands.

This kind of human intelligence was invaluable, and I encouraged our armed forces to take full advantage of it. When I took office, I noted that some of the military commanders had become overly enamored with technology—listening devices and the like—at the expense of good, old-fashioned human source building. The latter was clearly the path that would lead us to the hostages and allow us to take down the leadership of the armed groups, among other necessary advances. So we changed the trend, in part by putting as many soldiers in the field as possible. This was done not just through new recruits, but by making more effective use of the troops we already had. For example, when we visited Cartagena, we found that some naval officers were holed up in their relatively comfortable social club in the city's core—at a time when the paramilitaries, the ELN, and the FARC were wreaking havoc on the outskirts of town. So we requested that the navy move their command post to the suburban areas of El Carmen and San Jacinto. The results came quickly—San Jacinto was the same place where the woman got her "store" back.

We applied this philosophy everywhere. I told my generals that I wanted to see them in camouflage as much as possible—meaning that I wanted them out on the front lines among their men, rather than in dress uniform in their headquarters. We even got rid of the honor guard of soldiers who traditionally greeted the president when his plane landed in a Colombian city. On one of our first trips, as we deplaned from FAC-001 and saw the array of buttoned-up soldiers waiting for us with flags, Lina turned to me and said, "This is ridiculous, given the reality of the country."

I agreed. I told Captain Amaya and Alicia Arango, "This government is going to travel around the country so much that if they put an honor guard at each arrival and departure, we won't have any soldiers or police left over." And that was the end of that: Those soldiers were deployed to the field.

As for me, I spent as much time as possible out in the field among the troops. Just as I had done as governor and as a presidential candidate, I spent almost every Christmas Day and New Year's Eve either at military barracks or visiting needy communities, trying to lift morale and express our gratitude. I would share cake with them and toast them, expressing our best wishes for the year ahead. I attended every officer promotion ceremony, military academy graduation, or inauguration of new barracks that I could. I went jogging alongside the troops; I engaged in swimming races with them in our rivers and oceans. Every river, every ocean in Colombia is simply spectacular. Stepping out of the water after a good swim is one of nature's biggest pleasures. If one day the readers of this book have the chance to visit the river Vaupés, which I swam across, or the river Guatapurí, they will remember this book. I have always been inspired by Abraham Lincoln's proximity to the army that preserved American unity. He was in constant contact with his generals and soldiers, often sharing their tents on the battlefield.

One street, one jungle canopy at a time, we moved to extend the legal reach of the democratic state. We moved into areas such as Comuna 13, a Medellín suburb that had long been a chaotic mix of the FARC, ELN, the paramilitaries, and other drug dealers. But the first year of my presidency was like a boxing match: We would land two punches, and the *narcoterroristas* would respond with a punch of their own. It was clear to me that, to continue advancing, we would need additional material assistance.

16

Over the years, many countries offered Colombia their condolences. But only one country ever stepped forward to offer us real, tangible military aid that helped us address our problems. The Colombian people will forever be grateful to the United States, and to presidents Bill Clinton, George W. Bush, and Barack Obama, for providing us with many of the tools we needed to defeat terrorism and extend the reach of the democratic state. I made numerous friends and allies in Washington during my presidency, and I enjoyed good relations with Republicans and Democrats alike. So it is easy to forget, all these years later, the way that it all started—inauspiciously, to say the least. Indeed, my first trip to the U.S. capital following my election was like walking into a buzz saw.

I arrived in Washington as president-elect in June 2002 with very few connections in the upper realms of power. I was a bit of an outlier in that sense—Colombian presidents are often fluent in both English and the ways of Washington from the moment they arrive on the job. While it was true that I had spent about a year at Harvard, I was almost forty by the time I studied there—and I relied to a painful extent on the little Franklin pocket translator that I still carry around with me today. I could give reasonably fluent speeches on policy, but I wasn't comfortable in the cocktail circuit on K Street or on Capitol Hill. My only deep acquaintances in the United States were Colombia's enormously talented and dedicated ambassador in Washington, Luis Alberto Moreno, plus Professor Fisher from Harvard and a few other good friends from 1991, including Sandra Ceballos and Francisco Sánchez. For the most part, I didn't know Washington, and Washington didn't know me.

In the months leading up to my election, a steady stream of Colombians filed through the offices of Congress and the State Department, spreading the usual baseless allegations about me—that I supported the paramilitaries, that I didn't care about human rights, and so on. Many of these lies were then repeated elsewhere. For example, the first time my name ever appeared in the *Washington Post* was in December 2000, when an article flatly stated, "Uribe has been tied in the Colombian media to the paramilitaries." That was it. There was no independent reporting, no specific attribution, no attempt to seek a reaction from me—just a vaguely sourced attack on my name, repeated as fact. Three months later, I was once again mentioned in the *Post*: "Uribe, who is viewed as the presidential candidate most favored by paramilitary groups and their supporters."

My arrival in Washington on that June day in 2002 coincided with the United States government's publication of the extradition request of Colombia's paramilitary leaders. The Embassy officials remained silent, but I could see the fear in their eyes. In response to the barrage of questions I received on whether or not I would extradite them, the only thing I said was "Colombia is a nation of laws."

Two year earlier, President Clinton and President Pastrana had implemented "Plan Colombia," a counternarcotics initiative designed to reduce the amount of cocaine and other drugs flowing from our country into the United States. In the United States, it received decisive support, which we will always be thankful for, from politicians such as Denny Hastert, Speaker of the House of Representatives. The program essentially recognized that shared responsibility of industrialized nations where there is a high demand for narcotics. Despite my reservations regarding President Pastrana's peace plan, I did not hesitate to support Plan Colombia. I remember that before I was elected president, I traveled to Ecuador where I encountered vehement protests against the Plan. It seemed to me that the FARC were causing Colombians to move to our brother nation under the pretext of the fumigation of coca crops, all in order to destabilize Plan Colombia. I did not hesitate to address the Ecuadorian media in order to explain the plan's many virtues.

I believed that in order to be effective, Plan Colombia needed to change in the context of Colombia's security policy. The United States, with President Bush at its helm, agreed that fighting drug trafficking without facing cartels such as the FARC and the ELN was pointless The U.S. government offered us valuable intelligence and logistics help but it did not involve combat operations in Colombian territory. All efforts fell on our soldiers and police officers.

My first visit to Washington was about building confidence: I simply repeated the same things I had said to my fellow Colombians throughout the campaign that led me to victory. Since I hadn't yet taken office, I wasn't supposed to see President Bush on that first trip—I was scheduled to meet several members of his cabinet, including Defense Secretary Donald Rumsfeld, Secretary of State Colin Powell, and Bush's national security adviser, Condoleezza Rice. I was in Rice's office at the White House when, all of a sudden, President Bush decided to drop in on us.

He shook my hand and smiled amiably. We exchanged pleasantries for a moment or two—neither of us was really into small talk. Then, as is his style, President Bush leveled his gaze at me and got right to the point: "Mr. President, how do you intend to deal with the FARC?"

I replied: "What is your recommendation?"

President Bush looked caught off guard for just a moment. He probably thought that I was trying to dodge his question. That was not the case; I had spent years elaborating a detailed plan of my own. But I was eager to hear President Bush's perspective; we were less than a year removed from the attacks of September 11, 2001, and I admired the way he had conducted both his policies and himself as a leader. At that moment in history, perhaps no one in the world understood the fight against terrorism like President Bush did. I was genuinely curious to hear what he believed.

Quickly recovering from his surprise, President Bush explained his view that the world had changed after September 11, and that terrorism was now the main threat to security around the globe. He said that previous Colombian governments had engaged in a policy of appeasement by ceding territory to the FARC and taking other steps that allowed the armed groups to grow. He said he believed that stance needed to change.

"Mr. President," I said, "that is exactly what we're going to do." I then proceeded to explain to him the tenets of democratic security, and how we were going to confront the terrorists in our country.

Building a productive relationship with President Bush, the senior figures in his administration, and members of both parties in the U.S. Congress would require transparency and time. It did not happen overnight. But President Bush and I talked for a good while that first day, and in subsequent meetings after I became president—at the White House, at regional meetings, and even driving around in his pickup truck on his ranch in Texas. President Bush also visited Colombia twice.

Near the end of one of those first conversations, as I explained our intentions, President Bush started to seem just a bit uneasy. It was as if a disturbing thought had occurred to him that he dared not say out loud. Only later did I find out what was on his mind.

That same day, President Bush called his ambassador in Bogotá, Anne Patterson, a great friend to Colombia.

"We need to help Colombia," President Bush told her. "But to do that, we've got another mission to worry about. We've got to help keep Uribe alive."

17

"Mr. President, be careful! There's a very powerful criminal in Caucasia, just as powerful as Pablo Escobar. His alias is 'Macaco,' and he's telling people that he's going to kill you because you're *pisando muy duro;* you're causing too much trouble!"

A group of us were sitting in my office, listening to a source provide us with this information via speakerphone. I hung up, frowned, turned to my high peace commissioner, Luis Carlos Restrepo, and asked, "Who is this 'Macaco'?"

When I took office, no one realized just how extensive the tentacles of criminality were in our country. Vast swathes of Colombia were under the total dominion of the *narcoterroristas.* As we expanded the reach of the state and moved into areas of the country that the government hadn't fully controlled for decades—if ever—I was personally shocked by the extent of the reach of the paramilitaries in particular. By 2002, most estimates put the number of paramilitaries in Colombia between ten thousand and fourteen thousand—but as we soon discovered, there were far more. In his first conversation with commissioner Restrepo, the paramilitary kingpin Carlos Castaño said that he alone had fourteen thousand people under his control.

In portions of the country, the paramilitaries controlled, or had penetrated, elements of our institutions: some of our courts, some local governments, and some individuals within our security forces. In this respect, they were following the path of the armed left, who had also sought to broadly infiltrate the state as part of their doctrine of the "combination of forms of struggle." Salvatore Mancuso, a paramilitary leader, famously declared that 30 percent of the Colombian national Congress had some kind of connections with the paramilitaries. Such declarations roiled our society—the uproar over the ties between some politicians and paramilitary kingpins became known as the *"para-politica"* scandal. While Colombians knew who some of the paramilitary leaders were, such as Mancuso and Castaño, we soon learned new names: *capos* such as Rodrigo Tovar Pupo, alias "Jorge 40," Julián Bolívar, and Carlos Mario Jiménez, a.k.a. "Macaco," none of whom I'd ever heard of before.

One of the organizations that was penetrated by paramilitaries prior to my presidency was the intelligence agency DAS. The organization had suffered numerous problems in previous years, despite the efforts of some good individuals who worked there. When I took office, I had the idea that, because of the DAS's deteriorated reputation, it would be best to just close the DAS and start a new intelligence agency from scratch. In those early days of my presidency, with the massive security challenges that faced us, the DAS's leadership convinced me that reforming the organization was better than shutting it down. The reforms weren't enough. In retrospect, I believe I made a mistake by not following through sooner on my original instinct. Allegations of improper or illegal actions by the DAS would be a constant issue throughout my presidency. Toward the end of my administration, we introduced legislation to shut down the DAS—legislation that was approved shortly after I left office.

The armed forces, the analysts, the general population, and I were unaware of the size and penetration of the terrorist organizations that operated in our democracy. A third of the country was under the reign of the paramilitaries, another third was controlled by the guerillas, and the last third was at risk. Despite the attacks on the day of my inauguration, Bogotá authorities refused to believe in the existence of these groups in urban areas where, along with the FARC militia and paramilitary organizations, they were causing much damage to our cities.

We pursued the paramilitary bosses with the same vigor with which we pursued senior leaders of the FARC and ELN. I was explicit in every speech, every interview, and every private conversation that my government would make no distinctions among the criminal groups, that they were all equally subject to arrest and prosecution, and their activities would not be tolerated. The Colombian state had to recover the monopoly of the rule of law in Colombia. We never considered the possibility of coordinating with the paramilitaries in our operations against the FARC and the rest of the armed left; perhaps it would have resulted in faster military progress, but it would have caused extraordinarily severe damage to our democratic institutions. All criminal groups were equally corrosive to the rule of law.

That's why, when I learned of Macaco's existence, I wanted to capture him and bring him to justice as soon as possible. I gave an order privately, to a small circle of security officials, to try to obtain an arrest order from the courts. Within days, Macaco's lawyers came to Restrepo's office and asked, "Why did the president order Macaco's capture if our client is willing to negotiate?" This was one of the first occasions when I realized just how extensively the illegal groups had penetrated our institutions in certain areas. A short time later, when we increased our focus on confiscating property that had been illegally obtained through drug trafficking, I learned that Macaco's opulent ranch in Caucasia was extremely close to a military installation. The law called for us to confiscate his ranch; we did so. It wasn't until my government, with our single-minded and indiscriminate policy of recovering the exclusive monopoly of power, that the Macacos of Colombia began to feel intense, sustained pressure.

Their numbers were enormous—which presented a dilemma of its own. In addition to the paramilitaries, there were approximately eighteen thousand FARC, six thousand ELN, and several thousand urban militia for both of those groups at the time we took office. We were determined to put all of these criminals, and especially their leaders, under as much duress as possible. But we also knew that a classic "military victory" over such a large, diffuse, and powerful number of criminals was simply not feasible, even if we tripled or quadrupled the size of our armed forces (which we could not do). Instead, we believed our best available option was to pursue a multipronged strategy. We would use our troops to regain territory in the name of Colombian democracy, while simultaneously looking for ways to convince as many of the groups' "foot soldiers" as possible to put down their weapons. Put another way: We would pursue the illegal armed groups and their leaders with all our determination—but we would be generous with those who were willing to rejoin productive society.

We extended an offer to all of the armed groups—we would offer them a path to peace, but first they had to cease their criminal activities. Some groups, such as the FARC, rejected this offer out of hand. The ELN, meanwhile, was engaged in a separate set of talks that dated from the previous government, and took place in Cuba. But as our government's security policies showed signs of progress during those first months in power, things started to change. In a nutshell, people began to realize that we were serious. The rules in Colombia had fundamentally changed: My government would pursue all criminals, no matter their ideology or affiliation. *Narcoterroristas* of all stripes figured out that they could either spend the rest of their lives on the run, constantly facing the imminent likelihood of arrest or death, or they could talk to us and possibly negotiate some kind of middle ground. As the stark reality of that choice became more evident with each passing day, some groups began to drift toward the negotiating table—among them some of the paramilitaries, but also substantial segments of the armed left.

We clearly had their attention. But figuring out a solution that would entice these criminals to voluntarily give up their weapons and their drug-trafficking empires, which in many cases were worth millions of dollars a year, posed a considerable challenge. Previous agreements of this kind, in Colombia and elsewhere, had granted sweeping amnesties and pardons to those who agreed to demobilize. By the time I took office, the world had changed. It was no longer possible to grant amnesties in most cases, especially when it came to particularly atrocious offenses and crimes against humanity. Such treatment was explicitly forbidden by Colombia's constitution and complementary legislation, as well as international treaties that my predecessors had signed. We would have to explore other solutions.

How to balance the dueling needs of justice and peace, in a country such as ours, where thousands upon thousands of graves were still fresh in the ground? I agonized over this question as much as any other during my government, spending long nights discussing it with Restrepo and with members of the Colombian Congress, which would need to approve any arrangement. I drew on the experience of my family's own struggles, and consulted many history books.

Ultimately, we decided to pursue several paths. On the one hand, we leaned on some of the reconciliation strategies I observed during my post-graduate studies at Harvard and Oxford. I had watched with great interest from Oxford in April 1998 as the various parties signed the Good Friday Agreement, a landmark step in Northern Ireland's long peace process. With that agreement, those responsible for severe crimes were given a kind of conditional freedom or parole, but not a pardon. The distinction might seem technical, but it was, in fact, very important—the criminal recovered his or her freedom, but continued with the consequences of the punishment, in both the eyes of society and in practical matters. In Colombia, this meant the person was not eligible to hold elected office ever again. And, critically, if they ever committed another crime, they would be rearrested and charged with even more serious offenses.

For the senior ringleaders—for the Macacos of Colombia—the terms were more onerous. They would have to confess their crimes, dismantle their criminal organization, and hand over their personal fortune as compensation to their victims. They would also have to cooperate fully with the state's investigation. If they complied with all of these conditions, then instead of a forty-year prison sentence, they might get eight, for example. But if they failed, they would face even longer sentences, and potentially the punishment that scared them most of all—extradition to the United States.

Some people protested, arguing that even these terms were too lenient, given the scope of the massacres of recent years. I took this debate deeply to heart, and spent countless sleepless nights wrestling with the various arguments. Ultimately, I believed that my greatest responsibility was to put Colombia on a path to sustainable security and peace. That was why I had become president.

In 2005, Congress passed the legislation codifying the terms for demobilization—known as the Justice and Peace Law. A great many Colombians took advantage, and ceremonies celebrating the demobilization of hundreds or thousands of people at a time became a relatively common occurrence. By the end of my first term in 2006, more than forty-three thousand members of the various armed groups had demobilized.

Meanwhile, the ringleaders—the men like Macaco—began the long process of turning themselves in. In order to successfully participate in our offer, they would have to hew to a narrow path: cooperating fully with our investigations, while ceasing all of their criminal activities. The lure of returning to their past lives of opulence and impunity—to the glories of their ranch just outside the military barracks—was ever present. For some of them, the temptation would eventually prove too strong to resist.

18

As the first year of my government drew to a close, we could point to several tangible signs of progress: Kidnappings were down by a third. Murders fell 21 percent nationwide, with even more dramatic progress in areas that our troops now fully controlled, such as greater Medellín. We had expanded the security forces by more than twenty-five thousand people, and we had undertaken major military operations against the armed groups in areas such as Cundinamarca, greater Cartagena, and in the mountains surrounding Bogotá. As security improved and investment began to return to Colombia, our economy also started showing signs of life, with 3.8 percent GDP growth in the first quarter of 2003. I also noted that my approval rating was above 70 percent—testimony to the hard work of all members of my government, and a sign of the incipient, fragile confidence that Colombians were beginning to feel in our policies.

"Mr. Uribe's programs have for the first time given people in this country of 42 million a glimmer of hope," *The New York Times* wrote shortly after the first anniversary of my inauguration. Polls showed that 60 percent of Colombians believed I had kept my campaign promises. Others noted, correctly, that we had barely begun to solve our problems. "The best thing the president has done is to remind us that we can indeed save the *Titanic* with teamwork and much sacrifice," read an editorial in *El Tiempo*. "These are days of arduous plowing, tough planting, patient harvests and painful pruning."

For all our progress and political will, the capacity of the armed groups to sow terror remained formidable. The FARC still spurned our offer of talks and continued to massacre soldiers and innocent people with equal savagery. Overall, more than eleven thousand people were killed throughout Colombia in just the first six months of 2003, including Guillermo Gaviria Correa, Gilberto Echeverri, and the nine soldiers at Urrao. The scourge of kidnapping was still awful; there had been more than a thousand abductions in that same six-month period. A study released in mid-2003 by the World Markets Research Centre still ranked Colombia as the most likely country in the entire world to experience a terrorist attack. No, we had not yet forged the Colombia we all dreamed of. Not even close.

We knew that many of the worst attacks were directly coordinated by the committee of seven people—the so-called "secretariat"—that centralized almost all decision making for the FARC. Yet, despite intense work by our military, and our network of informants, we still had precious few leads on the whereabouts of men like Manuel Marulanda or Raúl Reyes. They continued to order attacks with impunity—and an ever-increasing disregard for civilian life.

Late one Friday night in February, I was in a meeting with members of my high military command when we received word that El Nogal, a well-known social club in northern Bogotá, had come under attack. I immediately rushed to the scene with Defense Minister Ramírez and several commanders from the security forces. What I saw there exceeded even my worst expectations.

The FARC set off a car bomb at eight fifteen at night, when they knew El Nogal would be the most crowded—the club was hosting a wedding, a ballet class, and a children's party at the moment of the blast, media reports later said. The explosive charge weighed more than 350 pounds and was made from a mixture of ammonium nitrate, fuel oil, and TNT. The explosion was so deafening that some people in the neighborhood thought an airplane had crashed; pieces of the car were found as far as five blocks away. Debris sprayed onto the street and caved in the roofs of passing vehicles. It took firefighters two hours to get the blaze under control. The final toll: thirty-five dead, including six children, and more than 160 people injured. The whole front of the building looked like it had just melted away, drawing some comparisons abroad to the bombing of the U.S. federal building in Oklahoma City a decade before. Some media called it the worst attack on a Colombian city since the days of Pablo Escobar.

The symbolism of the bombing could not have been clearer. El Nogal was a favorite gathering spot for several of my ministers and aides, as well as the business community of Bogotá. "The message to Mr. Uribe," *The Wall Street*

Journal wrote the next day, "is that if the guerrillas are not free to roam rural Colombia and terrorize peasants, they will attack the country's leadership." President Bush issued a statement calling the attack a "barbaric act of terrorism." Central American countries met in Panama, denounced the attack, and referred to the FARC as a terrorist group. Kofi Annan of the UN also condemned "this cruel bombing."

When I arrived at the scene that night with Defense Minister Ramírez, we saw blood splattered all over the sidewalk, and families standing around crying, holding one another in grief. We spoke with them first—offering our solidarity and our condolences. Minister Ramírez was extremely graceful that night in her compassion. As the rescue workers began digging through the wreckage, some of the journalists and other people present urged me and other officials to reverse our policies, arguing that the terrorist threat was too much to bear.

Shortly after midnight, I gave a televised speech from the scene of the bombing in which I acknowledged our pain and suffering but urged the country, yet again, not to give up in our fight against terrorism. "I know that the violent ones are making every effort possible to bend the will of the Colombian people," I said. "Despite all the pain we feel . . . I ask all of our compatriots not to cede before terrorism, and that we reach just one decision: to defeat the violent ones and capture all of them."

The next day, thousands of demonstrators across the city took to the streets, chanting the slogan *"Bogotá llora, pero no se rinde"*: "Bogotá weeps, but it won't surrender." The phrase was first uttered by Fernando Londoño, my interior minister, and then repeated by many other Colombians, including myself, in the aftermath of the El Nogal bombing. Lina participated in the march, accompanied by Vice President Santos. The demonstration was a clear sign that the people would, indeed, not be deterred in their quest for security. No, Bogotá would not surrender; nor would Colombia.

There was another plea I made outside El Nogal that night that received less media attention, but was just as important. I pointedly asked "the democratic world for help to defeat terrorism." I said there were countries "that take the terrorists' money for safekeeping . . . that tolerate drugs and money laundering . . . that acknowledge the terrorists as legitimate interlocutors and encourage them to commit heinous crimes against the people of Colombia."

I concluded the speech with a clear call to action: "Please," I said, "no more indulgence, and no more complicity."

Following through on this call would be difficult. It would be controversial. But we had seen more than enough tragedies. We could no longer ignore reality. It was time to act, and act boldly.

SECTION FIVE

Accountability

"Everything that man does as a mere individual . . . for the sake of his own preservation, and at the expense of society, is bad; and everything that he does as a social person, for the sake of the society in which he himself is included, for the sake of its perpetuation and of the perpetuation of himself in it, is good."

—MIGUEL DE UNAMUNO, *TRAGIC SENSE OF LIFE*

1

One evening, after wrapping up a meeting near Medellín, I invited the attendees to a nearby riding arena to see some horses. I remember there was a stallion that caught my eye—it possessed an elegance and a smooth gait that are particularly desirable in Colombian show horses. I felt inspired. I turned to the group of people with me and I declared, "I'm going to ride that horse around the arena while carrying a cup of coffee—and I won't spill a drop!"

President Hugo Chávez of Venezuela smiled. "Are you *really* able to do that, Uribe?"

I grinned and replied, "Let's bet a few barrels of oil and see."

President Chávez laughed heartily and agreed.

We alerted the horse's rider to our interest, and he brought the stallion over. As I mounted the steed, I asked my bodyguards to go get me a cup of coffee. They brought it back extremely full—right to the very lip of the cup. "*Muchachos,* how could you do this to me?" I said under my breath, smiling. "It's like you're in the opposition!"

I took a tiny sip to give myself just a little margin for error, and then began riding around the ring. After two laps, I finished—as advertised, without having spilled so much as a drop.

President Chávez beamed from ear to ear and applauded me. "Uribe!" he yelled. "You . . . you're like a centaur!"

We laughed and laughed. He still owes me the oil.

During the moments we were face-to-face, my relations during eight years with President Chávez were almost always civil. Much of the time they were spontaneous and warm. Even on the occasions when we disagreed, I believed that our disputes were not personal in nature—we were presidents, interacting on a state-to-state level. Meanwhile, I never lost sight of the fact that our countries are like family in many ways. Whatever issues I had with the Venezuelan government, I always took great effort to emphasize the brotherly ties between our two nations, which will never be shaken.

I tried to help President Chávez, and the Venezuelan people, on a great many occasions. During my first term, I met with him eight separate times. In a few instances, when President Chávez escalated his criticism of Washington to an unsustainable level, he asked me to put in a good word on his behalf with President Bush to help defuse the tensions—and I complied. During the Venezuelan economic crisis of 2003, we helped supply our neighbor with food, manufactured goods—and even, somewhat incredibly, Colombian gasoline, which was running short because of massive strikes there. Similarly, when the global food crisis broke out in 2007 and 2008, some Colombian businessmen asked me to halt or reduce our food exports to Venezuela because they were worried about the possibility of runaway inflation at home. I refused. I said publicly—and I told President Chávez himself—that if Colombia had a liter of milk left, we would share it with Venezuela. I always believed that international trade cannot just be a utilitarian exchange. There must be an element of solidarity and brotherhood, too.

Ultimately, though, my overriding responsibility as president was to bring security, prosperity, and the rule of law to the Colombian people. To accomplish these goals, we desired the full cooperation of our neighbors. At a minimum, we needed them to refrain from sheltering the terrorists and other criminals who were personally responsible for many of the deadliest attacks on Colombian soil. I worried that all of our security initiatives would be for naught if the *narcoterroristas* were able to cross over the border and find a safe haven on the other side, where they could continue planning and staging attacks in Colombia with impunity.

As I took office, I remembered President Chávez's comments at Oxford in 1998: that he would remain "neutral" between Colombia and the FARC. There were worrying signs well before I took office that his rhetoric had real-world consequences. In February 2002, six months before my inauguration, the head of President Chávez's counterinsurgency force resigned after declaring, "[The] Venezuelan government gives protection to Colombian guerrillas." Our security forces stationed near the border frequently came under fire from FARC and ELN terrorists operating in Venezuelan territory. In one such incident in 2002, terrorists just on the other side of the Arauca

River attacked our forces using twenty homemade mortars—gas canisters packed with screws, nails, broken glass, and human feces. One of the most egregious attacks came in March 2003, just six weeks after El Nogal, when terrorists crossed over from Venezuela and detonated a bomb in a busy shopping mall on Ash Wednesday in the border city of Cúcuta, killing seven people and injuring dozens of others, and then retreated back to the other side.

When pressed about the Colombian terrorists operating in Venezuela, President Chávez always responded that when his government found out about them, he took appropriate action. He also argued that Venezuela couldn't possibly contain every inch of its 1,400-mile border with Colombia—and he blamed us for not doing more to keep the violence from spreading into *his* country. After the Cúcuta bombing, I declared that the ELN and FARC had "fooled the people and government of Venezuela" by "hiding on the other side of the border and . . . disguising themselves as good citizens."

Still, we had our doubts. We had intelligence indicating the existence of terrorist training camps in relatively open view in Venezuelan territory. FARC operatives who had demobilized or been captured told us they received training in explosives and military tactics from Venezuelan soldiers. I tried to broach these issues as diplomatically as possible in my initial meetings with President Chávez, while also prodding him to end his "neutrality" and explicitly back Colombia's democratically elected government. When I landed in Venezuela for one of my first presidential visits there, and President Chávez received me at the airport, I gave him one of my ponchos. *"Presidente,* please accept my poncho as a gift," I said. "It's much better than Marulanda's towel!" I was referring, of course, to the FARC leader and his trademark red towel that he kept slung over his shoulder. President Chávez laughed, but we both knew the gift had deeper meaning.

In November 2004, when President Chávez visited Colombia for a summit, journalists asked him directly whether he or anyone in his government was in any way providing support to the FARC. His response was unambiguous.

"It's a big lie!" he exclaimed. "We do not support the FARC."

A month later, we received clear, unambiguous intelligence regarding the whereabouts of one of the FARC's most senior leaders—Ricardo González, alias Rodrigo Granda, who was living in a comfortable two-story house with a swimming pool in a posh mountain community about two hours southwest of Caracas. *The New York Times* noted that the town was also a well-known retreat for Venezuelan army generals.

2

Granda was an unusual figure within the FARC. He didn't often dress in camouflage, and he wasn't known to participate in military operations—instead, he advertised himself as the group's "foreign minister," and he traveled the world wearing polo shirts and blazers. Since 1994, Granda had reportedly visited at least sixteen countries, including Muammar Gadhafi's Libya, seeking financial and material support for the FARC. He served as a supposedly civilized face for the group abroad, a key role for an organization that depended on foreign largesse for much of its money and political sustenance.

Yet this was no "diplomat"—this was a criminal in flesh and blood. According to the Colombian police, Granda had helped orchestrate several kidnappings over the years, and he was also a key nexus in the FARC's narcotics trade. He had brokered meetings between the FARC and other criminal organizations, such as Mexico's Tijuana cartel. He was deeply involved in arms smuggling, including a landmark 1999 deal in which the FARC acquired ten thousand assault rifles via Peru. He also participated in efforts to export the FARC's brand of terror to other countries. Paraguayan authorities accused Granda of providing advice and logistical support that led to the 2004 kidnapping and subsequent murder of Cecilia Cubas, the daughter of a former Paraguayan president. In other words, Granda was a critical figure in the arming and financing of one of the world's most notorious terrorist groups. We had been searching for him for years.

Colombian intelligence indicated that Granda would be in Caracas attending two meetings of well-known leftist organizations in December 2004—the first World Meeting of Intellectuals and Artists for the Defense of Humanity, and a convention sponsored by President Chávez's government, the Second Bolivarian People's Congress. For us, specific information of this nature was virtually unprecedented—we rarely knew with advance notice where the FARC's senior leadership was going to be. None of the organization's top figures had ever been captured.

This revelation left us without any easy options. By late 2004, after two years in office, I was convinced that alerting Venezuela's army or police to Granda's presence through traditional channels carried a certain risk even if President Chávez knew nothing of sheltering the FARC, as he assured us, we knew that some elements within his security forces were. Granda could therefore be tipped off, which would allow him to disappear back into hiding. We had issued an international arrest warrant for Granda more than a year previously, to no avail. Media reports later said that Granda enjoyed the privileges of Venezuelan citizenship and had even voted in a recent local election. There didn't seem to be a legitimate institution to capture Granda in Venezuela. We would have to find another way.

Via our intelligence networks, we communicated Granda's whereabouts to individuals within the Venezuelan security forces who were sympathetic to our shared battle against the terrorists. A group of Venezuelan officials then contacted us in Bogotá, offering to bring us Granda—alive and unharmed—in return for a cash reward.

We considered the offer with care. I knew that such an operation could upset the Venezuelan authorities and pose diplomatic problems. I had worked very hard to cultivate good relations with all of our neighbors and other countries around Latin America, believing that doing so was important to our long-term security and economic prosperity. But I was also deeply disturbed that a notorious terrorist was being allowed to openly operate and hold political meetings in the capital city of a neighboring country, at an event under the auspices of the government. United Nations resolutions, such as number 1373 passed in September 2001, prohibit the provision of shelter to terrorist organizations. Meanwhile, the use of cash rewards to capture terrorists was consistent with international law and practice. I noted that, at that moment, the United States was offering up to $25 million for information leading to the capture of Osama bin Laden. And this was a truly unique, even historic opportunity—it was the first time we had such specific information regarding the location of a FARC senior leader, and an opportunity to take him into custody.

I had spent two long years watching how the FARC's leaders strategically plotted and planned massacres of civilians such as the ones at El Nogal and Cúcuta. I had cried with the victims' families; I had seen the splattered blood when it was still fresh. I knew that, for us to take the next significant step in improving Colombia's security, we would have to decapitate the FARC's leadership. Going after Granda would show the FARC's leaders that they would be held accountable for their crimes, no matter where they were. In the final balance, I made a decision: I would assume the responsibility of offending people's sensibilities, or creating a storm in the world of diplomacy. The steps we were taking were legal and they significantly advanced our goal of creating a safer Colombia. When our defense minister, Jorge Alberto Uribe Echavarría (no relation), warned me about the potential problems our decision could cause abroad, I nodded and said: "Send them my way, and I will assume all the responsibility." I could tolerate a few days of sensationalistic newspaper headlines; I could not tolerate any more funerals.

On the afternoon of December 13, after he attended one of the Venezuelan summits, Granda was having coffee with a journalist in a Caracas café when his cell phone rang. Granda excused himself and walked outside to the sidewalk to take the call. Within minutes, he was in a car, handcuffed, on his way to the Colombian border—and a high-security Colombian prison.

3

For three weeks, there was precious little communication from Caracas. When we released a statement saying that we had Granda in our custody, hardly anyone in Venezuela complained. A few days later, more details leaked out to the public after I held an off-the-record briefing with senior journalists in Bogotá, one of whom violated our good faith by publishing much of what was said. Even so, we heard nothing from Caracas. Finally I called President Chávez on New Year's Eve to give him my best wishes for the year ahead. I am certain that he knew all of the facts of the case by that point, but he was very calm. "Uribe, I'm hearing some talk out there," was the most direct thing he said.

And then, suddenly on January 3, everything changed.

The FARC's senior leadership issued a statement that sent President Chávez into a rage—and also inadvertently answered many of our questions about Venezuela's relationship with the FARC. In the statement, the FARC complained about Granda's arrest and essentially criticized President Chávez's government for allowing it to happen. With no apparent irony or sense of shame, the FARC stated that Granda had been in Venezuela "with the approval of government authorities" and called on the Chávez administration "to define its position" regarding the FARC's ability to operate in the country. The letter concluded by demanding a guarantee of security for the FARC at future meetings in Venezuela.

Having now been embarrassed in front of the international left, President Chávez abruptly sprang into full crisis mode. He recalled Venezuela's ambassador in Bogotá, and began shifting troops toward the Colombian border. In speeches, he called Granda's capture a "violation of (Venezuelan) sovereignty," and, taking a page from his usual playbook, he blamed the entire incident on the "imperialist" policies of the United States. Apparently opting to ignore the content of the FARC communiqué, President Chávez denied that his government had ever provided shelter to Granda or to any terrorist leader. Speaking on Venezuelan television, but addressing his words directly to me, he demanded an apology and said the incident would not be resolved until I made amends.

"Otherwise, Mr. President, my friend, this just becomes the law of the jungle," he said suggestively.

I was not going to apologize for Colombia's legitimate action to protect itself. But I also did not want to cause unnecessary damage to our relations with the Venezuelan government or its people. I refused to engage in a war of words. I limited my public statements to a dry, factual accounting of our actions, and my hopes for a quick and definitive resolution. "The problem of Granda isn't with Venezuela, but rather with the FARC," I said. "Our interest with Venezuela is to have a constructive and positive relationship."

Soon the FARC issued another statement, calling Granda's capture a "kidnapping" and a "serious transgression of international law." Though I had been exposed to the FARC's propaganda for many years, I was still struck by the hypocrisy of this comment, coming from an organization that kidnapped thousands of people a year, massacred civilians, trafficked in narcotics, and flagrantly broke the law in myriad other ways in Colombia every single day.

As we looked for ways to defuse the crisis, some people yet again proposed the typical solution: that I request the resignation of the commander of the National Police, which was responsible for the operation, as a symbolic gesture. One person suggested that police commanders were like "fuses"—that once they burned out, it was the president's responsibility to change them. I refused, saying that such a move would undermine the confidence of our security forces. I took the opposite approach: I assumed full responsibility and congratulated the National Police, thanked its director, and sought out ways to normalize relations between Colombia and Venezuela. I also telephoned leaders around the region, including President Luiz Inácio Lula da Silva of Brazil and President Alejandro Toledo of Peru, communicating the rationale for our actions and asking for their help in defusing the confrontation.

Nevertheless, President Chávez continued to escalate the crisis. He ordered a partial closure of the border, which had an immediate and chilling effect on bilateral trade. This was more painful for us than for them. Venezuela was our second-biggest trading partner, and we export labor to them. Venezuela's

exports, meanwhile, consisted mostly of raw materials and oil-related prod-
ucts, which they could just sell to somebody else with relative ease. I later
found out that President Chávez declared that he would "bring Uribe to his
knees" by restricting trade. Yet I remained resolute: We would not sell out
our national interests because of money. Several business groups issued statements of support for my government. As they realized, our future economic
prosperity was directly tied to our ability to defeat terrorism—backtracking
in this case might provide a short-term financial benefit, but it would cost us
dearly over time.

On January 23, more than a month after Granda's capture, President
Chávez convened a rally of tens of thousands of his supporters in Caracas.
He emerged triumphantly, to the sound of a bugle playing reveille. He called
the Granda incident a "fresh attack of U.S. imperialism" that "comes from
Washington, not from Bogotá." He then insulted the U.S. Secretary of State,
Condoleezza Rice, calling her "illiterate," according to media reports.

"I have been told she dreams about me," President Chávez told the crowd.

Some in the gallery started chanting, "Chávez has a girlfriend! Chávez has
a girlfriend!"

"Should I propose to her?" he asked the crowd, seemingly delighted.

"Noooooo!" they bellowed.

It was clear to everyone why President Chávez was acting this way. These
confrontations—whether with me, the United States, or others—were always
political theater designed to rally his base of support in Venezuela and abroad,
many political analysts said. I understood this. The problem was that the
underlying issue—the support of terrorists—was extremely serious. This was
not a game. We were presidents, and there were lives at stake. The Granda
affair had escalated to such a fevered pitch by this point that I had no idea
how it would be resolved. Until one evening, after midnight, my phone un-
expectedly rang.

4

"Uribe?"

"Yes?"

"Aaaah! I knew you'd be awake! You're a night owl, just like I am!"

The voice on the telephone belonged to Fidel Castro.

President Castro and I had spoken on a few occasions over the years, and people were always surprised by how well we got along. Despite our ideological differences, I always treated him with respect. I remained grateful for the frankness of the message that he had conveyed to me in 1997, via Gabriel García Márquez, regarding the FARC's true intentions during the so-called peace process. When President Castro and I finally met in person, we discovered that we shared a common passion for the intimate details of governing— we came at things from different perspectives, but at the end of the day we were both policy wonks. At the inauguration of President Nicanor Duarte of Paraguay in 2003, President Castro and I were seated at the same table for lunch, and we spent several hours enthusiastically trading ideas on topics such as dairy cooperatives and Colombia's enormous potential for electricity generation. Years later the prince of Spain, who was seated between the two of us at that lunch, recalled the whole conversation with a bemused smile. "Congratulations," he told me. "The two people in the world who have the most information stored in their heads are Fidel Castro and you."

On this troubled night in 2005, President Castro was calling in his capacity as peacemaker. The second I heard his voice, I realized the possibilities— President Chávez looked up to him as a kind of role model, and his influence in Venezuela was enormous.

But first President Castro wanted to talk about history. He spoke, not for the first time, about his long-standing interest in Colombia, and how it had evolved over many decades. In an odd twist of history, a twenty-one-year-old Fidel Castro happened to be in Bogotá attending a conference of Latin American students on the day in 1948 when Jorge Eliécer Gaitán was killed, triggering the infamous escalation of *La Violencia*. A decade later, when Castro became a household name, the coincidence fueled conspiracy theories that

Gaitán's death had been an international Communist plot. Castro wasn't even a Communist in 1948, and historians generally agree he wasn't involved. But the experience had clearly stuck with Castro, in the way that seminal events during one's young adulthood often do. He clearly relished the opportunity to chat with someone who not only knew Colombia, but had studied much of his own oeuvre in assiduous detail.

"President Uribe," he said, "I know that during your youth, you used to read everything I wrote. But I'm a much better person now than I was in that era!" Then he erupted with one of his gregarious laughs, and he continued talking.

I lay there in bed listening, with Lina asleep next to me. At one point, President Castro spoke for more than thirty minutes, uninterrupted. "Are you still there, Uribe?" he'd ask, and then he'd soldier on.

Finally, in the hours just before dawn, he shared with me his idea for resolving our situation. Both parties would move on by focusing not on what had happened, but on the future: Venezuela would vow to better police its borders, while Colombia would declare its intent not to engage in any more operations like the Granda case.

I had some doubts—I thought we needed to leave our options open, in case we ever discovered another senior terrorist leader hiding in plain view. But I told myself that, after this incident, perhaps our neighbors would be less likely to shelter the FARC.

In the end, President Castro's proposal paved the way to a temporary solution. A few days after our conversation, Lina and I were paid a secret visit on a Sunday afternoon at our residence in Rionegro by the Cuban vice foreign minister and Cuba's ambassador to Bogotá. We served our visitors Colombian *arepitas con quesito,* and they presented me with a very well-written letter from President Castro providing a more detailed framework for defusing the crisis. I gave the Cubans my reaction, and they traveled to Caracas the following day with news of my response.

On February 16, two months after Granda was delivered to our custody, I visited Caracas and met with President Chávez at the Miraflores presidential palace. The goal was to show the world that the situation between our countries was now back to normal. Venezuela's ambassador was back in Bogotá; trade had resumed. President Chávez told the press that we had both "decided to turn the page, to clear things up." And for the most part, he was right.

President Chávez was very charming and polite as he showed me around his palace. We had a lunch in his small office, accompanied by Venezuelan vice president José Vicente Rangel and my skilled foreign minister, Carolina Barco. I always believed it was important to have witnesses present during delicate conversations. But in this case, the conversation was almost like a chat among friends—President Chávez talked at length about his passion for Simón Bolívar. He spent the majority of our conversation asking me for my help in rebuilding better relations between Venezuela and the Bush administration. All told, we spoke for more than six hours. He mentioned the Granda affair only in the most oblique fashion:

"I don't protect the FARC," he told me almost apologetically. "But some of my followers are FARC sympathizers, and I can't do anything about them. Please understand, *Presidente*. It's not my fault!"

I departed Caracas that day relieved that the whole episode was over, but with a distinct feeling that we'd soon be back, dealing with these same issues again. How right I was.

5

As we neared the end of my first term, the progress we had made in changing Colombia was indisputable. Kidnappings fell by at least 80 percent from 2002 to 2006, and likely even more due to underreporting during those most troubled years. Homicides declined 40 percent during that same period. The economy had also returned to healthy growth. Colombians began asking how we would continue this progress—and deepen it. In theory, my presidency was going to draw to a close after just four years. Although reelection of presidents had been allowed during much of Colombia's history, the 1991 constitution forbade the practice due to short-term political considerations.

Public opinion on the matter was resounding. Polls showed that my approval rating remained above 70 percent, while about two-thirds of Colombians favored that the constitution be amended so I could run for a second term. Yet the idea of extending the term limits was by no means mine alone—previous Colombian governments had made similar attempts since 1991.

I was well aware of the pitfalls of concentrating too much power in one man's hands, but above all, I believed that we needed more time to ensure that the transformation of our security policies and our economy took hold. Otherwise, I feared they could be quickly undone—just as they had following my three years as governor of Antioquia. I also remembered the published comments of Raúl Reyes back in 2003: "Uribe's serious problem is that he only has three years left, and the FARC has all the time in the world." I was determined that the FARC and the other *narcoterroristas* not be allowed to simply stall until my presidency was over, and then strike back with renewed vigor. I believed that another four years of my policies would be devastating for them.

Ultimately, the Congress approved the amendment that allows for presidential reelection and our constitutional court declared it constitutional. A rigorous Law of Guarantees was introduced, specifying a series of obligations the President has to abide to while seeking reelection. In 2006, I ran for president again, and was reelected with more than 62 percent of the vote—

40 percentage points more than my closest challenger, who happened to be my old university professor, Carlos Gaviria Díaz. The margin was enough to ensure yet another rare first-round victory.

We would have another term. Years later, when Ingrid Betancourt was asked what the darkest moment was for the FARC, she said it was when the courts decided to authorize my reelection. There would be no waiting us out: the harsh new reality would unfold all too quickly.

6

Over time, the capture of Rodrigo Granda proved to be an important moment for Colombia. The intelligence we garnered was useful, and the FARC's leadership never again seemed quite as relaxed. But the next big breakthrough in our fight against the *narcoterroristas* was the one that, in retrospect, really began the chain of events that would transform our nation forever. It was also much more rewarding—in part because of how it happened, and where.

The Montes de María—literally, the "Mountains of Mary"—is one of Colombia's most unique areas, a low mountain range that begins near the Caribbean coast south of Cartagena and runs roughly ninety miles parallel to the sea. Lush, dotted with avocado trees, and possessed of good farmland, it has long been an important crossroads both geographically and culturally. During the last four centuries, the Montes de María has been a shelter for runaway slaves; a staging ground for government efforts at land reform; and a unique artistic melting pot that has produced luminaries such as the beloved Colombian musician and composer Lucho Bermúdez.

Unfortunately, the same characteristics that made the Montes de María such a rich crossroads also made it heaven on earth for narcoterrorist groups. Starting in the 1970s, the area became a major drug transit corridor between the mountains near Medellín and the secluded Gulf of Morrosquillo, where speedboats whisked freshly processed cocaine away to Central America, the Caribbean islands, and points beyond. The region's swamps, thickets, jungles, and low but steep mountain slopes made it a perfect place for secret hideaway camps; the terrorists could avoid "civilization" for years at a time. When I became president, control over the Montes de María was effectively split in half between the paramilitary groups in the north and the FARC and the ELN in the south. These groups grew fabulously rich off the drug trade, while most other residents remained mired in deep poverty. Despite the area's prodigious fertility, agricultural production essentially collapsed as the armed groups engaged in kidnapping and extortion, cut off highways, and forced thousands of helpless small farmers off their land. Meanwhile, the Colombian state hardly dared to enter the Montes de María at all. The area's security, roads, schools, and health care were either in abysmal condition or nonexistent.

So we got to work. One of my first major initiatives, implemented in September 2002, was to create an "area of rehabilitation and consolidation" that covered fifteen municipalities in the Montes de María. This measure essentially doubled the Marine Infantry presence in the region, while police also moved in en masse. Every day without fail, I telephoned the commanders in the region at least once—sometimes more often—to check up on progress. I asked them to hear the latest updates on kidnappings, murders, and other crimes in their district, and I listened to their general observations and requests. I also did not shy away from regularly calling colonels, lieutenants, and anyone else down the chain of command to ask for their view of conditions on the ground. Of course, this made some military leaders uncomfortable. Yet, by soliciting the views of our men and women in the trenches, I could be ensured of an accurate portrait of progress. I could also send a clear message that we would demand accountability from the very top to the very bottom of the organization.

Slowly, fitfully, and at enormous human cost, we made progress. We lost many brave members of the security forces in the Montes de María area during those early years, with many casualties from the antipersonnel land mines that the FARC had left saturated throughout the region. Yet through sheer persistence, we achieved a foothold. By the end of 2004, our forces had regained considerable territory and controlled almost all of the highways, including the main road north to Cartagena. The terrorists, who for years had driven around the area in broad daylight in luxury SUVs, mocking the authorities, were forced deep into the bush and were constantly on the run.

Meanwhile, we were moving in simultaneously with our "softer" forms of power. From child nutrition programs to an initiative called *madres comunitarias,* which began under President Virgilio Barco and paid a monthly stipend to the mothers of young children, we demonstrated to the people of Montes de María that the Colombian state had returned to stay. We greatly expanded the presence of our family welfare agency, the Instituto Colombiano de Bienstar Familiar (ICBF). Investment began to return to the region. I signaled my own commitment to the region by holding several of my Saturday town hall meetings there, as well as security councils open to the public.

As people began to have confidence in us, we started receiving a treasure trove of intelligence tips from the community. Residents of Montes de María discovered they could now talk to the police without risking death. Now that we had the terrorists on the run, many of the armed groups began to suffer mass desertions. We were able to "flip" some of them and turn them into government informants. Our demobilization program also attracted many adherents. In 2005, a notorious bloc of paramilitaries known as the Héroes de Montes de María put down their weapons. Two years later, we would see the total disintegration of the ERP, a fringe ELN group that had been particularly prolific in kidnapping in the region.

The Montes de María region was, in many ways, a microcosm of what we sought to do nationwide. This progress reaped a sufficient reward: hundreds of thousands of Colombians whom we welcomed back within the warm embrace of the state.

We didn't know yet that another victory was just around the corner.

7

Each captivity is cruel in its own way and the case of Fernando Araújo, a charming politician and career civil engineer, was no exception. Araújo had recently resigned as the minister of development in President Pastrana's government when, on December 4, 2000, he was kidnapped while jogging in his hometown of Cartagena. He instantly became the FARC's most prized hostage. For the first seven months of his captivity, Araújo was bound by a leash to a tree—retribution, his captors said, for resisting his abduction. They eventually untied him, but the following five years brought what, for Araújo especially, was the most inhumane punishment imaginable: isolation. The FARC forbade him from speaking to his captors, with the exception of basic requests such as food and permission to go the bathroom. Since there were no other hostages in Araújo's camp, this was the equivalent of a sentence to solitary confinement. And on it went for an almost inconceivable 2,224 days.

Yet, as the FARC would soon discover, Araújo was indomitable. He simply would not be broken. The man was so clever and so resourceful that I suspect the FARC's gag order against him was an implicit recognition that, if Araújo were allowed to speak, his words alone would somehow provide him a passport to freedom. In a sense, they were right.

Starting early in his captivity, Araújo begged the FARC for the right to make occasional "proof of life" videos, so he could show his family that he was still alive and in relatively good health. For a period of several years, his captors refused. But as our military campaigns increased the pressure on the armed groups, their calculus seemed to change. Weakened and on the run, the FARC began evaluating new ways to leverage their biggest remaining assets—Araújo, Ingrid Betancourt, the three American contractors, and dozens of members of the Colombian police and armed forces whom they also held hostage. By releasing videos showing their condition, the FARC cynically hoped to manipulate public opinion and increase popular pressure on my government to negotiate an asymmetrical prisoner swap or implicitly grant the FARC status as a "belligerent group."

In late 2005, Araújo's jailers came to him and told him to write a script for his first proof of life since the period shortly after his capture. The draft would then be submitted for approval to the FARC's "secretariat"—the seven-person council that ran the group. Araújo dutifully composed his script, and it was soon approved. On December 11, exactly one week after his fifth anniversary in captivity (and, coincidentally, two days before Granda's capture in Caracas), Araújo was finally permitted to speak.

In the video, Araújo appeared alarmingly thin but otherwise healthy, dressed in a clean white collared shirt lent to him by the FARC, which always tried to make its hostages look as crisp as possible in their public appearances. Araújo sat on a chair underneath a green FARC banner, as three uniformed terrorists with assault rifles stood sternly behind him. A small green parrot was perched on his shoulder. Speaking slowly but with strength, he encouraged my government to "show all the will necessary" to reach a deal for a prisoner swap with the FARC. He also assured his family that he was, for the most part, fine. *"A papá y mamá, que estoy bien, que los quiero mucho,"* he said: "To Dad and Mom, I'm fine; I love you a lot."

I never watched these videos myself—they made me too indignant—but our intelligence agencies pored over each word. To our regret, they found little of interest. So we were all shocked when Araújo's family contacted us and told us that the former minister had managed to reveal his location in the video.

As they explained to us, Araújo and his brother had gone to university with a man from Ovejas, a small town in the Montes de María. This friend had a way of speaking that was peculiar—he tended to omit possessive pronouns when he spoke, a habit that Araújo and others had gently mocked. By saying *"papá y mamá"* instead of *"mi papá y mi mamá"* in the video, Araújo was imitating his old friend's way of speaking—which, in ingenious fashion, communicated his general location in a way that only his brother would be able to decipher.

Fernando Araújo was in the Montes de María.

In ensuing months, we dramatically stepped up our military campaigns and surveillance efforts in the area. The FARC's so-called 37th Front, which was holding Araújo, was now constantly on the move in order to avoid air strikes and sweeps of our brigades. Araújo, for his part, had done his best to ensure that he would be able to hear any incoming messages. He was allowed to keep a radio—his only real contact with the world—in return for agreeing to write news summaries each evening so that the FARC's rank and file could discuss the important issues of the day. "They loved any kind of news about terrorist attacks against Western countries," Araújo later reported, "and also anything having to do with Hugo Chávez."

One night in September 2006, while quietly listening to one of the radio programs in which Colombian families spoke to their loved ones in captivity, Araújo finally heard the message he had been waiting for. *"Papá y mamá, muy bien,"* his brother said, practically winking at Araújo through the ether. "The cousins—Alfonso, María Jose, Guillermo, and Ana María—await more news from you."

Ana María, Araújo's cousin, was married to a man named Guillermo— who happened to be Admiral Guillermo Barrera, the commander of the Colombian navy.

At that moment, Araújo realized not only that his message had gotten through to his brother—but that our armed forces knew his general whereabouts as well. The meaning was clear: We were coming for him.

8

As it turned out, discovering Fernando Araújo's location wasn't the only unexpected bonus we got for reestablishing control over the Montes de María.

Few cities in the world are as fascinating or as beautiful as Cartagena, a port founded by Spanish sailors in 1533 and, for centuries, the most important outpost of Spain's overseas empire. Its colonial center, a UNESCO World Heritage site, is characterized by cobblestone streets, balconies overflowing with red and pink bougainvillea, and towering churches and museums with views of the nearby Caribbean Sea. Eight miles of stone walls encircle the old city, ensuring over time that its distinct architecture and culture remained perfectly preserved. If there is a finer window into what life must have been like in the Americas in the seventeenth and eighteenth centuries, I am unaware of it. In later years, immigration by Italians, Jews, French, and Lebanese ensured a cosmopolitan character that makes Cartagena that much more vibrant and unique.

I was saddened to see during my first presidential campaign and the early years of my government that tourists had largely deserted Cartagena. Colombians visited in minuscule numbers, and foreigners hardly came at all. Cartagena had a reputation as one of the safest cities in Colombia—but even that apparently wasn't safe enough. There were several headline-grabbing terrorist attacks within Cartagena's city limits during the late 1990s and early 2000s, including Araújo's kidnapping off the streets and a foiled FARC bomb attack prior to a visit by U.S. president Bill Clinton in 2000. In August 2002, just two days before my inauguration, explosives hit the governorship building. Meanwhile, Cartagena's woes were emblematic of a national problem—foreign visitors had been avoiding Colombia for both tourism and business for years. Some international life insurance companies refused to cover travel of any kind to Colombia. Famous foreign travel publishers such as Fodor's and Frommer's had never even published a guidebook about our country.

I was determined to bring foreigners to Colombia so they could witness its beauty, and also invest and spend their money. This was an obsession of mine. So I decided to set specific, audacious goals—and I made it my personal mission to convince huge cruise operators such as Royal Caribbean to come back to Cartagena.

Cruise ships were a particularly lucrative form of tourism. While the ships didn't always bring overnight visitors, they did deposit hundreds or even thousands of tourists at a time who were eager to eat, buy souvenirs, and spend their money in other ways. Our data showed that each cruise passenger spent between $100 and $150 per day while in port. Cruise passengers were also, as a general rule, more conservative in their choice of destinations than many other tourists—their threshold for risk was low. So I knew that, at the beginning of my presidency, we wouldn't be able to pursue this goal immediately, because the security situation didn't yet allow it.

Yet by 2004, we had made significant inroads in Cartagena. Why? Among other reasons, because we had retaken control of the Montes de María, just south of the city. Many of the criminals who had terrorized Cartagena during the previous decade often descended from the mountains to commit their crimes, and then fled back there once they were done, out of reach of the authorities. Once we controlled the highways leading in and out of the area, those shenanigans largely ended. It was another example of the multiplier effect of our security policies.

Our ambassador to the United States, Luis Alberto Moreno, arranged a personal meeting for me with senior executives from the cruise industry. I traveled to Miami and told them our story. They said that our progress sounded impressive. Before long, an emissary of the cruise industry—Michele Paige, the executive director of the Florida-Caribbean Cruise Association—came to have a look at the new Colombia.

My government was willing to do virtually anything to create the conditions for investments that created jobs and raised Colombians' living standards. The redistribution of wealth was just as important as its creation; stimuli created more wealth which in turn generated more taxes that would allow more security and social policies. I believed that tourism had huge growth potential, but there were countless other sectors, too: software, biofuels production, medical tourism, pharmaceutical and cosmetic manufacturing, and business process outsourcing, among others, could also be key to Colombia's future if we could create confidence and find the right investors. I established a rule with my cherished confidante, the private secretary of the presidency, Alicia Arango: I wanted all foreign investors coming through

Bogotá to come to the Casa de Nariño to meet with me personally. We created and maintained a database of contacts for these investors—we would track their activities over time and stay in contact with them before and after their investment was made. As elsewhere, follow-up was absolutely key.

Improved security was usually the common thread that made investors start looking at Colombia again, but we knew we couldn't stop there. Security merely leveled the playing field with other emerging market countries, but did nothing on its own to create competitive advantages. Under the guidance of our three finance ministers—Minister Junguito, Alberto Carrasquilla, and Óscar Iván Zuluaga—as well as many other leaders, including our tourism and trade ministers, Jorge Humberto Botero and Luis Guillermo Plata, we took bold steps that would make our economy more productive and a more attractive place to invest. From the first year of my administration, we instituted significant tax incentives for companies that made long-term bets on the economy: the only way, in our view, that Colombia would be able to create high-quality jobs and make our country competitive in the global economy. We introduced a new law that authorized special tax deals for companies making large investments, and also provided a twenty-year guarantee whereby any future Colombian government would have to pay a penalty if they tried to modify the terms of the agreement.

We worked on security, investment, and social policy. However, it was important to observe certain austerity measures: our government needed to be more efficient by keeping costs down, limiting bureaucracy and showing its commitment to the people. All told, we implemented reforms at more than 460 state entities.

I never thought that, considering the obstacle of the radical left, we could go from being a country condemned to producing less than two hundred and fifty thousand barrels of oil a day to being a country that currently nears two million barrels a day. Another key initiative was the overhaul of Ecopetrol, the state-run Colombian oil company, thanks to the courage of our ministers and the company's presidents such as Isaac Yanovich. We introduced reforms in the company's work and pension structure. We floated 20 percent of the Ecopetrol's equity which, through a joyful and democratic process, allowed almost half a million Colombians to buy the company's stocks.

The risk of being unpopular never stopped us from undertaking any reform. The only reforms we didn't tackle were those for which we didn't have enough time. We stuck to our purpose of staying clear of demagoguery and maintaining constant dialogue with the community, which allowed us to introduce these reforms without much public disapproval.

But through all these long-term reforms, we never forgot about our specific goals. When the cruise industry representative Michele Paige came to Colombia, Minister Plata met her in Cartagena. The next day, I rendezvoused with them and we continued on the presidential plane to San Andrés, a gorgeous island off of Colombian's Caribbean coast, and another potential cruise destination. Minister Plata informed me that Ms. Paige did not seem too interested in Colombia but that over dinner the night before, she had mentioned her love of horses and how we both shared that passion. So during the flight, I engaged her on the subject and the look on her face immediately changed. I mentioned how horses don't take flattery or sadism, how, much like politics, horses require absolute balance. After we visited the island of San Andrés, back on the plane, I came back to the topic of horses and Ms. Paige mentioned that she would be interested in seeing a native Colombian horse.

I thought, *Well, for the fatherland, no task is too large.* Shortly after the plane left San Andrés for the return flight to Bogotá, I jumped up from my seat and asked the pilots to change course and make a stop in Rionegro.

I had an ironclad rule against using the plane for personal, recreational purposes—but this was clearly in the interest of the nation. We landed in Rionegro after dark, and made our way to my house. The house was totally closed up for the season, so we had to have food delivered from local restaurants. We ordered up a wide range of Colombian specialties, from *chicharrones* (fried pork rinds) to *arepas* (a dish of ground corn dough or flour). I took out a bottle of *aguardiente* liquor, found some cups, and poured it for our guests.

I escorted Ms. Paige to the barn, and together we brought my horse Juguete ("Toy") over to the grass area just outside the riding arena. I did several laps, riding Juguete bareback, without a saddle. Later, we returned to the topic of the cruises and I personally committed to guarantee visitors' security during their stops in Cartagena, Santa Marta and San Andrés.

It seemed to me that Ms. Paige was now more open to the idea of including Colombia as a cruise stop.

Shortly thereafter, Ms. Paige invited us to St. Kitts for a meeting with several senior executives from the cruise industry, including Richard Fain, the CEO of Royal Caribbean Cruises. I traveled there myself, and helped convince Mr. Fain to bring Royal Caribbean back to Cartagena. Several other carriers soon followed suit. I'm sure it was the facts on the ground—that is, the dramatic improvement in security—that were most critical in their decision making. But it's possible that my demonstrations of how important their business was to us, as well the firsthand proof that my government was willing to go the extra mile for investments, may have also played a role.

Toward the end of my presidency, as security showed more dramatic improvement, we launched our new ad campaign for Colombian tourism: "The Only Risk Is Wanting to Stay." The number of foreign visitors to Colombia, including tourists and businessmen, jumped from 1.1 million in 2002 to 1.9 million in 2006 to about 2.8 million in 2010—a rise of 154 percent during my presidency. I set the specific goal of improving Colombia's standing in the World Bank's annual Doing Business survey, which ranks countries according to a variety of factors, from the simplicity of their tax regimen to their openness to trade. By the end of my government, we were the top Latin American country in the Doing Business rankings, ranked thirty-seventh out of 183 countries, ahead of Spain, Portugal, and Taiwan, among others. Foreign direct investment soared from an average of about $2 billion a year prior to my presidency to consistent levels of $8 billion and above during the final years of my government. Even more important, domestic investment increased from $10 billion in 2002 to approximately $57 billion in 2010.

Meanwhile, I kept my promise to Ms. Paige—as the tourists streamed back to Cartagena and other tourist sites such as the Sierra Nevada, the Pacific coast, and Medellín, among others, I made myself personally accountable for their security. When Cartagena hosted the annual convention of the World Tourism Organization in 2007, I gave the keynote speech and provided all two thousand attendees with my cell phone number, with instructions to call me if they had any problems. The only calls I received were from delegates thanking me. I personally took every call.

During the final December of my presidency, in 2009, we had three cruise ships land in Cartagena on the same day, bringing more than ten thousand mostly foreign visitors to the city. Starting that morning at four a.m., I began calling the Cartagena police chief and mayor, asking for regular updates on security. All day long, I monitored the visitors' safety. By nightfall, as most of the passengers were back aboard their ships, we had one complaint—from a pair of German ladies who were upset that they were charged $50 for having their hair braided. The police looked into it. But it was certainly a far cry from just nine years before, when people were being snatched off of Cartagena's streets and dragged into the jungle for years at a time.

9

Over the years, I constantly urged the Colombian military to do everything within their power to rescue Fernando Araújo, along with all the other hostages. In my daily phone calls to my commanders, I always asked for Araújo by name and explicitly asked what they knew of his whereabouts. But for reasons that were not fully clear at the time, going after Araújo proved especially problematic. In the early years of his captivity, we launched several operations to rescue him—yet the FARC was either gone by the time we arrived or, worse, they were waiting to ambush our forces. It appeared they knew exactly when we were coming, and by what means.

Meanwhile, I did not close the door to a negotiated solution for the hostages' release. On December 14, 2005, three days before the FARC released Araújo's proof of life, I formally agreed to a proposal for talks put forth by mediators from France, Spain, and Switzerland. The international delegation called for both Colombian forces and the FARC to temporarily withdraw from a seventy-square-mile zone near the village of El Retiro in southwest Colombia. We would then use the area as a staging ground for formal talks. The stated goal of the talks was to negotiate an agreement under which the FARC would liberate Araújo, Ingrid Betancourt, and roughly fifty other hostages. Our government was willing to consider releasing about five hundred FARC prisoners from our jails, upon the condition that they leave the FARC and take up residence abroad, or that they agree to participate in one of our formal reinsertion programs.

My agreement to hold talks surprised many people: I had, by then, acquired a reputation at home and abroad as a "hard-liner" who was not at all interested in negotiation. This reputation was simply not accurate. We were always open to talking to the FARC, under certain conditions. What we could not tolerate under any circumstances was a demilitarized zone similar to the one during the previous administration, in El Caguán, that would allow the FARC to rebuild their military capabilities and continue their criminal activities while pretending to be interested in peace. Since this new proposal contemplated the withdrawal of both Colombian forces *and* armed

FARC operatives from a relatively small area with no civilian population, I was willing to try it. I did have misgivings—I believed the Colombian state should be constantly expanding its remit, not reducing it—but I put my objections aside because the hostages' lives were such a priority. Meanwhile, the international mediators assured me their proposal had a good chance at success.

"I confess this is a concession on the part of my government," I said at a press conference on December 14. "We accept (the proposal) because we want to understand the anguish, the pain, the suffering of so many Colombians who have family members who have been kidnapped." My consent to the deal met with immediate, enthusiastic approval from many of the hostages' families, including Ingrid Betancourt's mother, who declared, "[Uribe] has taken an important step, and we hope that the rebels do the same."

When the moment of truth arrived, the FARC showed its true colors yet again. To my disappointment, as well as that of the international delegation, the FARC at first remained publicly silent about our offer. And then they responded to it in their own characteristic way: On December 16, two days after I extended my olive branch, the FARC launched a major offensive in our northeast near the Venezuelan border. They kidnapped three civilians near Sardinata, set buses and trucks on fire near Durania, and blew up electrical towers, leaving more than three hundred thousand people without power. On December 17, the FARC raided a military outpost near the Panamanian border, killing eight police officers and taking twenty-nine others prisoner in what Reuters described as "one of the biggest blows against the security forces in years."

Just ten days later, in the La Macarena National Park on the opposite end of the country, in southern Colombia, about three hundred FARC fighters ambushed an army unit that was destroying the only thing the FARC really cared about anymore—its coca crops. Twenty-nine of our soldiers died—and Reuters now called this newest assault "the worst blow against the military for years." We immediately went to the site of the tragedy and vowed that we would return in weeks to personally oversee the continued manual eradication of coca crops—a commitment that we kept.

Finally, late on December 30, 2005, the FARC officially confirmed what was already abundantly clear: They had no interest in talks. They falsely declared that they had never even received the international facilitators' proposal. Raúl Reyes, the group's second in command, declared that the FARC would never agree to a hostage swap as long as I was president. This was a transparent, cynical, and ultimately ineffective attempt by the FARC to influence the election the following year.

Despite these setbacks, I did not give up—ten months later, I consented to yet *another* attempt at compromise. In October 2006, shortly after I was reelected president, I again offered to withdraw armed troops from the area around Florida and Pradera, two towns in the southwest, for the purposes of creating a "corridor" for the FARC to release hostages. This was another proposal made by European negotiators, who assured us that the FARC had agreed to the release of at least one hostage. We opened the corridor, but not one hostage appeared. Just a few days later, a FARC terrorist dressed as a naval officer drove an SUV into a military academy in northern Bogotá and blew it up. The bomb injured ten people and forced the evacuation of more than two thousand students.

We were outraged. Our patience and good faith had been abused once again. These events reinforced, yet again, the main lesson of the last two decades: The FARC would treat any offer of compromise as a sign of weakness, and would attempt to strengthen its power accordingly. They had no interest whatsoever in genuine negotiations. The day after the military academy attack, I declared an end to talks for a hostage swap. "We cannot continue the farce," I said.

Shortly thereafter, we advanced with a new plan for a military rescue of Fernando Araújo.

10

For a year after we received Araújo's ingenious proof of life, we hunted for him in the thickets and swamps of the Montes de María. We installed hidden microphones and other high-tech surveillance equipment to track the movements of the FARC's 37th Front. As usual, though, it was human intelligence that ultimately allowed us to determine his exact location—an informant whom we paid in return for the information. Araújo was being held in a camp in the area of Aromeras Norte, in the custody of about two hundred men. With his specific whereabouts in hand for the first time, we had to act very quickly, since we knew the FARC, under enormous pressure, was changing campsites every few days.

The time had come to call the former minister's father, Alberto Araújo Merlano, and inform him that we would soon be launching a military rescue.

We scheduled the operation for New Year's Day, 2007. As we planned the details, the shadow of the 2003 massacre in Urrao hung over us. We sought to avoid a repeat by overwhelming the FARC this time with numbers and a display of force—nearly eighteen hundred members of the Colombian navy, air force, army, and police would participate in the mission—twenty-four times the manpower we had employed at Urrao. They would be backed up by multiple Black Hawk helicopters and a navy command-and-control aircraft. As a precaution, we greatly increased the frequency of helicopter flights in the area during the days prior to the operation, so that the FARC would become desensitized to their presence—and avoid the kind of confusion that led to the deaths of Gaviria Correa, Echeverri, and the others. We also put together a special team of long-distance snipers, whose objective was to approach the camp and neutralize Araújo's guards as the assault began.

The day before the rescue was scheduled to take place, I was at the airport in Rionegro, preparing for my usual ritual of spending New Year's Eve with the troops or with Colombia's neediest. We were bound for Bojayá—the small town where the FARC had destroyed a church during the presidential campaign in 2002, leaving 119 civilians dead, including many children. Virtually the entire town had been devastated in that attack, and we had made rebuilding Bojayá a special priority—part of an ongoing commitment to the worst-hit areas of Colombia that we intended to reinforce publicly with our visit.

As we waited for bad weather to clear, my new defense minister, Juan Manuel Santos, said he had to speak to me urgently. He pulled me aside and informed me there was a complication—we had received intelligence that the FARC unit holding Araújo was preparing to move out, probably later that same afternoon. Unless we scrambled to launch the rescue twenty-four hours early, we would almost certainly lose them, warned General Freddy Padilla. However, Santos said, some of the last-minute preparations for the assault, including the arrival of the special team of snipers, had not yet been completed.

I gathered other senior officials, and canvassed their opinions on how we should proceed. Some of those present recommended we cancel the rescue attempt. Surely the ghosts of Urrao were a factor in everyone's thinking. Yet I had followed the progress of the armed forces closely during the previous four years, and I knew firsthand how they had made dramatic strides in training, firepower, and special operations. I also thought of the five full years it had taken us to get a bead on Araújo's location as well as the failed attempt to negotiate a staging ground for talks, which had made it painfully clear that the FARC was never going to voluntarily release any of its high-value hostages. The decision was clear to me; I didn't hesitate.

I turned and looked at General Padilla.

"Proceed," I said. "Proceed under my responsibility."

11

Shortly after ten a.m., I telephoned Alberto Araújo Merlano and informed him that our attempt to rescue his son was under way, a day earlier than planned.

"The helicopters have been in the air for twenty minutes," I said. "We are all praying for a successful result."

I felt Don Alberto's pain across the phone—a palpable conflict between stoic patriot and afflicted father. Very judicious and brief in his words, he thanked me and said he would wait by the phone for the result.

For much of the morning, we were not fully aware of the developments—cell phone service was spotty in Bojayá, and we had to rely on a single satellite phone for information. But soon the news began pouring in: Our helicopters had arrived, a rocket attack had been launched to stun the terrorists, and our troops flooded the camp. We received immediate reports of casualties. And then, at long last, we got the final word from our commanders in the field:

The camp was secure.

But Araújo was nowhere to be found.

12

We discovered several of Araújo's belongings at the campsite—evidence that he had, indeed, been there at the moment of the assault. But we didn't know for certain why he had vanished—had the FARC managed to flee with him? Had they executed him, and then concealed the body? There was no physical evidence at the scene to discount any of these possibilities. We were alarmed to discover that the FARC unit's leader, Gustavo Rueda Díaz, a.k.a. Martín Caballero, was also missing—even though we discovered some of his belongings as well as the dead body of his partner, which confirmed that he, too, had been at the campsite. Had he escaped into the jungle with his prized hostage in tow?

We did the only thing we could—we launched a massive manhunt. We had already ringed the area around the camp with thousands of soldiers. Now we tried to close the circle in the hope that we would be able to find Araújo before the FARC did. We knew this was a race against time: The FARC would be pursuing him with just as much urgency.

As one day passed, then two, then three, then four, I can honestly say that I never lost hope. But the human sacrifice of the operation continued to mount. One of our valiant Infantry Marines, Tayron Almanza Martínez, was killed during the search operation. Two others were injured.

Several times a day I called Araújo's father, assuring him that we were doing everything within our power to find his son. Our conversations rent my heart. Apart from him, though, we wanted to keep the operation secret from the public for the moment. We didn't want the FARC to know that we were also looking for Araújo; for all they knew, this was just another army raid. Thanks to the discipline of our armed forces and my inner circle, we were able to keep any hint of the incident from appearing in the press.

Day and night, I telephoned our commanders and kept track of our troops' movements to ensure there would be no gaps in the slowly collapsing ring of forces. I told them I had confidence in their abilities, and to inform me the moment we had news, good or bad.

For five full days I barely slept. And I prayed that this fine man, this symbol of everything that was good and resilient about Colombia, would somehow be clever and resourceful enough to find his way to freedom.

13

Fernando Araújo had, in fact, been devising an escape plan for years. He was certain that one day a moment would come when he would have to flee—or be killed by his captors. Based on years of listening to the radio as well as his captors' conversations, he was aware that the FARC executed its hostages rather than allowing them to be liberated. He knew all the details of the massacre at Urrao. He had also heard about Consuelo Araújo Noguera (no relation), a former Colombian culture minister whom the FARC abducted in 2001—and then murdered with two bullets to the head when she couldn't keep pace with her kidnappers. Once Fernando Araújo heard the coded radio message from his brother, and realized that a rescue was likely coming, he stepped up his physical and mental preparations.

Through it all, he was fully aware that no hostage had *ever* successfully escaped from the FARC—but he believed that he had no choice but to try.

An excellent athlete, Araújo stayed in shape while in captivity by running in place and doing push-ups. He worked hard to ingratiate himself with the FARC—following every order, and being as docile as possible in his interactions—to put his captors at ease and to ensure that he would not be chained up again. That way, a fast getaway might be possible when the crucial moment came. And, finally, he prepared for failure, writing in his journal, "I understand what the family is doing with me"—his way of saying that he agreed with our decision to stage a military rescue, even if he perished in the process.

The morning of the operation, Araújo heard our helicopters buzzing overhead—but this had been going on for days and, as we had hoped, both he and the FARC had stopped paying much attention to them. Araújo continued listening to his usual Sunday-morning radio program until he realized there was, in fact, something unusual about the sounds these helicopters were making. He quietly began to pack up his journal and his few other earthly goods, his eyes alternating back and forth between his small backpack, what he could see of the sky through the jungle canopy, and the two FARC terrorists who stood guard with assault rifles some ten yards away.

With a fireball and a flash of brilliant orange light, the assault was under way. Araújo instantly threw himself to the ground. As bullets flew all around him, he began crawling away on his hands and knees—certain that a full-out sprint would earn him a volley of bullets in the back. Out of the corner of his eye, he saw one of his jailers shooting up at the sky—as if in slow motion, screaming and pointing as bullet cases cascaded to the ground. Araújo dragged himself along for several hundred yards, pausing only once, when he dropped his radio—and he briefly doubled back to retrieve his most beloved possession, his only real outlet to humanity for the previous six years.

Araújo had observed during his long captivity that, when a FARC unit arrived at a new camp, the first thing it did was to identify an emergency exit—the escape path it would take in the event of an army assault. The FARC hardly ever engaged in direct combat, knowing they would be overwhelmed by our troops. At this particular site, Araújo knew that the FARC's only planned escape route led south. So he had already mapped out, in his mind, his own escape in the opposite direction. Once he crawled past the latrines on the edge of the FARC camp, he rose to his feet and, surprised to still be alive, he headed north, hoping to arrive at a nearby town called El Guamo.

In the ensuing hours, Araújo walked as quickly as he could—again not quite running, so he could stay aware of his surroundings. On more than one occasion, he saw our helicopters through the jungle canopy and frantically jumped and waved to get their attention—no luck, given the thickness of the vegetation. As night fell and he continued his journey toward what he hoped was north, he realized he was in for a long haul.

For five full days, Araújo survived on water from cactus plants, waded through swamps with muck up to his shoulders, and tracked small *jabalís*— wild boars—in the hope they might lead him to food. He had to abandon his northward march when he came across a thicket of thorns so thick that there was no way through or around it. Finally, on that fifth day, he came across a man on a donkey who he feared might be FARC—but by this point, Araújo was so exhausted and hungry that he decided to try his luck. The man turned out to be friendly—and he directed him to the nearby village of San Agustín.

At first, the townspeople were hesitant to help this strange, sunburned, bearded, sick-looking man who had wandered in from the bush. Finally, someone pointed him down the street, where two uniformed soldiers were on patrol, completely unaware that the biggest prize in four decades of struggle against the FARC was about to land in their laps.

Araújo ran over to them—really running now, for the first time in six years—and told the soldiers who he was. As they radioed their superiors with the glorious news, Araújo could not stop looking over his shoulder, fearful that the FARC would somehow materialize at any moment and drag him back into captivity. For a long time, he stared expectantly into the savanna, not quite believing what was happening. During captivity, Araújo had experienced recurring dreams in which he was free, and then woke up, devastated, to find he was still a prisoner.

As if sensing his thoughts, one of the soldiers put his hand on Araújo's shoulder, smiled, and gently assured him, "Don't worry, Dr. Araújo. Nobody's going to take you away from us now."

14

Four days later Araújo came to see me at the presidential palace, he shook my hand, beamed, and said, "Mr. President, I want you to know that I was never kidnapped."

My eyebrows arched in surprise. "What do you mean?" I asked.

"I infiltrated the FARC," Araújo said with a wink. "My mission was to learn everything I could."

He was joking, of course—his captivity had been all too real. But Araújo's point was very serious: After more than six years living among the FARC, he was a treasure trove of intelligence. This was a brilliant man who had closely observed every tactic, every movement, every aspect of the FARC's doctrine and its day-to-day operations. Over the following days and weeks, he shared numerous insights with me. In turn, I convened our senior military commanders and asked Araújo to repeat to them the central points of his message:

1. Life had changed for the FARC since our government began. In the early days of his captivity in 2000 and 2001, the FARC kingpins had driven around the roads of the Montes de María in broad daylight in luxury Toyota SUVs, often with Araújo in tow. Araújo told us that once our military began moving into the area, the FARC couldn't travel by vehicle at all anymore, and they were constantly on the run.
2. The FARC had infiltrated portions of our military. While I remained fully confident in the overall integrity of our armed forces and its commanders, Araújo confirmed what some had suspected: The terrorists knew well in advance when we were launching both land and air operations in the Montes de María. Days or even hours before air strikes, Araújo reported, the FARC would simply move their camp, sometimes just five hundred meters away from the original site. They returned as soon as the bombardment was over.
3. Similarly, the FARC was taking advantage of the set duration of some of our military offensives. The Colombian military would deploy its resources into a new area with a defined timetable of, say, two months.

Fully aware of the duration of the offensive, the FARC would gather enough supplies for those two months and then move in a circle from one camp to another. A separate FARC unit was then designated to cover their tracks and deploy antipersonnel mines to kill or maim any Colombian troops who might be trailing them. Once the two months were over, life for the FARC went back to normal.

4. Our current strategy for air strikes, in general, did not seem to be effective. Araújo reported that, among the many bombardments that he personally saw or heard during his six years in captivity, none had hit its target. While the air strikes did serve to keep the FARC on the run and occasionally intimidate them, Araújo said he had never seen a FARC terrorist injured, much less killed, in such an attack. We needed to make some kind of shift.

As we spoke, I fully realized for the first time what a huge coup Araújo's escape truly was. Some of these issues our military was already aware of. But to hear them articulated in such lucid and authoritative fashion from a man who had spent the last six years living and breathing daily life with the FARC was something entirely new. I didn't yet know how, but Araújo's contributions would be absolutely critical in the chain of resounding victories that were soon to follow.

15

We were just weeks away from the 2006 election when my advisers came to me and said, "We have a serious dilemma."

For the previous two years, we had been negotiating a free-trade treaty with the United States, hoping that it would help us in our quest to create high-quality jobs at home. Although both the Clinton and Bush administrations had once harbored dreams of a huge free-trade area encompassing most of the western hemisphere, I helped convince President Bush that, because of resistance from countries such as Venezuela and Brazil, the best path to regional integration for the foreseeable future was through bilateral deals. We quickly began moving toward a free-trade deal between the United States and Colombia and we'd later work on similar deals with several other countries and trade blocs around the world, such as the European Union and Canada. Many people worked hard on the negotiations, including Luis Guillermo Plata, Jorge Humberto Botero, Luis Alberto Moreno, Carolina Barco, Diego Palacio, Andrés Felipe Arias, María Consuelo Araújo, and Hernando José Gómez.

So here was the supposed dilemma that had my advisers so concerned in 2006: Our polls showed that the free-trade deal was unpopular in Colombia. Some people harbored a deep-seated suspicion of the United States, while others had reservations, some of them quite reasonable, about the terms of the agreement. As a result, some of my political advisers suggested that we should wait until after the election to advance in our negotiations with the United States, since otherwise my opponents might be able to use the free-trade deal as leverage against us during the voting.

My response was blunt: we'd move forward with the negotiations and we'd stick to the timeline we had planned; our next step would be to close the deal.

I have never been willing to put my own electoral or political considerations ahead of the country's best interests. The trade deal with the United States was good for Colombia, even if it might be bad for me in the short term. I also believed that the agreement would have to be negotiated as transparently as possible, hiding nothing from the Colombian people, in order for it to have long-term success. I thought elections should constitute an opportunity for people to take into account every issue, and cast their votes accordingly. If we held our talks in the shadows, people's suspicions would only grow; and future governments might feel compelled to renegotiate its terms. This agreement had to endure for it to be effective.

So rather than try to somehow camouflage or slow-pedal the free-trade deal until after the election, we decided to take the opposite approach. That said, we needed to explain to the public what it was about and thus gain the people's support by making an effort to educate everyone. My aides approached one of Colombia's biggest broadcasters, RCN, and asked whether I could host a marathon television debate regarding our negotiations with the United States. I would bring the relevant ministers and officials on TV with me, and we would accept any and all questions—totally uncensored, totally unscripted. RCN was willing to do so, but only at a time of low ratings—their previous engagements wouldn't allow them to preempt their regular programming.

So we asked RCN when their period of lowest ratings was—and when they said it was from ten p.m. to six a.m., we agreed to do it at that time.

RCN decided to call the program *The Trade Deal Marathon: Uribe Responds.* We provided a toll-free number and a special e-mail address for Colombians to ask questions, and I gave strict orders for the network not to monitor or otherwise screen incoming calls for content. I was joined by much of my cabinet, including my ministers for trade, tourism, and agriculture, as well as the chief negotiator of the free-trade deal.

The vast majority of the questions were excellent. We answered queries about the deal's effect on our domestic production of corn, whether there would be special tariff regimens for agriculture, whether Colombia could start exporting wood pulp like Chile did, and so on. Someone asked me via e-mail: *If you were a Colombian entrepreneur, what kind of business would you go into if the U.S. agreement is approved?* I replied that I would export biofuels produced from Colombian sugarcane, yucca, or African palm. Meanwhile, I sincerely shared my misgivings about the plan—I admitted, for example, that I was worried about the deal's potential impact on Colombian rice and poultry production. Somewhat predictably, a few political leaders also telephoned in to ask hostile questions. One of my opponents in the presidential election called, challenging me to put the whole trade deal to a popular referendum— I replied that the constitution that he himself helped write in 1991 gave the president clear jurisdiction over matters of foreign policy, making a referendum unnecessary.

At two a.m., RCN took a quick commercial break as we all ate some *arroz con pollo*. And then we charged ahead.

At the start of my presidency, Colombia's trade was very limited. Previous governments had made unilateral openings of our market, and the country had enjoyed temporary trade preferences from the United States and Europe. But the only formal trade agreements in place were with the Andean Community (which comprised Colombia, Venezuela, Peru, Ecuador, and Bolivia) and the so-called G3 of Colombia, Venezuela, and Mexico. By the end of my presidency, we had negotiated free-trade agreements with forty-five countries, including the European Union, Chile, several Central American countries, and Mercosur—the South American trade bloc, of which Brazil is the largest member—and Switzerland and its allies. We negotiated investment protection treaties with China and India. With Japan we strengthened our commercial relations since they had been weakened by the great deal of kidnappings. We started negotiations with Korea, Panama, and others. We signed treaties with Honduras, El Salvador, and Guatemala in Medellín. We were unable to move forward on the treaty with Costa Rica because this sister nation's priority was to advance on a referendum that would ratify its agreement with the United States. We met with all the heads of states belonging to the Pacific association in order to ask them to lift the moratorium to include Colombia. Our minister of foreign relations, Jaime Bermúdez, opened the doors to the "Arco del Pacífico" treaty with Mexico, Peru, and Chile. In many of those places, I personally traveled to address questions in the same comprehensive and transparent fashion that I did on Colombian television that night in 2006. In 2009, I visited Canada and addressed its parliament, fielding some very pointed questions from legislators in an effort to ensure passage of our free-trade deal there. The Canadian agreement was approved a few months later.

Our trade deal with the United States was approved by the Bush administration in 2006 but it's approval in the U.S. Congress would come only a few years later.

I had positive relationships with many Democrats in Washington, including then-senator Hillary Clinton and Senator Christopher Dodd. But many political analysts in the United States said that final approval of the trade deal with Colombia became delayed by domestic politics. The Democrats opposed several of President Bush's initiatives, including other trade agreements with Panama and South Korea. Some Democrats justified their opposition to the Colombia deal by citing violence against labor union leaders, but that argument had lost much of its force.

From the first day of my government—not because of foreign pressure, but because it was the right thing to do—I always emphasized that democratic security meant security for everyone—including opponents of my government and the most vulnerable members of our society. In addition to the overall security gains that we experienced, we took special steps, such as creating new units within the justice system that were dedicated to investigating rights violations. In several areas, with the strong leadership of Vice President Santos, we made substantial progress. For example, ten journalists were killed in Colombia in 2002; by 2010, that number fell to one.

On the subject of union leaders, we were able to make major improvements. Leaders of organized labor had been persecuted for years in Colombia, often by the paramilitaries. In fact, during the 1970s, Marxist guerillas introduced a "combination of different forms of struggle." They would kill, kidnap, and penetrate different layers of society by posing as students and labor organizations. The paramilitaries began assassinating workers, accusing them of collaborating with the guerillas, and the guerillas would do the same to take revenge, calling their victims traitors. During our administration the number of union deaths fell from around two hundred in 2002, the year I took office, to about twenty in 2010. We also made progress in overcoming impunity: we went from having one person sentenced for the assasination of workers, to over two hundred. The number was still too high; but we kept pursuing the problem with all our efforts. The progress was significant enough that in 2010, just before the end of my government, the International Labor Organization removed Colombia from its list of sanctioned countries—for the first time in more than two decades. In sum, while a great many challenges still remained in the area of human rights, just as in other areas of our security, I believed we had made every effort to address the problems.

Secretary of State Rice wrote in her memoirs: "Yes, Colombia had a history of violence toward labor, but the level of violence faced by union members was now less than that faced by the general population, in part because of special protection for labor leaders. The fact is that the opposition to the United States–Colombia Free Trade Agreement was thinly disguised protectionism." In the end, the U.S. Congress would approve the Colombia trade deal, along with the South Korean and Panamanian agreements, on the same day in 2011—after both President Bush and I left office.

Throughout these processes, we were never able to satisfy everyone. Yet by patiently answering questions with attentiveness and good faith, we were able to address the doubts of most people. Perhaps more important, we also showed Colombians that we would be absolutely transparent about any deal's risks as well as its benefits. They could be confident that we were acting in their best interests, and they could hold us accountable for our actions—the very essence of democracy.

As the all-night TV program on RCN came to a close at six-oh-two a.m., and I began to collect my notes and papers, the announcers asked me whether I was tired.

"Don't you get enthused by this?" I asked. "This is important. No, no, eliminate the word 'tired' from the Colombian dictionary when it comes to opportunities like this."

The broadcaster switched to a camera with a live shot of the capital's skyline.

"There's a look at Bogotá," one of the announcers said.

"Wow, the sun is out," the other one murmured. "We hadn't even noticed."

And then we all decided to do one more hour. You always have to go the extra mile.

16

It took us about nine months to start putting Fernando Araújo's advice to good use.

By the beginning of my second term, our growing relationship with the United States was paying dividends. The U.S. Congress had extended the mandate of Plan Colombia to include all drug-trafficking groups, including the FARC. Over time, we worked in partnership with the Bush administration and members of both parties to extend the cooperation between our two militaries in other ways as well.

Some accounts have exaggerated or otherwise distorted the role that Plan Colombia played in our country's turnaround. Over the course of my eight-year presidency, the amount of money that Colombia spent on defense far exceeded the amount of military aid from the United States. Many of our police and soldiers gave the ultimate sacrifice—their lives—for which we will be forever grateful to them and to their families. The work of our defense ministers—Marta Lucía Ramírez, Jorge Alberto Uribe, Camilo Ospina, Gabriel Silva, and Juan Manuel Santos—was instrumental to our success. Colombia's turnaround was primarily the result of Colombian blood and treasure.

American contributions were of immense importance, especially in key areas such as intelligence gathering, military training, and tools that boosted our airpower. One critical decision was President Bush's move to restore a program called Air Bridge Denial, which tracked aircraft suspected of carrying narcotics and alerted Colombia's military to their presence so we could force them to the ground. President Bush had suspended the program prior to my presidency because of a tragedy in Peru, but the program was implemented again in Colombia in 2003. By 2007, suspected drug flights in Colombian airspace had declined by 86 percent, according to U.S. government data; I saw "before" and "after" satellite images that clearly showed how the beehive of air traffic in our skies shifted to Venezuela during those years.

Yet the most important development of all—the one that really marked a before-and-after in our fight against the terrorists—was the Bush administration's authorization to sell Colombia smart weapons. These targeted munitions, which could be guided via GPS and other advanced tracking systems, allowed us to greatly improve the precision of our attacks. They proved to be the best way for us to address Araújo's observation that the FARC had been unbothered by our air strikes over the years, in part because they lacked accuracy.

We first used the smart weapons in a successful air strike on September 1, 2007, against Tomás Medina Caracas, a.k.a. Negro Acacio, the head of the FARC's 16th Front and a major player in its drug-trafficking activities. Our missiles hit their mark, and Caracas was killed. Some eight weeks later, in a stroke of fate, we had an opportunity to use them for a second time—to take down Araújo's main kidnapper.

I've always tried not to excessively personalize the terrorist threats that faced Colombia. Demonizing individuals accomplished little and could be counterproductive, because it raised their profiles in both life and death. Nonetheless, it is fair to say that Gustavo Rueda Díaz, a.k.a. Martín Caballero, had committed more than his share of misdeeds during twenty-five years with the FARC. Apart from masterminding Araújo's kidnapping, and then personally supervising his captivity, Caballero had a sadistic streak that was best typified by his use of antipersonnel mines. Araújo told us that when one of Caballero's mines killed a Colombian soldier or policeman, Caballero would cut the victim's name out of his uniform and sew it onto his own hat. According to our armed forces, units under Caballero's direct command on the Caribbean coast were responsible for the deaths of 218 police and soldiers, as well as 420 civilians. He blew up around fifty electrical towers and executed numerous attacks on the Caño Limón–Coveñas oil pipeline, a critical conduit. He was also the suspected author of the infamous bomb attack in Barranquilla during my 2002 campaign, which left four people dead and forced my campaign to suspend public events. Araújo described him as "robust, disciplined, very studious, but cynical and a psychopath."

With much dexterity, Caballero had had somehow been able to escape the FARC camp when we tried to rescue Araújo. His female companion and his eldest son died during that assault. Over the ensuing months, we captured his cousin, his other two children, and his niece, all of whom Caballero had recruited into the FARC's activities. We clearly had him on the run.

In October 2007, ten months after Araújo's escape, we received Caballero's location from an informant, whom we paid the equivalent of $850,000. But we knew we needed to be especially guarded—Araújo had also warned us that Caballero seemed to always find out beforehand about coming air strikes, and escape at the last moment. Caballero had been under constant duress since our New Year's Eve raid, and we believed that his communications capacity had eroded as a result. We also hoped that, with our new technology, things would be different. But there was no way to know for certain.

On October 24, Caballero was in a camp in an area known as Aromeras Sur, in the vicinity of El Carmen de Bolívar. We launched an air strike using smart weapons that obliterated his camp, killing Caballero and nineteen other terrorists.

Our troops arrived at the scene and found Caballero's body—and his cell phone, which was switched off. Defense Minister Santos later reported that, when our soldiers turned on Caballero's phone to examine its contents, a new text message popped up: *Tenga cuidado que le van a caer.* "Careful, they're coming for you."

If the message had arrived just a few minutes earlier, the outcome might have been different. The lesson was clear: While we were making progress, we still had considerable work to do. If our goal was to strike down the FARC's remaining leadership and rescue the other hostages, we would need to further improve the quality of all of our institutions and bring to justice those who aided the criminals—no matter where they were.

17

Late one evening, Defense Minister Santos and General Padilla came to my office with some of the worst news of my presidency: There was evidence that rogue Colombian soldiers had been abducting innocent civilians, murdering them, and passing them off as members of illegal armed groups.

In some cases, our soldiers had dressed the cadavers in FARC uniforms and then transported the bodies to areas where the FARC operated. The euphemism for this abominable practice was known as *falsos positivos,* or "false positives." Some people alleged that the soldiers engaged in such practices to inflate their units' so-called "body count" so that they could claim to be making progress in extending security. While there had been allegations of false positives as far back as the 1980s, and other reports of military abuses during my government, the cases presented by Santos and Padilla suggested that the practice could have been more widespread within our armed forces than we previously believed.

When I learned of these allegations, I felt physically ill. The murders were a violation of every principle that my government stood for, and every order that I had ever given to the armed forces. From my first day in office, I had given explicit instructions that violations of human rights or democratic principles would not be tolerated. In public and in private, my message was always the same; I never winked at any illegal practices, and I did not intentionally look the other way or otherwise remain willfully ignorant of any abuses. When I was presented evidence of criminal behavior in any government institution, I acted decisively and transparently to hold the responsible parties accountable for their actions. Democracies do not tolerate abuses against their citizens. This incident would be no exception.

We had, in previous cases involving alleged criminality in our security forces, established a clear record of moving quickly—with no regard whatsoever to politics or to our public image. In 2006, just a few days before the presidential election, we learned of a particularly loathsome incident in Jamundí. A group of our soldiers was accused of killing Colombian police who were in hot pursuit of drug traffickers—who were, in turn, allegedly under the protection of the soldiers. Horrified, I made the decision with Camilo Ospina—our defense minister at the time—to request that the case be investigated by the civilian justice system rather than military courts. We reacted in similarly expedient fashion following other incidents of alleged atrocities in Guaitarilla, Cajamarca, and elsewhere.

My government also passed a rule early in our administration in which, every time a military mission resulted in the death of someone believed to be a terrorist, our soldiers were not allowed to move the body until a prosecutor or someone from the civilian judicial system appeared on the scene. The purpose of this rule was both to protect human rights and enhance the reputation of the armed forces by making their activities more transparent. Paradoxically, the measures we took since 2003 were not noted by our human rights critics, but they did lead to overprosecution on behalf of the ordinary courts, which in turn led to the military's complaint over the removal of military courts.

That night, Minister Santos and General Padilla came to the meeting with judges and the government's advisor for human rights. At midnight, having reviewed the key points of the evidence, we decided to fire members of the security forces who had not strictly followed the protocols we had implemented in order to prevent such atrocities. Under the circumstances, we were obliged to act quickly. The next morning at seven a.m., I went on television, explained the results of the investigation to a shocked and saddened nation, and communicated our decision to fire those responsible. There were twenty-seven immediate dismissals in total from throughout the chain of command, including three generals. The decision pained me immensely, given my great love and respect for the armed forces, but it was necessary. The Colombian newspaper *El Tiempo* called it "the biggest military purge in the country's history."

"The investigation has found that members of the armed forces could be involved in murders, and there have been failings in procedures, in protocols, and in vigilance," I said. "These findings require us to take drastic decisions. We cannot allow any violation of human rights. . . . For us, truth and transparency are just as important as overall effectiveness for the success of democratic security."

Punishing the guilty wasn't enough. We immediately took steps to ensure that such crimes would never be committed again in the future. We again asked our civilian justice system to look into all allegations of false positives. We invited our military commanders to join my defense minister and me in regular public hearings on live television so that they could field any allegations from the community of human rights violations.

I met with many of the victims' mothers to offer my most profound regrets and better understand how the crimes took place. They told me heartbreaking stories of how their children had been lured away by promises of jobs—only for their bodies to be found days later, hundreds of miles away from home. The cases included a homeless man, a young epileptic, and street vendors. According to press accounts, the casualties even included a veteran who had left the army following the amputation of his left arm, and was then murdered by individuals from the institution he had once participated in and revered. I expressed my condolences and my horror at the crimes, and vowed to prosecute those responsible.

Several of the mothers told me their children had been involved in drug trafficking. This added on to other information we had linking these crimes to connections between drug dealers and certain members of the armed forces. We were already aware of some cases, such as the incident at Guaitarilla at the beginning of my administration, in which individuals within our armed forces were allegedly compromised by money from drug-trafficking groups. We knew of cases in which drug traffickers paid Colombian soldiers to kill their rivals, and then pass them off as members of the FARC or other groups. A declassified 1994 CIA report stated that this practice had occurred in Colombia since at least the 1980s. I personally interviewed a witness at the UN headquarters in Bogotá who told me that the main purpose of the killings was so that soldiers could give the impression that they were making progress against drug traffickers, while they were in fact protecting the real kingpins. I came to believe that drug trafficking had played an important role in the case of the false positives another horrific consequence of the drug trade.

In the years since the false-positives scandal erupted, I have been asked whether I believe my policies or my leadership style in some way contributed to the murders. Some of these questions are derived from misinformation. For example, the notion that soldiers received extra pay or other financial incentives in return for a higher "body count" is totally false. Meanwhile, others have said that by placing heavy pressure on my commanders, I created a culture in which such abuses could take place. Others have argued that our uncompromising pursuit of armed groups generally elevated the security forces to a level where they believed they could operate with impunity.

I respectfully but firmly disagree with all of those contentions. Evidence collected during my government, anecdotal and otherwise, suggests that military leaders were *less* likely to commit abuses in an environment in which morale was high and their institution had the clear support of the Colombian government. We went public immediately with cases that came to our attention. Finally, I reject the notion that a demand for results somehow leads to criminal behavior. In my appearances at military academies and officer promotion ceremonies, and in my speeches to the nation at large, I consistently combined my clamor for results with a demand for efficacy and transparency, clear instructions that human rights needed to be fully respected, and warnings that criminals inside and outside the military would be punished for any deviations.

Ultimately, as was our duty, we reacted to the false-positives cases by making it easier for civilians to denounce crimes while simultaneously implementing safeguards to eliminate the number of abuses in the armed forces and hold accountable any criminals in our midst. Our data showed that cases of false positives rose in the 1990s, peaked during the years immediately before my presidency, and then declined. Other cases continue to make their way through the Colombian justice system, and several of the accusations have turned out to be false, in many cases several years after the fact. One such instance was a case involving members of the 4th Army Brigade in Medellín, in which individuals were exonerated from all charges—eight years after charges were filed. But to my great regret, there were too many other cases that were far too real.

Shortly before the end of our government, a delegate of the United Nations High Commissioner for Human Rights paid me a visit, bearing good news: He informed me that in the past eighteen months, he had only received four complaints and only one looked serious. I replied that those weren't good news; we need to reach zero cases. The continuation of democratic security depends on its credibility, which in turn is based on its efficiency and transparency.

18

Following Fernando Araújo's escape, the aura of invincibility that had surrounded the FARC and its hostage camps was forever shattered. Just four months later, Jhon Frank Pinchao, a Colombian policeman whom the FARC had held in the jungle for nearly nine years, fled during a rare lapse in attention by his captors amid a driving rainstorm. Pinchao made a makeshift life preserver out of a plastic jug, and floated down muddy rivers for days. He survived by eating palm hearts and bird's eggs that he found on the ground. At night, he shoved leaves into his clothes to try to insulate himself from bug bites, and he jogged in place during rainstorms to avoid hypothermia.

Within days, our police had intercepted FARC radio traffic that one of their hostages had escaped somewhere in the south, in the state of either Guaviare or Vaupés. We didn't know exactly where the escape had occurred, but the assumption was that the prisoner would attempt to flee by river. Yet again, we were engaged in a frenetic race with the FARC to see who could track down an escaped hostage first. We dispatched helicopters and police to the area, and put all of our intelligence assets on full alert. Finally, miraculously, on the seventeenth day of his odyssey, a police unit discovered Pinchao, gaunt, hungry, and with a festering infection in his left hand, on the banks of the Apaporis River deep in the Amazon.

Pinchao's escape bolstered morale within our security forces and throughout Colombia. It was the first time a captive soldier or policeman had ever escaped from the FARC. Hours after we found him, Pinchao was in Bogotá giving a giant hug to the eight-year-old son he had never met, a scene that caused people to break down in tears all over the country. Yet there was another reason that his escape was so important: Pinchao had been held in the same FARC camp as Ingrid Betancourt, the three American contractors, and several other hostages. Like Araújo, he was a treasure trove of intelligence, and he sat down with me and my military commanders as soon as he was able.

We were immediately struck by Pinchao's resilience, and by his loyalty to the police and the armed forces—he said that he had never given up hope, even during the darkest hours of his captivity. While he was unable to give us much more than a general location of the camp—which had surely changed since his escape three weeks before—Pinchao was able to provide us with several new details about life with the FARC, and confirm several things we had suspected for years. He told us about the physical and psychological condition of the Americans (pretty good) and of Ingrid (much less encouraging). He told us about the hostages' daily routine, and was even able to draw us a rough map of their sleeping arrangements while in camp. Finally, Pinchao was able to corroborate one of the most sensational and disturbing pieces of intelligence we had: that one of the hostages had given birth while in captivity.

Clara Rojas, Ingrid's campaign manager during the election, had accompanied her on that ill-fated trip to former FARC territory back in 2002. Rojas was taken hostage as well. She was thirty-eight and had never had a child. Clara became pregnant. Having babies was forbidden among the FARC's rank and file—the group often forced its female members to have abortions—but an exception was apparently made for Rojas.

When the time came for Clara Rojas's delivery, the FARC could have done the humane thing and set her free—or at least taken her to a hospital or clinic. Instead, they kept her prisoner in their jungle camp. The birth became complicated. The FARC's leader at the camp realized both Rojas and the baby were in danger and decided to perform a cesarean section. The surgery did not go well, and the FARC "doctor" had to open the incision even wider and forcibly extract the child. In doing so, he fractured the baby's left arm. Rojas needed forty days of bed rest before she was able to walk again. Pinchao told us that the child was named Emmanuel, and that his left arm never fully healed from the trauma of his birth. As a baby, he seemed to be in constant pain, and struggled with typical jungle maladies such as leishmaniasis—the wasting sores caused by sand flies.

When Pinchao held a press conference and revealed the full details of Emmanuel's existence to the Colombian public, the outrage was unlike anything we'd ever seen before. Some people had become jaded over the years about the FARC's misdeeds, but the thought of a sick baby held hostage seemed to universally repulse even the biggest cynics and apologists in our society.

Two other tragic events that year would ratchet up the public pressure on the FARC even further. The first was related to the twelve lawmakers from Valle del Cauca whom the FARC had kidnapped in Cali during the spree of violence immediately preceding my election. For five years, the legislators suffered in the deepest reaches of the jungle. In June 2007, the terrorists holding the legislators came into contact with another FARC unit—which they mistook for members of the ELN, and commenced attacking. As combat raged, the terrorist leader gave the order to execute the hostages—just as they had done with Echeverri, Gaviria Correa, and the soldiers at Urrao. Eleven of the twelve legislators were murdered. In a cynical ploy to cover up their deed, the FARC blamed the Colombian army for the confusion and then waited eighty days to turn over the dead bodies to the Red Cross. Their deception was futile—a forensic investigation showed that the eleven cadavers had received a total of ninety-five bullet wounds, most of them in the back. I was personally devastated by this crime, and Colombian society was outraged at the FARC for yet another reprehensible massacre of innocent civilians.

When the FARC broke the news of the murder of the deputies, they did so from Europe via a website, stating that the incident occurred by confrontation with the army. Before addressing the nation I waited 11 hours to confirm that the military had not clashed with guerrillas in the area around that time. By revealing the truth, our good faith was rewarded.

The second event took place toward the end of the year, our police intercepted a video containing footage of the hostages including an emaciated Ingrid, along with letters she had penned to her mother. The images of Ingrid showed just how badly her physical condition had deteriorated over the years, and her words revealed a person who had suffered for far too long. "It's very difficult for me to continue to hope," she wrote, adding that the suffering of her children as a result of her captivity "makes death seem like a sweet option."

"Aqui vivimos muertos," Ingrid wrote. "Here we live like the dead."

Even for the FARC, which by then had a popular approval rating of less than 2 percent in polls, these revelations before a disgusted Colombian public were too much to bear. For the FARC to maintain even the slightest degree of credibility as an "army of the people" in the eyes of their few remaining die-hard supporters at home and abroad, some kind of face-saving gesture was necessary. We expected them to make some kind of dramatic move. And we weren't particularly surprised when they identified their preferred interlocutor.

19

I was on a helicopter, lifting off from a park in the Chicamocha Canyon in Santander, when my phone rang.

"Uribe?"

"Yes?"

"*Presidente,* I'm calling because I want to help you."

President Chávez was speaking from Caracas, accompanied by Piedad Córdoba, a leftist Colombian senator with whom he had good relations. I had recently authorized Senator Córdoba as a facilitator to try—yet again—to broker an arrangement that would lead the FARC to release its hostages. She had traveled to the Venezuelan capital to meet with President Chávez, who said he now wanted to join the negotiations himself. "I can help you reach an agreement," Chávez said.

My first thought was: *If I authorize this, it's a political risk. If I don't authorize this, it's a human risk.*

By that point in my presidency, I knew that President Chávez did not always have Colombia's best interests in mind. I had numerous questions about what his involvement in negotiations would imply. What if this was an attempt by President Chávez, who had just lost a major referendum at home, to portray himself as a peacemaker on the world stage? What if it was a ploy to undermine my government and put the focus back on negotiations, in which the FARC seemed to have no sincere interest?

On the other hand, I also realized that President Chávez was in a unique position. "The FARC don't even listen to *me* anymore," President Castro had told me. It was clear that President Chávez was the only global head of state that still retained any influence with the FARC and their leadership. Meanwhile, the FARC was coming under increasing pressure from both the military and Colombian popular opinion. If the FARC was looking for a relatively dignified path to reconciliation, or at least a modest improvement in their public image, President Chávez might offer them just the kind of high-profile figure that would allow them to save some face.

Our government had already shown that we would go to great lengths, and consider all kinds of options, if it might result in the hostages' freedom. Earlier that same year, in 2007, our government decided to unilaterally release about 150 FARC prisoners as a gesture of good faith. Immediately after we announced this decision, I received two phone calls from Nicolas Sarkozy, who had just taken office as the president of France. He asked me whether I still planned to release the FARC members; I said yes. He called me back and asked me again, to which I responded that I always fulfill my word. He then asked if he could request something else of me: whether I would consider releasing Rodrigo Granda, the FARC "foreign minister" whose capture had triggered the diplomatic crisis with Venezuela. I accepted, as long as the law would allow me. I did not ask the President, but I figured he would have some sort of agreement with the FARC. I preferred to trust him rather than to express my curiosity. As soon as we released Granda, he immediately returned to the FARC and resumed his criminal activities. The last photos we have of him showed him in Venezuela dressed in camouflage and undertaking criminal activities. None of the hostages were released: either there was no agreement, or they had failed Sarkozy.

Such experiences did not deter me; I always reminded myself that the hostages' lives were at stake, and any good-faith effort to free them could end in the solution we had spent years yearning for. So as President Chávez waited on the telephone for my response to this latest offer, I took a deep breath. I remembered the sage advice of the late Colombian president, my deeply admired onetime boss, Julio César Turbay Ayala: "Never react on your first impressions." Yet, despite my reservations, I decided once again to put the hostages' lives first. I told President Chávez that I would consent to his participation, and that we would discuss the details a few days later, at a regional summit in Santiago, Chile. There, I thanked President Chávez for his offer and told him I would make just one request of him—that he conduct the process with maximum discretion and privacy. He smiled and agreed.

In retrospect, this was like asking a cat not to chase birds. An absolute circus ensued. Over the course of several weeks, President Chávez discussed the state of the negotiations on several occasions on his nationally televised weekly talk show. He met with the FARC leader Iván Márquez in Caracas, and then held a press conference with him on the steps of the Miraflores palace—the first time a FARC leader had ever appeared in public with a foreign head of state. While on one of his world tours, he told President

Sarkozy that I was willing to meet right away with the FARC's supreme leader, Manuel Marulanda—a gross distortion of what I had personally told President Chávez. Through it all, I was patient—perhaps unreasonably so. Finally, when I received word that President Chávez had attempted on several occasions to directly call one of our senior military leaders and that through Senator Córdoba he had finally reached the head of the Army in an unacceptable and dangerous breach of protocol, that was the last straw. I issued a statement the next day putting an end to President Chávez's role as a facilitator, drawing a furious response from Caracas and dismay from the disappointed families of the hostages.

By mid-December 2007, with negotiations for a larger prisoner release still going nowhere, the FARC apparently decided to yield before the clamor of Colombian public opinion. They announced plans to unilaterally liberate three of their most prized hostages: Clara Rojas; her child, Emmanuel, who was now thought to be three years old; and Consuelo González de Perdomo, a former congresswoman who had been held hostage since 2001. Their one condition: They would turn the hostages over to only the Venezuelan government.

Despite everything that had transpired, I didn't give the matter a second thought; I agreed immediately to the FARC's terms. I even authorized the entry of Venezuelan helicopters into Colombian territory so that they could collect the hostages themselves. The FARC set December 28 as the date for the release. A delegation led by the Venezuelan foreign minister Nicolas Maduro traveled to the Colombian city of Villavicencio, where we set up a logistics center to receive them. The delegation included camera crews and an entourage of foreigners: the former Argentine president Néstor Kirchner, the American film director Oliver Stone, who was a friend of President Chávez's, and representatives from several other countries, including Bolivia, Brazil, Cuba, Ecuador, France, and Switzerland.

Everything was now set to go forward. Except for one big problem.

20

When the big day arrived, the team of international visitors and dozens of journalists were eagerly waiting in the tropical heat of Villavicencio for word on how to proceed. At any moment, the FARC was due to radio in coordinates for the location where the hostages would be set free. The Venezuelan helicopters flew in as anticipated, painted in the colors of the Red Cross, ready to go pick up the three captives. Minutes turned to hours, and the day ended with no word from the terrorists. Speaking from Caracas, President Chávez blamed the delay on bad weather and the FARC's poor communications. But no one really knew for sure.

A second day passed. And then a third. Still no news. The delegation was growing nervous, as was the rest of Colombia and the world.

Finally, on the fourth day, New Year's Eve, the FARC issued a statement blaming the delay on their favorite scapegoat: me. In a letter addressed to President Chávez, the FARC said the release of the hostages had been sabotaged by "intense military operations in the area," and that staging the handover in such circumstances would place everyone's lives at "grave risk." "As soon as we can find a place that offers us security," the FARC said, "we . . . will make possible the safe return of Clara, Emmanuel, and Consuelo."

The delegation, and the international community in general, erupted with furious recriminations. Foreign media lamented that Álvaro Uribe, the warmongering hard-liner, had struck yet again. President Chávez angrily accused me of "dynamiting" his rescue plan, adding that the communications breakdown could be due to radio interference from secret U.S. forces operating in Colombia.

None of this was true. We had halted major military operations in the areas where we believed the FARC had the hostages. Instead, we suspected that something else was afoot. Something else was preventing the FARC from handing over the two women and the young child as promised to the Venezuelan delegation. And with each passing moment, as our intelligence assets reported in, we became more and more certain as to the reason behind the delay.

The situation had now escalated to the point where I needed to personally intervene. Luis Carlos Restrepo, our honest and hardworking high commissioner for peace, called me from Villavicencio and asked whether I could travel there urgently to help refute the accusations being made against us. So I suspended my usual trip to spend New Year's Eve with the soldiers—ironically, I was headed to the Montes de María—and traveled instead with Defense Minister Santos and General Montoya to Villavicencio. When we arrived, we were again besieged by outraged questions about why we had "sabotaged" the handover.

We gathered the international representatives in a small room, and kept the journalists outside. First, General Montoya patiently assured those present that the army had not staged any operations that would have spoiled the handover. And then I took the stage and told the delegation our theory on what had really happened.

"We believe that the FARC have not liberated the child Emmanuel," I said, "for the simple reason that the FARC no longer have Emmanuel in their custody."

Silence.

Finally, former president Kirchner voiced what was surely on many minds: "If that's true," he exclaimed, "we're all going to look like fools!"

21

Emmanuel had posed a problem for the FARC from the moment he was born. Traumatized by the brutal circumstances of his birth, the child was frequently sick. He shrieked and wailed constantly, leading the terrorists to either cover his mouth or sedate him when they went on long marches, so that any army patrols in the vicinity wouldn't be able to hear his screams. Emmanuel's arm, so badly mangled during the botched C-section, never fully healed. Finally, when the boy was eight months old, and he developed a particularly horrid case of leishmaniasis, causing a sore on his face that would not close, the FARC apparently decided they'd had enough.

Over the screams of an outraged and heartbroken Clara Rojas, the FARC took Emmanuel from her. Days later, they delivered the child into the custody of a peasant family in the southern town of El Retorno. This happened in early 2005. They instructed the father of the household that they would come back for Emmanuel one day—and that in the meantime, he should try to pass the child off as his nephew. Emmanuel Rojas became known as Juan David Gómez Tapiero.

Emmanuel was now out of the jungle, but his health failed to improve. Within a few months, the "uncle" took him to a nearby health clinic, which referred them to a hospital in the city of San José del Guaviare. The doctors were so repulsed by the child's malnourished condition, the sores on his face, and the unhealed wound in his arm that they remanded the boy into state custody. To the horror of the "uncle," who had been instructed by the FARC to guard this child with his life, Emmanuel was then sent to a foster home in Bogotá. No one involved—not the peasant family, not the doctors, not the foster home—had the slightest clue as to the child's real identity, or the fact that an entire nation was looking for him.

In addition to the information provided to us by Jhon Pinchao, our security forces had long suspected that one of the hostages had given birth. Several years earlier, an army patrol had come across a hostage camp and found a crib. Various possibilities circulated as to who the mother might be. We intercepted FARC radio messages in which one of the parties lamented that

Clara Rojas had become "unstable" after her child was taken from her. This alerted us to two critical pieces of information: the true identity of the child's mother, and the possibility that Emmanuel might no longer be in the FARC's custody.

Our intelligence agencies had dramatically expanded their reach and their sophistication in the years since I took office. By the middle of 2007, their hard work paid off with a major coup. They learned of the existence of a boy with a lame left arm, matching the description we had of Emmanuel, in a foster home in Bogotá. Two of our agents, posing as a young couple, subsequently rented a home across the street from the foster home, so they could keep an eye on the boy. Still, we couldn't be certain as to his identity. In a proof-of-life video that the FARC released around that same time, one of the hostages in Clara Rojas's camp explicitly talked about how he carried Emmanuel on his shoulders during marches—this, obviously, turned out to be classic subterfuge by the FARC. But our doubts were compounded by a basic question for which we had no answer: Why would the FARC offer to free Emmanuel if they didn't have him?

Minister Santos theorized in his memoir, *Jaque al Terror,* that it was a classic loss of "command and control" by the FARC's leadership. That is, as our military offensives and intelligence intercepts put the FARC under constant pressure and disrupted their ability to communicate, the FARC's senior leaders failed to realize that Emmanuel was no longer in their custody, or at least accessible to them. I believe it was also possible that the FARC had too much faith in their ability to find the boy, no matter where he was. Whatever their reason, just as the delegation of international observers began to converge on Villavicencio, we received word that the "uncle" from the small town of El Retorno was now frantically searching the foster homes of Bogotá, whispering to people that the FARC would kill him unless he located the boy right away. We detected the presence of FARC operatives who were searching for the boy in Bogotá as well.

There could no longer be any doubt: "Juan David" was Emmanuel.

After addressing the international delegation, I walked outside and revealed what we knew to the press. "The terrorists don't dare to keep their promises because they don't have the boy," I told the shocked reporters. "The FARC terrorist group doesn't have any excuse. They've fooled Colombia, and now they want to fool the international community."

The whole charade quickly fell apart. Former president Kirchner and several others went home that same day. Even as they boarded their planes back to Caracas and other destinations, some still searched for a way to portray the episode as being our fault. "Shame on Colombia," Oliver Stone told reporters. "Shame on Uribe."

The FARC had been deceiving Colombia, and the world, for decades now. Some of us had understood their true nature for many years. But the episode with Emmanuel exposed their tactics in the eyes of the international community in a way that people everywhere could understand. Ten days later, the FARC released Clara Rojas and Consuelo González—there was no delegation, no fanfare, just a pair of Venezuelan officials in the company of the International Red Cross. A DNA test was performed by two laboratories—one in Colombia, one outside the country—to confirm that Emmanuel was her real child. All of the world was heartened by the image of Rojas being reunited with her son—after nearly three years apart.

The FARC's decision to release Clara Rojas was clearly an attempt to save face. It didn't work. The next mortal blow to the FARC would be struck not by the government, but by the Colombian people.

22

As 2008 dawned, a major transformation had taken place: Colombians no longer feared the FARC. The Emmanuel case, the escapes of Fernando Araújo and Frank Pinchao, and the now-dramatic improvement in Colombia's security had all combined to cause a major change in the way people saw our country. For the younger generation in particular, the fear had been replaced by something else—disgust and repudiation.

Using the then relatively new medium of Facebook, a group of young people organized a march they called *Un millón de voces contra las FARC*— "A million voices against the FARC." The goal seemed like a pipe dream at first. But in one of the first global demonstrations of how social media could reflect the popular will and mobilize it, word quickly spread. Many were attracted by the march's apolitical origins, and its elegant, damning slogan: *"No más secuestros. No más mentiras. No más muertes. No más FARC"*: "No more kidnappings. No more lies. No more deaths. No more FARC."

On Monday, February 4, 2008, demonstrators took to the streets to demonstrate their rejection of the FARC—not just in Colombia, but around the world. As far afield as Japan and Australia, protesters braved freezing weather to show their sentiments. In Colombia, people filled the streets, waving flags and wearing white T-shirts printed with the march's slogan. The march was totally peaceful—a civilized nation, united in its message. The turnout was truly overwhelming: millions of people marched in protest.

I participated in the march, but as just another Colombian among multitudes. As fate would have it, I was in Valledupar—the once-troubled northern city that I had visited on the very first trip of my presidency, to launch our first highway convoys. Here, too, things had changed. Instead of cowering inside their homes and watching the proceedings in intimidated silence, as they had in 2002, people took to the streets here, too. I thanked the demonstrators around the world for joining "this chain of spiritual energy against kidnapping and against crime."

The *narcoterroristas* had never been in a more fragile condition. They were weakened militarily, their mystique of invincibility was gone, and the whole country was visibly united against them. Plus, we had now compromised them in ways that no one, at that point, could have dared to imagine.

The endgame was now upon us.

SECTION SIX

Loyalty

"The horrible night is over."
—COLOMBIA'S NATIONAL ANTHEM

1

By the middle of 2007, the principal supplier of food, fuel, and other goods to the FARC in southern Colombia was . . . the Colombian government.

Thanks to the extraordinary work of our police intelligence agency, the DIPOL, we had managed to infiltrate nearly every element of the supply chain for the so-called 48th Front of the FARC. Over the course of four years, we patiently acquired general stores, docks, speedboats, trucks, distribution companies, and pieces of property in the area near the border with Ecuador. We saturated the region with a network of secret microphones, cameras, tracking devices, and other cutting-edge technology.

There were more than a dozen undercover agents stationed permanently in the area, posing as merchants, motorboat drivers, and others. The full details of their work may never be made public, but it was nothing short of heroic; some of them spent longer than three years in the field without relief. They focused primarily on human intelligence—carefully recruiting sources, collecting information, and sending it back to central command for review. Soon there were more than two hundred civilians in the area providing intelligence, usually in return for financial incentives. Each of them was covertly administered polygraph tests in the field in order to ascertain the veracity of their contributions. The agents communicated the results and other information back to central command using a mix of new and old technology, including secret code in books and magazines.

In Bogotá, DIPOL agents worked around the clock to process the incoming data from the field. They supplemented this information with more than eight hundred interviews conducted with FARC members who were demobilized, captured, or otherwise removed from the group's rank and file. All told, we acquired more than seventy-five thousand pieces of information, each of which was exhaustively analyzed.

The sole purpose of this massive operation? Nothing less than the capture of Luis Edgar Devía Silva, a.k.a. Raúl Reyes, the number two figure and, crucially, the internal communications guru for the FARC.

2

Reyes was the key. We believed that if we could get to him, we would strike a mortal blow to the FARC's operational ability and maybe—just maybe—open up a clear path to rescuing the so-called "high-value" hostages, including Ingrid Betancourt and the three Americans.

Reyes had been notorious to the Colombian public for more than a decade. He was one of the FARC's most prominent faces during the peace process, famous for his obstinate obstruction of progress during the talks, as well as statements that justified kidnapping and the drug trade. He referred to hostages as "detainees," and extortion payments as a "war tax." He was also perceived as a possible successor to the FARC's supreme leader, Manuel Marulanda, who was in his seventies and reportedly in ill health. The prospect of a new generation taking power within the FARC offered us no relief whatsoever; Reyes was part of a hard core that had no interest in making peace, as indicated by his comments back in 2003 that the FARC was willing to just wait out my presidency. As long as Reyes and others like him were still at large, the FARC would remain a serious threat to peace in Colombia.

"After forty-four years of fighting, the FARC's seven-man secretariat remained intact, like some unholy priesthood," the American journalist John Otis wrote in *Law of the Jungle,* a book about our pursuit of the terrorists. "And with Manuel Marulanda and the rest of his top commanders still calling the shots, the FARC, though battered, seemed poised to survive and regroup."

There was another, perhaps even more compelling reason for wanting to get Reyes—his role in the FARC's communications structure. By the mid-2000s, Reyes was the nexus for virtually all of the group's most critical internal communications. He was like a midpoint in the triangle—if the FARC's various "fronts" wanted to communicate with one another, they usually went through Reyes. If Marulanda and the rest of the "secretariat" wanted to issue orders to terrorists in the field, they usually went through Reyes. For this reason, we believed that neutralizing Reyes could lead us to the cells that held Ingrid and the other hostages. At the very least, his removal from the field would throw the FARC's internal communications into utter chaos.

In December 2004, I made a decision that may have prevented Reyes's elimination. We received information that several FARC leaders would be gathering at a house in Quito, Ecuador. The FARC were constantly moving through Quito, where they owned several businesses, mainly for the purpose of laundering drug money. Our intelligence indicated that Reyes would be arriving at a house accompanied by Juvenal Ovidio Ricardo Palmera Pineda, a.k.a. Simón Trinidad. Like Reyes, Trinidad had been a lead negotiator for the FARC during the peace process. Once that charade fell apart, Trinidad resumed his identity as one of the group's most ruthless drug traffickers and kidnappers, sowing mayhem with particular zeal in his hometown of Valledupar. A curious character, he was the son of a family connected to the farming and livestock sector, had studied economics briefly at Harvard, and was wanted by the United States on multiple charges of international drug smuggling. We coordinated with Ecuadorean security forces to be ready to make the capture.

At the last moment, I received an urgent phone call from General Jorge Daniel Castro Castro, one of our finest police commanders. *"Presidente,"* he said, "Trinidad is at the house, but there's no sign of Reyes yet! Should we wait or should we make the capture?"

We worried that if we waited too long, Trinidad might leave the house. "It's better to have the small fish than no fish at all," I told the general.

The operation was a success, thanks to the work of the Ecuadorean security forces and the government of Alfredo Palacio, which was always helpful with our joint efforts to fight terrorism. Within hours, the Ecuadorean government deported Trinidad to Colombia. Once he was in our custody, I offered to abstain from extraditing Trinidad and another FARC operative known as "Sonia," who had been arrested by our commandos in the jungle, if the FARC agreed to release the hostages. The FARC didn't say a single word in response. So we sent them both to the United States, where they were judged and sentenced.

Getting Trinidad was a triumph, and a severe blow to the FARC's operations. Yet, more than three years later, we still didn't have the big fish.

Thanks to the hard work of our intelligence services, we knew Reyes's general location: southern Colombia, where he was moving back and forth across the Ecuadorean border. On at least four separate occasions, our military staged special operations aimed at Reyes. Yet Reyes was extraordinarily well protected. Like all the FARC's chiefs, he was constantly on the move. On the occasions when he did briefly settle down in a fixed spot, the FARC erected numerous "satellite" camps on the perimeter in order to ensure his protection. Breaking through these rings of security, and distinguishing the central camp from the others, proved extremely difficult. We staged unsuccessful air strikes. On one mission, we stationed sharpshooters in the trees, ready to take down Reyes when he passed by, but, in a stroke of extraordinarily bad luck, some of Reyes's guards passed underneath the very tree where one of our men was perched, and found him. A firefight ensued, and Reyes escaped. A separate operation resulted in the death of an army captain, who was shot by one of Reyes's men.

These close calls were extremely trying for members of our armed forces and my government, very few of whom fully understood the enormous manpower and treasure that we were sacrificing in the name of defeating this man. The near-misses were also hell for our intelligence agents in the field. They were spending years at a time in the jungle, under false identities, unable to tell anyone the truth about who they were. Their anguish was such that our police intelligence chiefs often ventured into the field personally to assure our operatives that they were performing an enormous service to our country, and that their efforts would soon bear fruit.

They were right on both counts.

3

Reyes had spent many years on the run, successfully evading some of the best-trained troops and intelligence agents on the planet. Yet our capabilities had advanced enormously since 2002. And in the end, he was just one man. Against a confident Colombian nation that was now thoroughly united against the FARC and actively pursuing its destruction, Raúl Reyes didn't stand a chance.

We knew that Reyes was migrating constantly among several camps in the border region. From one person among our growing roster of informants, we received a tip about a "special" camp that Reyes had begun using in recent months. At the camp, Reyes received delegations of visitors: journalists, students, foreign nationals, and others. The visitors were treated to long sermons about the virtues of the FARC's methods and its supposedly pure ideology. Some visitors reportedly received explosives training. One visitor called Reyes's camp "a public relations office for the FARC." It was, in sum, the closest thing the FARC had to a fixed base of operations since their halcyon days at Caguán during the peace process.

In early 2008, a group of visitors made its way to Reyes's preferred camp. One of these visitors was working with us. This person was equipped with a specially designed device that was activated upon entering Reyes's camp. The device was able to identify the frequency of the signal that Reyes was using to communicate with the rest of the FARC. From that point on, every time Reyes spoke with the outside world, his signal acted like a beacon that revealed his location to us.

Through this extraordinary coup by our intelligence services, we now had the exact location of Raúl Reyes. It was a historic achievement. The police and military commanders and Minister Santos came to me with the news, and asked for authorization to launch an air strike. The mission seemed airtight, with little risk, with the exception of one critical detail: among the many camps that Reyes was using on either side of the Colombia-Ecuador border, this one was on the Ecuadorian side, a very short distance from Colombia.

4

The news about Reyes's location wasn't a complete surprise: We had experienced issues on our southern border for years.

The main issue was the rampant drug trafficking and cultivation in the area. During the second half of my presidency, as we successfully reduced kidnapping throughout Colombia's territory, the FARC began to depend on drug cultivation and smuggling for an even greater portion of its income. This increased even further the urgency of our drug eradication efforts. As with other coca-growing regions in our territory, we had undertaken an aggressive aerial fumigation program in order to kill the crops on the Colombian side of the border. This, in turn, prompted complaints from the Ecuadorean government, which feared environmental damage from the chemicals that, they said, were drifting into their sovereign territory. There was considerable scientific evidence against these arguments, but in the sole interest of friendship between our countries, we responded to the wishes of President Palacio of Ecuador and stopped fumigating within a six-mile (ten-kilometer) band on the Colombian side of the border. Within a year, that strip of Colombian territory exploded with coca blossoms, and became one of the world's most concentrated narcotics-growing areas. I called President Palacio and told him we had no choice but to resume fumigation. He disliked the decision, but we proceeded transparently.

In January 2007, a year before we pinned down Reyes's location, Rafael Correa became president of Ecuador. A young economist who was just forty-three when he took office, Correa seemed eager to follow the path taken by President Chávez. During the first round of the presidential campaign, Correa had stated that the FARC was not a terrorist group. He even said that Ecuador's northern border was not with our government, but with the FARC. Correa spoke constantly of violence in Colombia, but laid the blame only at the feet of the paramilitaries. These statements were inflammatory enough that some moderate Ecuadoreans began fearing Correa was a radical leftist—so Correa toned down his rhetoric a bit during the election's second round. Nevertheless, I had seen and heard enough to be concerned. I reproached

Correa publicly during a *consejo* in Putumayo, near the border with Ecuador, repeating my case for why the FARC was a terrorist organization, and articulating why Colombian democracy could not accept the legitimization of the FARC in his speeches. I worried that Colombia was about to be hemmed in on two sides by governments that were sympathetic to the FARC.

As I had done at first with President Chávez, I tried to extend Correa an olive branch in the hope of winning his trust and collaboration on security-related matters. Shortly before his inauguration, we met at the inauguration of Daniel Ortega in Nicaragua, where Correa pressed me on the subject of fumigation. Despite what had occurred on prior occasions when the aerial spraying was halted, I told Correa that we would engage in one last round of fumigation and then stop, in a gesture of brotherhood and friendship between our nations.

The alternative to aerial spraying was so-called manual eradication, in which Colombian troops would go into the area and protect civilians as they destroyed the coca crops. This was easier said than done, because after all this wasn't just anyone's cocaine—this was the FARC's cocaine.

Soon after we began manual eradication, our troops began coming under intense fire from FARC operating on the Ecuadorean side of the border. On numerous occasions, the FARC made incursions from their camps on the Ecuadorean side, attacked our soldiers, and then retreated back to "safety" in Ecuador. In one such ambush, we lost two dozen men. I had the sad duty of traveling to the border region to receive the bodies. We made several entreaties to President Correa's government to help us control the border area more effectively; they were met with either silence or the boilerplate reply that any violence in the area was Colombia's problem alone.

This was the context in which we learned that Reyes's camp was in Ecuadorean territory, just a few hundred yards across our border. Reyes had felt confident enough to invite visitors to this camp precisely because of its location; Reyes believed he couldn't be touched as long as he was in Ecuador. Had the government in Quito been a more cooperative partner in regional security, we might have asked for their assistance in capturing Reyes, just as we had a few years before with Simón Trinidad under the previous Ecuadorean administration. Under the new government, evidence indicated that if we made such a request, Reyes would get tipped off.

I had always stated, publicly and privately, that we would pursue terrorists no matter their location. Our government's willingness to do so, even under difficult circumstances, had been clear to the international public since the Rodrigo Granda case some three years before. While I had hoped the Granda episode would lead the FARC to stop taking shelter in neighboring countries, it regrettably had not. Meanwhile, Reyes was a more important figure than Granda—critical to the FARC's day-to-day armed criminal operations and its control of the hostages. Crucially, I was also certain that we could comply with an ironclad rule of my administration: that there be no risk of innocent civilians dying in our air strikes. Reyes's camp was in an isolated area of jungle. It also appeared that we could launch the air strike without our planes ever leaving Colombian airspace.

The biggest risk was in the diplomatic arena. Some of my aides, including Defense Minister Santos, posed doubts about the operation because of the risk of creating a conflict with our neighbor. Indeed, I remembered the aftermath of the Granda case, and how difficult it was to put relations with Venezuela back on a relatively normal footing. I preferred to maintain good ties with all countries, particularly our regional partners. Yet here we were again, with one of our neighbors sheltering Colombian terrorists in relatively open view, possibly with the complicity of certain agents of the Ecuadorean state. This situation could not continue; if another bitter confrontation was necessary to eliminate this mass murderer and ensure greater long-term respect for Colombia's security, then so be it. I remembered a phrase from Shakespeare: "So foul a sky clears not without a storm."

When my commanders came to me with the plans for the air strike, I evaluated the pros and cons one last time. This was an operation that would eliminate one of the most wanted terrorists not just in Colombia, but in the world. It could provide us with a path to the hostages, who had been held now for more than five years. Our intelligence was excellent. Our military capabilities were up to the task.

"Proceed," I told the generals. "Proceed under my responsibility."

5

At twenty minutes past midnight, I placed the first phone call to General Padilla.

"We've launched the bombs, *Presidente*," he said.

"Very good, *mi general.*"

Shortly thereafter, another call: "We've hit the target. Preliminary reports are that the operation is a success."

"Very good, *mi general.*"

Minutes later after speaking with General Padilla again, I spoke to Minister Santos who said to me: "*Presidente,* we need your authorization to enter Ecuadorean territory and verify the results of the operation."

This carried a greater risk; Colombian special forces would be entering Ecuadorean territory. It would be a reconnaissance mission, rather than a combat mission, but it was daring nonetheless. Yet the stakes of this operation were too high for us to refuse: We had to know for certain whether Reyes was dead. I gave the authorization.

I sat there in my Rionegro residence where I had arrived around midnight, waiting for the phone to ring just once more. I tried to visualize the criminal camp and what it might look like at that moment: the tents, the jungle. The camps on Reyes's perimeter would be buzzing with panic and confusion; some of the rank and file would be running toward the site of the bombing in an attempt to save Reyes, if he was still alive. The central camp itself would be on fire, smoke billowing everywhere. There would be wreckage strewn about, broken trees on the ground, and computers.

The computers.

Reyes's computers.

An epiphany: Something about the juxtaposition of the wreckage, the flames, and the computers in my mind transported me back to December 1992, and the bombing I barely survived at the Hotel Orquidea Real. My laptop survived those explosions with no damage—the data was still totally intact. Something similar had occurred six months previously, when we conducted a similar attack using precision weapons on another FARC leader,

Tomás Medina Caracas, a.k.a. Negro Acacio. Acacio's laptops still worked, although none of the information in that case proved hugely useful. But Reyes, as the point man for all FARC communications . . .

When General Padilla called me back, I made an explicit request:

"*Mi general*, it's very important that you tell our men to look for laptops. If they find any, they must bring them back to Colombia!"

"Understood, *Presidente*!"

6

At approximately three a.m., my phone rang again.

"*Presidente*," Minister Santos said, "I can report that Raúl Reyes has been eliminated."

"Thank you, *Ministro*," I replied. My mind immediately turned to the remaining FARC kingpins. "And what about Mono Jojoy? When will we get him, too?"

7

I placed my first phone call to President Correa shortly after sunrise.

The call posed a risk of its own. Our forces were still in Ecuador at the moment of the call, attempting to complete the relatively short but extremely arduous journey through thick jungle back to Colombian territory. But I hoped that by calling President Correa and giving him news of our operation first, before the news broke publicly, I might be able to appeal to his democratic sensibilities and limit the ensuing fallout.

President Correa reacted calmly. "I see," he kept repeating. I communicated to him the broad contours of what had happened, but did not go into detail. At the end of our conversation, he quietly thanked me for calling and hung up. Yet I remembered how, with the Granda case, President Chávez had also been very calm in the beginning—until the FARC and his leftist base reacted with rage, pushing him to near hysteria. Similarly, I suspected this wouldn't be the last I'd hear from President Correa on the matter.

Per our usual protocol for news that was positive for the Colombian people, it was Minister Santos who informed the nation of Raúl Reyes's demise. Later that morning, we received word that the Ecuadorean military had mobilized its forces, and they were rapidly moving north to the scene of the operation. Luckily, our men were able to successfully return to Colombia in time to avoid a potential confrontation.

For a few hours, things stayed quiet. But everything changed once President Chávez got involved. Even though the situation did not involve Venezuela in any way, President Chávez's reaction to Reyes's death quickly took on apocalyptic and very personal tones. He went on television and condemned the "cowardly assassination" of Reyes, whom he deemed a "good revolutionary." He said that if Colombian forces ever entered Venezuelan territory in the same way, he would consider it a "cause for war."

"Don't be thinking you can do that here!" President Chávez declared, wagging his finger at the camera.

We then witnessed a kind of one-upmanship between Correa and Chávez to see who could rattle their sword the most. Correa withdrew his ambassador from Bogotá; Chávez expelled personnel from our embassy in Caracas. Chávez called our actions a "war crime," while Correa denounced us for attacking the camp as the terrorists "slept . . . in their pajamas." Some of this followed the pattern President Chávez had established during the Granda case. But this time he went *much* further. Speaking on live television, President Chávez ordered ten army battalions, including tanks and aircraft, to Venezuela's border with Colombia. President Correa soon mobilized Ecuadorean forces as well.

As the confrontation escalated, I went on television to make clear to the Colombian people and to international public opinion that our target had been the FARC, not the brother nation of Ecuador. I noted again that the bombing took place in an isolated area with no civilian population, with the sole purpose of eliminating a highly dangerous criminal. "We have taken another step toward defeating the celebrity of bloody terrorism, which fifty years ago was ideological, but today is a terrorism of mercenaries and drug traffickers," I said. Meanwhile, Colombia's military was under strict orders "not to move one single soldier toward the border"—a message that Minister Santos made a point of noting in public. Our actions were against the terrorists, never against our brother nations of Venezuela and Ecuador. Fernando Araújo—the former FARC hostage, whom I had recently appointed as our foreign minister—assiduously worked his contacts around Latin America to communicate to our regional partners that Colombia's only desire was for security and peace.

In truth, I never believed that a conflict was imminent with either Venezuela or Ecuador. We certainly would not have been the aggressor. The peace-loving people of our three nations would never have tolerated a war. We believed that the saber rattling was more about President Chávez and President Correa posturing in the eyes of the region than a harbinger of aggressive action. Our intelligence even indicated that, as they departed for the border, some Venezuelan soldiers had been asked by their families whether they could do some shopping in Colombia if they got the chance. Yet the confrontation was still very risky, as such escalations almost always are. Some military analysts pointed out that, with tensions running so high because of the incessant rhetoric from President Chávez, nerves could fray, and sporadic shooting could break out among young and untested soldiers.

Through it all, President Chávez continued to escalate his rhetoric and actions. Drawing yet again from previous experience, he closed our border to commerce—a move that he knew would hurt Colombia more than it did Venezuela. He held a minute of silence on his television program to mourn Reyes. Meanwhile, he used language that was strong even by his usual standards, describing Colombia as "the Israel of Latin America"—a comment that some commentators said seemed tinged with particular ugliness, especially given President Chávez's growing associations with Hezbollah, Hamas, and Iranian president Mahmoud Ahmadinejad. "We're all going to have to reflect, all of us," Chávez said. "Will we choose war or peace?"

In fact, President Chávez's reaction was so totally over-the-top that some people openly began questioning why he was behaving this way. President Vladimir Putin of Russia called Chávez and urged him to climb down from his confrontational stance and seek a diplomatic solution, according to media reports. President Sarkozy did the same. A former Venezuelan ambassador to the United Nations said in the international press: "Chávez is effectively supporting narcoterrorists who take refuge in Venezuela and Ecuador while saying a democratically elected leader of Colombia cannot fight back." Even the Bush administration, which had long ago adopted a policy of discussing President Chávez's actions as little as possible so as not to provoke him any further, felt compelled to describe his actions as "odd." Indeed, no one understood why President Chávez was acting so rashly.

But I understood perfectly. Both Chávez and Correa must have known exactly what was coming.

8

"Uribe?"

The voice on the telephone this time belonged to a very senior Colombian politician. Out of respect for our private conversation, I will not disclose his name. He was calling me with a request that I heard on several occasions during those tense days: that I should defuse the crisis with Ecuador and Venezuela by asking Defense Minister Santos to submit his resignation as a gesture of Colombia's contrition.

"*De ninguna manera*," I said. "Absolutely not. The responsibility for this operation was mine and mine alone."

"What about General Padilla?" The head of the armed forces.

"Absolutely not."

"*Presidente*," he intoned, exasperated, "you are facing an unprecedented crisis. You have two neighboring countries who have closed their borders and are in a state of near war."

"We acted defensively, to protect ourselves from terrorists," I replied. "We did nothing wrong."

There was a long pause.

"At the very least, Álvaro, solicit the resignation of the head of the air force," he said. "He leaves, and you can say that this whole incident was an abuse by the air force. That would be enough to resolve the diplomatic situation."

"That may very well resolve the diplomatic situation, as you say," I replied. "But the country will be worse for it. We will lose the confidence of the armed forces. We won't have enough trust for future operations that could free us from the problems of terrorism."

"You're making a grave mistake," he warned.

"Loyalty," I replied. "Loyalty let us reach this point. Loyalty will take us forward."

I didn't realize it at the time, but that conversation would prove to be one of the most important moments of my presidency.

The armed forces, with General Padilla at their head; General Mario

Montoya, head of the Army; and General Jorge Ballesteros, Air Force commander—as well as the Police, led by its Director, General Oscar Naranjo—did an exemplary job in the name of our country. When I addressed the nation, I publicly thanked them and assumed full responsibility for the diplomatic difficulties that had ensued.

9

In the end, the crisis would be defused not by an apology, nor by a forced resignation—but by the words of Raúl Reyes himself.

The files we found in those computers at his camp were not only intact—they were a treasure trove. The hard drives included thousands of e-mails that Reyes had sent and received over a period of several years. In essence, they provided a near-complete historical record of the FARC's most recent activities. The e-mails contained explicit details about the FARC's activities and its relations with foreign governments, including Venezuela and Ecuador. In the e-mails, Reyes and the rest of the FARC's leadership, including Manuel Marulanda, discussed their plans to stage new, even more horrifying attacks against the Colombian population.

At the Colombian government's request, the authenticity of the laptop's content was immediately verified by Interpol. The international police organization's chief, Ronald Noble, traveled to Bogotá to testify that the e-mails had not been modified, erased, or altered in any way.

Among the more relevant pieces of information:

- The FARC was in negotiations abroad to get 110 pounds of uranium, possibly for the purpose of exploding a "dirty bomb" to terrorize the Colombian population.

- President Chávez's government had promised the FARC at least $300 million in direct support in 2007.

- President Correa's own presidential campaign had been financed with several hundred thousand dollars in FARC money.

- FARC leaders had met with senior members of President Correa's government, and were given permission to set up permanent bases in Ecuador's territory.

These were damning, unequivocal pieces of evidence. To me, they explained the behavior of President Chávez and President Correa not just with respect to the Raúl Reyes incident, but going back some time. The hard drives also contained information about the FARC's drug-smuggling activities, its efforts to conceal the truth about the massacre of the Cali legislators, and many other atrocities. The content has been studied in further detail in the years since then. A book published in September 2011 by the International Institute for Strategic Studies, an independent London-based think tank, concluded, among other things, that President Correa had "personally requested and illegally accepted illegal funds from the FARC in 2006."

The weight of the evidence was such that I wanted to present it in the court of public opinion. An opportunity presented itself. On March 7, 2008, a few days after the operation against Raúl Reyes, presidents from around Latin America were due to gather for a regional summit in Santo Domingo, Dominican Republic. President Chávez and President Correa were both set to attend. Foreign Minister Araújo received messages from diplomats and other leaders in the region who offered to broker private meetings on the eve of the summit that could possibly have defused the confrontation. Yet by that juncture, we believed it was important to air our grievances in an open and transparent fashion. I wanted to do so not out of personal spite or a desire for confrontation. Instead I believed that, by presenting the truth about the FARC and identifying those who had collaborated with terrorists, we could prevent future such incidents and make a long-term positive contribution to Colombia's security.

That morning, I sat at a long table with President Chávez, President Correa, and almost every other head of state from around Latin America. As cameras from dozens of television networks aired the meeting live, I calmly read the content of Raúl Reyes's e-mails to a stunned and silenced audience. I did not raise my voice; I did not become angry. I simply recited Reyes's own words: his letters to Manuel Marulanda, his correspondence with individuals in Colombia and abroad, and his own description of the special relationship that the FARC enjoyed with the Ecuadorean and Venezuelan governments. All around the world, people watching their televisions learned the truth about the FARC, its disregard for human life, and its ties around the region.

As I spoke, President Correa slumped in his chair, glaring at me. When it was his turn to speak again, he had little of substance to say, apart from an ad hominem attack on me. "How difficult it is to believe someone who has lied so much!" he declared.

President Correa's words were of no use. The charade was over, and everyone knew it. As the meeting progressed, I was passed a note from President Manuel Zelaya of Honduras, who was part of the contingent of leftist leaders in the region. The note said that President Chávez was willing to discuss a deal. Meanwhile, other presidents from around Latin America, including President Felipe Calderón of Mexico and President Leonel Fernández of the Dominican Republic, who was hosting the meeting, gave conciliatory speeches urging us to maintain the unity of the region for the sake of peace.

Finally, at the end of the day, I accepted these efforts at mediation. The truth had been exposed to public opinion; we had accomplished our goals. As cameras flashed, I shook hands with President Chávez, and we publicly declared the confrontation over. I sensed that President Chávez was accepting the resolution in good faith; he seemed eager to move on. The situation with President Correa was more difficult. We also shook hands, but I perceived clear hostility from him. On that occasion, and on many others, I asked for Ecuador's forgiveness for the bombing, explaining to the public that it was an extraordinary measure due to our fight against terrorism.

In the ensuing months and years, we would work very hard to heal our relationship with Ecuador, with the valuable assistance of the Carter Center. We never sent our troops to the borders, closed our market, or imposed visas on Ecuadorean visitors. When I saw President Correa at a Presidents' summit in Mexico in 2010, I offered him every bit of evidence except the names of the pilots, hoping to disabuse of him of his false belief that the United States had somehow orchestrated the strike against Reyes. President Correa said he wasn't asking for the names of the pilots.

On the conciliatory tour undertaken by the Secretary of the OAS, José Miguel Insulza, in order to respond to his concerns regarding the operation, I offered to show him the video. Late at night, he called me to thank me and said that he was satisfied. I was hoping that on his visit to Quito the next day he would be able to clear all doubts and resolve the diplomatic impasse. But wounds are slow to heal. Formal relations between our countries would not be restored until after the end of our administration.

Despite the problems, I am glad to say that the tensions never boiled over. The talk of a conflict among our countries in early 2008 ceased almost as quickly as it had begun. And we were free to watch as, with Reyes gone and the kingpins' forty years of seeming invincibility punctured, the FARC began imploding with a speed that we could have only imagined.

10

Only three days after Reyes's death, Colombian police in the town of Pácora, north of Manizales and south of Medellín, received a tip: The bodyguard for Iván Ríos, another member of the FARC's so-called secretariat, wanted to turn himself in—and he had something in his possession that might interest us.

Ríos, whose real name was José Juvenal Velandia, was the leader of the FARC's central bloc and oversaw an enormous share of its drug trafficking. The U.S. government was offering as much as $5 million for his capture. Members of Ríos's unit, including his female partner, were responsible for hundreds of kidnappings across Colombia. Ríos was also, notably, just forty-six years old—one among just a few FARC kingpins below retirement age. In previous months, we had obtained Ríos's location from a deserter among his inner circle. Ríos and his unit had come under intense pressure as we cut off his supply lines and tightened the noose around him.

Three days after the phone call, Ríos's bodyguard emerged from the jungle as planned. He carried with him a large satchel. The bodyguard was escorted by our police to a nearby military base for a meeting with a Colombian army colonel.

"So," the colonel asked, "where is Iván Ríos?"

The bodyguard reached into his satchel. Out came a severed human hand.

"Here is Iván Ríos," the bodyguard replied.

The bodyguard reported that the pressure exerted by our military on the FARC had become unbearable; he knew the game was up. So, a few nights before, the bodyguard had entered Ríos's tent and shot dead both him and his female companion while they were sleeping. The bodyguard ran out of the tent, screamed that the army was attacking, and urged the remaining FARC to run for their lives—which they promptly did. The bodyguard then went back inside the tent and calmly used a knife to sever Ríos's right hand, hoping the evidence would permit him to collect the cash reward. In his satchel, he also carried Ríos's passport, ID card, and laptop computer.

This incident posed an ethical and moral dilemma for me. It was one thing for a criminal to abandon a terrorist group, confess his crimes, and reintegrate into Colombian society. But it was entirely different for a criminal to murder another criminal and then try to collect money for his deed. While the result was the death of a dangerous terrorist, the circumstances did not otherwise advance our critical goal of regaining the monopoly of the use of force.

About three weeks later, we received news that was unequivocally positive: alias Manuel Marulanda, the FARC's supreme leader since 1964, had died of a heart attack at the age of approximately seventy-six. Marulanda had spent his final days on the run, never able to sleep more than one night in the same place, as our military conducted constant air strikes and other operations targeting him. The FARC, stunned and demoralized by such a rapid series of setbacks, was able to keep his death secret for a short period. But this news, too, eventually became public. The symbolism of his demise was poignant. Marulanda was not only a ruthless kingpin, but an example of the FARC's backwardness and total disregard for the Colombian public.

Meanwhile, the pressure exerted by our military continued to take its toll among the FARC's rank and file. In just the first quarter of 2008, more than two hundred FARC members demobilized. In May, the leader of the FARC's so-called 47th Front—Nelly Ávila Moreno, alias "Karina"—turned herself in after months of running from the military that left her scarred and on the brink of starvation. At its peak, Karina's gang of terrorists had some three hundred people—by the end, there were fewer than fifty, some media reports said. We had set Karina's capture as a particular goal, given her ruthless activities in Antioquia and other places. Here, as elsewhere, the most important goal was to remove her from the field by any means possible—we made a point of publicly guaranteeing her safety if she turned herself in. She did so two weeks later.

With the FARC's leadership in tatters and its rank and file profoundly demoralized, we knew the time had come to make a renewed push toward an even greater goal. That meant going after Ingrid, the three Americans, and the other hostages. The timing was ideal, and we finally had the information we needed. The death of Raúl Reyes had given our operations a very important advantage.

11

In all of our endeavors, whether we were fighting terrorism, improving the economy, or strengthening social cohesion, I believe there was one element that explained our successes.

That element was loyalty.

The way in which we analyzed and discussed problems and solutions among the members of our administration, the commanders of the Armed Forces, and the community was rooted in a sense of teamwork, a community state, or of high civilian participation. Every meeting we had with the community, whether they were employers, workers, or any other group, became a dialogue and ended with a record of findings in order to guide the government's actions. I'm deliberative, vehement, I look for causes, I propose objections, yet finally yield to the arguments, never under pressure. I selected my team with the utmost care. I wasn't necessarily aware of everyone's political affiliation, but I decided to focus on their moral and professional competence, as well as their commitment to our government's objectives. Several of them reached some of the highest government positions before they were 35 years old, my goal being to groom the future leaders of our country. I confess that I put all my trust in those who work with me; not only do I defend them professionally, I defend them personally. I'd rather err on the side of too much loyalty rather than not enough, and for the most part, I've received high returns. There is a paradigm of loyalty: *Operación Jaque* or "Operation Check."

In the aftermath of Raúl Reyes's death, some people in the Colombian press speculated that one or more of our military commanders would be forced to step down. But I stood by my commanders publicly and assumed full responsibility, just as I had after the massacre near Urrao in 2003, and ever since. Once the storm passed, these same commanders felt empowered—they saw once again that they had the confidence and support of the president and the Colombian people. This showed them that they could think in daring and creative—and risky—terms without fear of losing their jobs or being otherwise undermined. It is impossible to overstate how important this security was to them. So it was no coincidence that, within weeks of Reyes's demise, they came to me with an extraordinary, highly audacious plan for the rescue of the hostages.

The rescue plan had begun to take shape a few months previously, in February 2008. A special unit of twelve Colombian troops, covered in camouflage and equipped to survive in the jungle on their own for up to a month, had been tracking the hostages on the shores of the Apaporis River near Cornelio. One morning at about nine a.m., they saw a group of four FARC terrorists appear on the other side of the river. The FARC stripped to their underwear, left their weapons on the shore, and bathed in the river for half an hour or so. Our men stayed perfectly still. Around one thirty p.m., the terrorists returned, leading five hostages at gunpoint—two Colombian policemen and the three American contractors. According to the book *Operación Jaque* by Juan Carlos Torres, it was the first time in ten years that the Colombian military had laid eyes on FARC hostages in captivity. That was an accomplishment in itself. Unfortunately, there was no way to rescue the hostages at that moment—our troops estimated that there were between eighty and a hundred FARC in the vicinity, meaning our men were badly outnumbered. The river separating them from the camp was wide. Plus, a forced rescue of a small number of hostages could have put at risk the lives of any other captives nearby. So we limited ourselves to observation, and while we eventually lost track of the FARC's exact location, having even a general location was an enormous coup.

Now that we knew their general whereabouts, our military leaders had to figure out an effective way to extract the hostages safely from the jungle. Of course, this had never been done before. The FARC had long ago established, at Urrao and again with the Cali legislators, that it would kill its most prized hostages rather than see them liberated. The liberation of Fernando Araújo had shown us the risks of even the most massive and well-orchestrated military rescue operation. Jhon Pinchao, the Colombian policeman who escaped from Ingrid's camp in 2007, confirmed to us that the FARC unit holding her was under explicit orders to execute her and the Americans in the event of an attempted rescue. I suggested our troops also consider another option known as a *cerco humanitario,* a "humanitarian ring," in which we would surround the hostages with a large ring of troops, tighten the circle, and then send in an emissary to try to convince the FARC that they should hand over the hostages alive. But this presented obvious risks and difficulties. Faced with such obstacles, our commanders eventually decided to prioritize options that focused on deception. And this was where the death of Raúl Reyes opened a door.

As the midpoint in the FARC's triangular system of communications, Reyes had brought a degree of order to the group's operations. With him out of the picture, and Marulanda as well, confusion reigned within the FARC. In several cases, the terrorists simply did not know how to communicate with one another anymore. Meanwhile, Reyes's computers contained further clues to the FARC's internal communications methods. Our intelligence agencies had already been working for years to crack the FARC's secret code. Their exceptional efforts were just as valuable as the men and women working in uniform out in the field. By mid-April 2008, the understanding of how the terrorists communicated with one another had nearly been perfected.

With the code broken, our military leaders, led by General Mario Montoya, came up with a plan made possible by the absence of Reyes: By sabotaging the FARC's communications, we would try to trick the terrorists into voluntarily releasing the hostages, without our forces firing a single shot.

The concept was truly ingenious. It centered on intercepting messages between the FARC's "central command" and the FARC unit in the field that held Ingrid, the Americans, and the other hostages. First, a small group of our own intelligence agents were trained to precisely mimic the terrorists, using their slang and imitating their regional accents. In order to make it seem like these agents were speaking from the jungle, we then stationed them in a house that the military rented on an isolated mountaintop near Bogotá, which we determined had the same acoustic properties as the jungle. Finally, once everyone was in place and the training was complete, we used advanced technology to jam the radio frequency that was employed by the FARC unit with the hostages and seamlessly substituted our own people. From that point on, instead of talking to FARC central command, the unit with the hostages was talking to our own intelligence agents. We repeated the same technique on the other end; the FARC command still believed they were talking to their comrades in the field, when they were actually talking to our people instead. This ruse would go on for more than two months, undetected—a masterpiece of intelligence work, and a clear sign of how much our capabilities had advanced in recent years.

Once our agents made the "switch," they began carefully testing to make sure that the FARC unit with the hostages did not harbor any suspicions. Posing as the FARC central command, they gave the unit basic orders to move the hostages from one place to another. A few days later, the unit radioed that it had done as instructed. Our intelligence agents celebrated; we could now effectively control the hostages' movements.

Still, a huge question remained unanswered: How would we convince the FARC to actually release the hostages? Controlling the FARC's movements was one thing; getting them to voluntarily let go of their most prized possessions was another. Here, the fine men and women of the Colombian security forces and intelligence agencies put their heads together once again. Whatever answer they came up with, they knew they would have my support. Their final response was truly brilliant, rooted once again in the FARC's recent rash of mistakes and miscalculations. One of Colombia's finest hours was almost upon us.

12

Rescuing the hostages was a formidable challenge of its own. But throughout my presidency, the most severe crises had a strange way of coming in waves. We usually found ourselves dealing with several high-stakes issues simultaneously, which made having a skilled and empowered team of advisers that much more important. May 2008 was perhaps the most extraordinary example of this. At the exact same moment that we were putting the finishing touches on a plan to rescue Ingrid and the others, we were also dealing with two other huge challenges that threatened to tear down much of the progress we had spent six years trying to build.

For our government, the dismantling of terrorism comprised three elements: straightforward authority, generous reintegration without impunity, and social policy in order to stop young people from being attracted to terrorism. In 2005, we issued the Justice, Peace and Reparation Law, the first law in Colombia to demand justice and reparations for victims. We focused our efforts on demobilization; elimination was the least desirable of our options. By the end of our government, more than fifty-two thousand people had accepted some variation of an agreement to demobilize—among them some thirty-five thousand members of paramilitary groups and seventeen thousand guerilla members. Our intention was to act generously toward those who met the requirements of demobilization and severely toward those who violated them. Despite the human and financial efforts made to reintegrate them into Colombian society, about 7 percent of those who welcomed the offer relapsed into criminal activities.

Yet we soon realized that some of the *narcoterroristas* were trying to cynically take advantage of our generosity. In particular, there was a core group of paramilitary kingpins who had accepted the terms of demobilization but refused to meet their commitments under the law. They did not hand over their wealth as promised, they did not give up their landholdings, and, worst of all, they continued to commit crimes. We received numerous reports that they were still ordering murders and coordinating drug-trafficking activities. The paramilitaries ordered the death of one of their own kingpins, Carlos Castaño, as part of what was apparently a bloody internecine feud. In another incident, Rodrigo Tovar Pupo—the paramilitary known as "Jorge 40"—ordered the kidnapping of José Eduardo Gnecco, a former senator from El Cesar, at the same time he was engaged in negotiations to demobilize. I went on television and said I would send the army in pursuit unless Jorge 40 released Gnecco immediately; he reluctantly did so, but the message of gross defiance was all too clear. Another one of them, Diego Murillo, a.k.a. "Don Berna", was tied, by a judge, to the murder of a deputy from the state of Córdoba. I ordered General Castro Castro, director of the National Police, to personally enter the paramilitaries' demobilization zone in order to capture him there. After three days of searching for him, Don Berna agreed to turn himself in.

Perhaps these men believed that their enduring connections with some rogue individuals within Colombian politics and the Colombian judicial system would protect them from having to obey the rules we had established. Perhaps they thought that the Colombian state was not strong enough to force them to keep their word. On both counts they were wrong.

Gradually, and during the course of several months, we increased the pressure on these men to cooperate. On December 1, 2006, as I departed Colombia to attend President Calderón's inauguration in Mexico City, many from this group of core paramilitary kingpins were transferred to a high-security prison. To our dismay, we received word that these ruthless men continued to order murders and other crimes from behind bars. At the start of 2007, I told my commanders that these men had still not met their obligations to turn over their personal wealth, as clearly required by the Justice and Peace Law. As a result, I asked General Óscar Naranjo, the head of the National Police, to apply a special provision of Colombian law that, thanks to the work of Interior and Justice Minister Fernando Londoño, gave the state broad authority to forcibly seize their assets. Yet even this was not enough to deter the kingpins from continuing to commit crimes. Their actions were making a mockery of the principles that my government sought to uphold, and resulting in the deaths of many innocent people. As 2008 progressed, I realized we had to consider a more draconian solution.

Our government was deeply convinced, even though there had not yet been a legal ruling, of something that was obvious to most citizens: These individuals continued with their criminal activities despite the opportunity they had been offered. It was also clear, to my regret, that Colombian prisons were not sufficiently secure to prevent these criminals from continuing to terrorize the population from behind bars. I invited Minister Santos and my senior commanders to my office, and I asked them to begin proceedings to extradite a core group of fourteen paramilitary leaders to the United States, including Jorge 40, Salvatore Mancuso, Diego "Don Berna" Murillo, and several others among the most senior and feared kingpins.

Extradition was taken to be the worst punishment and it had to take into account the gravity of the facts.

When I privately told Lina of our intentions, her reply was: "Okay, Álvaro. But are you ready for the revenge? Know that these people will use every resource, lie, whatever, in order to take revenge against you, our family, government members, commanders, long after you are no longer president, forever."

I told her that I understood, but I had to fulfill my duties. She agreed.

We had already seen disturbing hints of what form such "revenge" might take. We received word via "Don Berna's" lawyers that a judge associated with the Colombian Supreme Court had offered his client unspecified benefits if he falsely accused me of crimes. The court never provided us with tangible proof of this offer. I could have delayed the extradition in order to get more information about the case, but I chose not to because I decided once again that my duties as president took precedence over any efforts to protect myself.

And so we proceeded. That day in my office, when I gave the extradition order, one of our top commanders said: "*Presidente*, I will obey your orders. But I ask you: Who will take care of us when we are no longer in these positions?"

"God will look after us," I replied. "For now, we must extradite them."

A few hours after the news of the extradition was released, a media circus ensued. The kingpins telephoned their journalist contacts, as well as their friends, in a last-ditch effort to rally public opinion to their side and possibly reverse the extradition order. They did not succeed. In the predawn hours of May 14, 2008, the fourteen paramilitary leaders, wearing bulletproof vests and handcuffs, were put on planes bound for the United States. I felt immense gratitude towards General Naranjo, director of the National Police, when he told me the extradited men were already in flight and outside the Colombian air space. In the ensuing days and weeks, other paramilitary leaders met a similar fate.

The extraditions prompted considerable criticism, and not just from the paramilitaries and their allies. Many of the critics who had said I was sheltering the paramilitaries from their crimes by refusing to extradite them in order to avoid having them voice their accusations against individuals who had supported my government in front of American judges. Now many of these same critics instantly turned. They began accusing me of extraditing the criminals so that they would not have to pay reparations to their victims or answer questions about their crimes.

In truth, I had one reason, and one reason alone, for extraditing these men: I thought it would improve Colombia's security. I believed that by removing these individuals from our country, we could not only prevent them from committing further crimes, but also show other individuals that they would face dire consequences if they did not cooperate with us. As Alfredo Rangel, a well-known security analyst, noted in the press: "There will be more pressure for those in the process to tell the truth and make reparations because now the risk of extradition is real, not hypothetical." The timing had nothing to do with Colombian politics, and the decision was in fact not abrupt at all; it was the culmination of a years-long, painstakingly incremental process of trying to convince these men to cooperate. Meanwhile, I authorized the extradition only after receiving guarantees from the United States that they would make all of the kingpins available for questioning by Colombian authorities so that we could continue to investigate their atrocities and seek reparations. There would be no impunity in this case, nor any other. In the Colombia we led, the law applied to everyone.

13

The third major crisis we simultaneously faced came not from within Colombia, but from abroad—and it was, in some ways, the most hazardous challenge of all.

As 2008 unfolded, the United States and other developed economies began experiencing a severe crisis. The crisis was the result of imbalances within these countries' financial systems, brought on by an unsustainable housing bubble, the substitution of speculation for production, and the enormous debts incurred by both governments and private citizens. We did not share these problems in Colombia. Our economy had notched years of robust, ever-greater expansion, thanks to the improvement in security and our tireless efforts to make it easier for businesses to create jobs and make investments that would help reduce poverty. We went from GDP growth of just 1.9 percent in 2002, the first year of my government, to growth of 4.7 percent in 2005, 6.7 percent in 2006, and 6.9 percent in 2007. This growth occurred without asset bubbles, thanks in part to the robust financial regulations that had been started by the previous government, and deepened under ours.

Yet even though we had been austere and responsible, the problems of the developed nations soon reached Colombia's shores anyway. Demand for our main exports dropped, and liquidity in the global financial system dried up. By the middle of 2008, in addition to all our other challenges, Wall Street analysts said we were facing a certain recession, and very possibly a severe one. In addition, the international financial crisis coincided with the closing of the market in Venezuela and the disaster of the financial pyramids created by drug traffickers in order to launder money.

In the end, though, Colombia's performance was almost miraculous—our economy actually grew in both 2008 and 2009. It was one of the few Latin American economies to do so, and our resilience stood in sharp contrast to the problems in Europe and the United States.

How was this possible? On the one hand, it was due to the hard work and wisdom of our economic team, including Finance Minister Zuluaga and Carolina Rentería, who was the director of the National Planning Agency.

They were able to skillfully implement a countercyclical fiscal policy, stimulating the economy by several different means. One of the most critical measures was to provide subsidized interest rates for the lower and middle-income sectors of the population in order to acquire new housing, a step that greatly stimulated construction. This was made possible thanks to the reforms, austerity measures, and savings from previous years. Fortunately, before the crisis, the government had sold nationalized banks due to the failures that occurred in the late nineties. The price obtained was very acceptable due to the confidence in investment that we had gained in Colombia. Throughout our government, our people worked hard to cultivate the confidence of domestic and foreign investors, and the value of the Colombian stock exchange multiplied by five during our administration. Our country, far from being a "failing state," was now considered one of the safest bets in the world for investors. Indeed, the private sector's investment confidence allowed it to perform a highly important countercyclical role.

Of equal importance, though, were the strides that we made throughout eight years to make Colombia a less unequal country. Perhaps the best safeguard against a crisis was to have a broad and deep pool of Colombian entrepreneurs of all sizes. During our government, more than a hundred and fifty thousand new small and medium-size companies were created, growing their share of the economy from 72 percent to 86 percent. Microlending, in which small amounts of money are lent to humble people, enjoyed such fast growth that the amount of outstanding credit expanded from $380 million to $4 billion by the end of our government. I am often asked why Colombia reacted so quickly to our new policies. I highlight only one point in my answer: the creativity and industriousness of its citizens.

I am aware that people, in the long run, may remember my government best for our contributions to security. But we put equal emphasis on social programs, which for us, are inseparable from security. They provide the resources that validate the need for security in the hearts of our citizens. It was not difficult, as a countercyclical measure, to expand social coverage in order to protect the most vulnerable from the crisis; these policies had been in effect since the beginning of our administration. Throughout the eight years of my government, we increased social spending by 85 percent in real terms—compared to a 65 percent increase in defense spending. By the final year of our government, we were spending three times as much money on social programs as we were on defense. Our intense focus on education—which we committed to without hesitation from that first troubled day of my government, in front of the worried mayors in Florencia—paid clear dividends in the short term, but will aid Colombia even more in the years to come. Thanks to the efforts of Education Minister Cecilia María Vélez who held her title for eight years—as opposed to more than 110 ministers from the previous 100 years—and her team, as well as the National Learning Service (Sena) headed by Darío Montoya, we made significant progress in coverage, quality testing, opportunities for college access, and creating databases to improve science and technology and vocational training. Thanks to the multiplication by eight of the number of trained citizens, Colombia became a prominent regional leader. For the sake of the country's future, with great enthusiasm we dedicated ourselves to education, knowing that we wouldn't see the effects during our government. This case illustrates the idea of offering officials stability regardless of political events, as long as they carry out their programs.

All told, poverty fell sharply during our administration. As measured by personal income level, it fell from 53 percent to 38 percent during those eight years. We were unsatisfied; I had targeted a 35 percent poverty level. We ultimately could not attain that goal because of the global financial problems, our disrupted trade with Venezuela, and a widespread crisis involving pyramid schemes, connected to money laundering, that I wish our government had acted sooner to contain. When adding social policy subsides to people's incomes, poverty dropped by 22 percent, which means thirteen million Colombians overcame poverty during our government—a number greater than the population of greater Bogotá—an accomplishment that changed many lives. There were other governments in Latin America that claimed to have a monopoly on helping the poor, and believed that the path resided in expropriating industries and bullying investors in an attempt to create "socialism." In the long run, these governments did indeed achieve greater equality—by making everyone poorer (except, of course, for their own friends and cronies). By contrast, we proved that it was possible to respect the rights of investors while substantially reducing poverty and creating actual wealth.

That we were able to tackle all of these major challenges at once was testimony to the skill and teamwork of thousands of officials in our government, and the importance we placed on all three corners of the "triangle of confidence"—democratic security, investor confidence, and social cohesion. Without all of these elements functioning at once, our country might very well have endured an extremely severe crisis in 2008–09. Without social cohesion, for example, the initial strains of the crisis may have destroyed the support for our government. Without investor confidence, we would not have had the resources for the military operations that strengthened our security or for the productive increases that allowed us to create jobs and taxpayers.

I spoke constantly of the "triangle" over the years—so constantly, in fact, that it led to an amusing but very revealing moment during the final months of my government. In May 2010, Cartagena hosted the World Economic Forum's annual meeting on Latin America—the first time that the gathering of global leaders, based in Davos, Switzerland, held their regional meeting in Colombia. This was considered a significant advance in our drive to achieve international confidence. During the conference, we moved part of the presidency to Cartagena and established a temporary office close to the convention center.

One afternoon, as I walked in the sunshine from the meeting site to our office, I stopped to talk with several pedestrians. A school bus of children drove by, and I was delighted when they leaned out the window and began shouting, "Uribe! Uribe!" As I prepared to go back inside, I saw a yellow taxi parked on the side of the street, and noticed that the driver was asleep. Wanting to say hello, I rapped lightly on the driver's window.

He awoke immediately, saw me, and his eyes nearly bulged out of his head. He rolled down the window and blurted out, "¡*Presidente!* Democratic security, investor confidence, and social cohesion!"

I began to laugh. "Hello," I replied. "Tell me, why did you just say that?"

"Because I hear you on the radio repeating the same thing every single morning!" he said, laughing now, too.

To me, it was a simple sign that the vast majority of Colombians were now on the same page, with a shared vision for our future. United, and with all three cylinders of the government firing at once, no task was impossible for us.

14

I stared at General Padilla for just a fraction of a moment, blinking.

I couldn't quite believe what I had heard.

He looked back at me and smiled. "Do we have your authorization?"

The plan to trick the FARC into releasing Ingrid, the three Americans, and the other hostages went beyond the plot of a Hollywood movie. I can claim no credit for the idea; it was entirely the creation of the dedicated men and women of our military and intelligence agencies. My role as president was to give them the support they needed, and to ask a few questions about the plan's viability and contingencies: what our alternatives were if the operation did not work, and how we would try to save the hostages' lives in the event of a mistake.

Minister Santos, General Padilla and I debated the risks. Minister Santos harbored prudent misgivings about the operation. He suggested that, if it failed, we should consider letting the FARC and the hostages escape back into the jungle. But I believed that, more than six years after Ingrid's abduction during the presidential campaign, we could not let the hostages out of our sights ever again. I suggested a plan B—a massive ring of troops to be ready to surround the area on short notice, so we could close the circle on the FARC and convince them to release the hostages peacefully, in case our deception-based plan failed. In a conversation with Bernard Kouchner, the French foreign minister, I asked whether he would be willing to fly to Colombia to cross a humanitarian military fence in order to enter into direct contact with the FARC and demand the release of the hostages. He accepted. I didn't give him many details, but I told him we might contact him on short notice. He gave me his home number and said he would be on standby.

Even with these precautions, we knew the operation was extraordinarily risky. The U.S. ambassador later said he believed that our plan had only a 50 percent chance of success. But the urgency was mounting; we simply couldn't wait any longer. We knew that the health of the hostages, particularly Ingrid, was extremely precarious. Meanwhile, even as we subverted the FARC's communications and prepared for the final step of *Operación Jaque*, we never ceased our attempts for a negotiated solution. On March 28, we made a new offer of cash, the possibility of reduced jail terms, and residence in a foreign country in return for the liberation of the hostages. On April 1, President Sarkozy declared that Ingrid was close to death, and that he wanted to send a medical team to treat her. We supported this proposal, but, to the surprise of almost no one, the FARC wouldn't allow it.

With the military operation now the only path available, we knew it required absolute secrecy in order to succeed. In the days leading up to the operation, knowledge of the detail was limited to a group of just four people—General Montoya, General Padilla, Minister Santos, and me. Not even the troops who were being trained to participate fully knew their purpose until just a few days before the plan's execution, set for July 2, 2008.

We made just one exception to the cloak of confidentiality. On July 1, we received a visit from two distinguished U.S. senators—Joe Lieberman and John McCain, who at that time was the Republican Party candidate for president of the United States. A former prisoner of war who had been held for five and a half years under brutal conditions in Vietnam, Senator McCain knew the cruelty of captivity all too well. When he inquired about the fate of the three American contractors, I told him that we would attempt to rescue them the very next day. He nodded and solemnly wished us the best.

As the troops participating in *Operación Jaque* made their final checks and were deployed to the staging area, our military commanders contacted me for one final authorization.

15

"The operation is ready, Mr. President."

"Then proceed," I said. "Proceed under my responsibility."

I closed my eyes. I said a prayer.

And then I saw their faces.

16

On the morning of July 2, the hostages awoke in a small, warehouselike building in the state of Guaviare—the same area that had once formed the core of the FARC's demilitarized zone. The mood of the hostages was restrained but hopeful. They knew that something was happening; their captives had offered them new clothes and decent food, and they had just spent the night sleeping on thin mattresses for the first time in several years. But they had no idea what was coming.

Neither did the FARC.

For weeks, the hostages had perceived mounting confusion and desperation among their captors. Via radio, they heard the news of the deaths of Raúl Reyes, Iván Ríos, and Manuel Marulanda. They noted that their captors, who had shown a degree of discipline for so many years, now seemed rudderless and adrift. The FARC's growing sense of paranoia had been further inflamed after they spotted mysterious metal tubes sticking out of the ground with cameras inside them. Certain that they were being pursued, the FARC had begun ever longer and more arduous marches through the jungle; food was now intermittent and limited to a few tablespoons of rice served with a little bit of broth. Keith Stansell, one of the three American contractors, called it "starvation marching." Most of the hostages now looked like "sticks that someone had taken a knife to and hollowed out our cheeks and necks," Stansell wrote. Ingrid Betancourt was in even worse condition. They had recently been joined in the camp by eleven Colombian soldiers and police, some of whom the FARC had held for more than a decade.

Now, as the sun came up, the fifteen hostages began to learn why they had been brought to this place, and why their treatment had suddenly improved somewhat. The details were sketchy, but the FARC told them that a delegation of international aid workers would be flying in that afternoon by helicopter. The delegation's mission was to check up on the health of the hostages—this was presumably why they were now being so well fed—and then fly them to another part of the jungle, where a different FARC unit was waiting to assume control of their captivity. This, some of the hostages believed, was a possible prelude to a negotiated deal for their release. "I figured that in about a year's time we'd be out," Stansell wrote. As the FARC prepared for the delegation to arrive, they donned new camouflage uniforms and assembled into receiving lines, indicating that something momentous was about to happen.

It all seemed very encouraging. But when the two helicopters finally appeared overhead, the hostages' mood abruptly changed. They looked on in dismay as one of the helicopters touched down next to a field of coca plants, while the other stayed airborne, and a group of strange, foreign-looking men streamed out. Some of the aid workers were wearing Che Guevara T-shirts. They were accompanied by a journalist from a Venezuelan TV network and a cameraman. "In the middle of the Colombian jungle," the journalist yelled, over the deafening roar of the chopper, "we are here for what will be a historic moment for Colombia and the world!"

The hostages instantly realized that this was not a humanitarian mission at all; instead, it seemed to be just another publicity stunt performed for the benefit of the FARC.

The fifteen hostages watched in mounting disgust as the aid workers began chatting and joking with the FARC's rank and file. The aid workers even presented the terrorists' leader with a small gift. Then, with the pleasantries over, the aid workers walked over and began to address the hostages. They produced plastic tie-wraps from their pockets, and told the hostages that in order to transport them to the agreed location, they would have to handcuff them first. Here, the hostages' disgust degenerated into outright mutiny. Instead of indicating the beginning of the end of their captivity, as they had hoped, this whole operation now seemed to herald a new and even grimmer phase. The Americans began furiously yelling at the aid workers, saying they wouldn't board the helicopter at all. One of the Colombian policemen threw himself to the ground and began writhing around in protest, refusing to get up. Through it all, the helicopter's blades continued to whir at full speed, adding a sense of urgency to events.

Ultimately, after much cajoling, the aid workers convinced all fifteen hostages to put on the restraints and they began loading them onto the helicopter. Two of the FARC kingpins also boarded the copter, joining them as escorts. As the chopper began to lift off, the aid workers became even rougher with the hostages, pushing them into their seats, pulling off their boots, and binding their feet with more of the tie-wraps. The FARC kingpins surveyed the scene, satisfied smiles on their faces. The helicopter banked to the west and soared high above the jungle.

Within seconds, mayhem erupted.

The hostages watched in utter shock as the aid workers pushed the two FARC kingpins to the ground and quickly subdued them. The group's "doctor" produced a hypodermic syringe and shot one of the kingpins full of a powerful sedative. Then the aid workers' leader turned to the hostages and declared, "We are the Colombian army, and you are free!"

The hostages looked at one another for a moment in astonishment, and then they began cheering and embracing one another.

It was an operation on a par with any other in military history. The fifteen hostages had been freed, and the FARC leaders subdued, without any casualties. Not a single shot was fired.

The final phase of *Operación Jaque* had been weeks in the making. Once our military decided on deception as the basis for their rescue, they found the blueprint in the terrorists' own recent actions. A few months earlier, the FARC had released Clara Rojas, Emmanuel's mother, to a Venezuelan delegation that arrived by helicopter with a TV crew in tow. Our military studied the video in minute detail, believing that what worked once in reality had the best odds of working again as a deception. For inspiration, they also watched other movies about great hoaxes, including the Hollywood film *Ocean's Eleven*. Once our commanders settled on a plan, a group of nine brave Colombian soldiers volunteered to participate, and they were given designated roles to play. They rehearsed their parts for days, going over every possible scenario. They even called in an acting coach to help them perfect their performances.

Our commanders took as many precautions as possible, aware of how many things could go wrong in a high-stress situation involving so many distrustful people. The plastic tie-wraps were necessary to dissuade the hostages from trying to revolt after they boarded the helicopter, but before they could be informed of the hoax. Since the hostages outnumbered the "aid workers" by nearly two to one, such a revolt could have been disastrous. At an air base in nearby Guaviare, trauma surgeons were on standby in case the mission went horribly awry. Through it all, the "cameraman" was transmitting live audio feedback to the pilots in the helicopters, so that they could monitor the events as they unfolded. If the "journalist" said the words, "I've lost my wallet," that was a code that the terrorists had discovered the deception—signaling the pilots to take off and save themselves.

Ultimately, though, the operation was blessedly free of major problems. From the helicopter's landing to the disarming of the two FARC terrorists on board, the total duration was twenty-two minutes and thirteen seconds.

The moment of greatest danger, in fact, may have been during the celebration. As the passengers jumped around, hugging one another, laughing and crying with euphoria, some among them worried that the old Russian helicopter might come crashing down. But providence smiled upon them one more time that day, and they were delivered from danger.

"Colombia! Colombia!" they chanted.

And then they sang our national anthem, overwhelmed with pride in our nation.

17

As events unfolded that day, I followed our customary policy: Business as usual, working for the community.

I traveled to an area in Santander state where severe flooding had occurred, hoping that I could help coordinate the disaster response. As fate would have it, there was no reliable mobile phone service in that area. I carried a satellite phone in case I needed to be reached in an emergency, but the connection was not reliable enough for me to follow the operation step by step. I proceeded normally, dedicating my full attention to the stories of the flood victims, trying to figure out how our government could help them. Their plight might not have seemed as dramatic to the outside world, but, in truth, their situation was just as dire as that of the hostages. Their lives were in danger, too.

Finally, as we were returning from the stricken area in a helicopter, I received a call from Minister Santos.

"Mr. President"—his voice crackled—"the operation was a total success! Ingrid, the three Americans, and eleven soldiers and police are safe and sound."

"Thank you, Minister, and thanks to God," I replied. "Congratulations. Please give my regards to the commanders and to the Colombian armed forces. Today is a proud day."

The call ended, and I shared the news with the other occupants of the helicopter. None of them had any inkling of the operation. Alicia Arango burst into tears of joy and gave me a giant hug. I shook hands with Minister Andrés Uriel Gallego, General Flavio Buitrago, and Admiral Amaya. Horacio Serpa, who was one of my opponents during the 2002 and 2006 presidential campaigns and was now the governor of Santander, celebrated with us as well.

Per our usual protocol in such cases, it was Minister Santos who went on television and shared the news with the Colombian people and the world. In the ensuing hours, I received phone calls from many leaders. President Bush called and complimented us on the operation, and commented on how it

symbolized Colombia's dramatic turnaround. President Sarkozy expressed
his joy. Ban Ki-moon, the head of the United Nations, welcomed the operation and publicly called on the FARC "to immediately and unconditionally
release the remaining hostages." Barack Obama, then the Democratic Party
candidate for president of the United States, issued a statement saying he
supported our "steady strategy of making no concessions to the FARC," and
pledged that if elected he would do "everything I can . . . to defeat this terrorist organization."

Minister Santos asked me whether I wanted to come with him to the military base in Tolemaida to receive the hostages before the eyes of the nation.

I declined. "You go alone, *Ministro*," I said. "We need you to go, for the
sake of your political future."

I wanted to signal to the nation that, in moments of great joy and moments of tragedy alike, our will to work would remain constant—our emotions would remain steady. We would proceed normally with the business of
the Colombian nation, fulfilling our duty. So I kept the rest of my scheduled
agenda for that day, which included the reopening of the San José hospital in
Bogotá. This was another project that had been extremely important to us;
prior to my government, many public hospitals had gone bankrupt and
closed. Under my administration, we overhauled the structure of 224 public
hospitals. Thanks to more efficient management, the hard work of Ministers
Juan Luis Londoño and Diego Palacio and many other people in my government, plus the influx of revenues that came from the successful reawakening
of the Colombian economy, we were able to save many hospitals from bank-
ruptcy, and attend to a great many sick people. When I arrived at the hospital,
many people were standing and applauding us. I acknowledged them, but
carried on. Our business was most important.

Finally, that evening, I met the hostages at the Club Militar in Bogotá.
Ingrid wept, and profusely thanked the Colombian military. "They got us
out grandly," she said. "I never expected to get out of there alive." She also
urged neighboring countries to stop interfering with Colombian democracy.
"Colombians elected Álvaro Uribe," she said. "Colombians did not elect the
FARC."

The Americans were already airborne, on a flight back to Texas. They were
escorted by the U.S. ambassador, who had brought a case of beer to share
with them on the plane. When the contractors spoke to the media, they were

grateful as well. One of the hostages, Marc Gonsalves, called *Jaque* "the most perfect rescue that has ever been executed in the history of the world."

I invited all the Colombian hostages to the Casa de Nariño, and invited every one of them to deliver some words to the nation via television. When it was my turn to speak, I began my address by giving thanks to God and the Holy Virgin. I congratulated Minister Santos, General Padilla, General Montoya, and other members of the high military command. As Ingrid and the policemen and soldiers looked on, I congratulated the families of the hostages, who had shown just as much bravery over the years as the prisoners themselves. I vowed that we would not rest until all of Colombia's hostages were freed, and then I read aloud the names, one by one, of those who were still deprived of their freedom.

"In the middle of all our weaknesses and limitations, let's not forget for a single day the families of those who are still kidnapped," I said. "This is our commitment: We won't forget you for a moment until you are *all* back in freedom."

18

The next day, at the airport in Bogotá, Ingrid was reunited with her son and daughter. They had been apart for more than six years. Ingrid was so overjoyed that she ran up the steps of the Jetway and embraced her children before they could even disembark from the plane. They reemerged hand in hand, smiling from ear to ear. "These are my babies, my pride, my reason for living," Ingrid said, wiping away tears. Both children had barely been teenagers when she was abducted; they were now young adults of nineteen and twenty-two. "They look so different, but they look so the same," she said. "They're so beautiful. I think they're beautiful."

For the American contractors, the reunion with their loved ones had to wait just a little longer, but it was just as sweet. After they landed in Texas, the Americans were received at first by military doctors, who helped prepare them mentally for their reinsertion back into civilian life, a process they later described along with the rest of their ordeal in their bestselling book *Out of Captivity*. After they'd been held prisoner for so many years, many things had changed; life for all of the former hostages would bring complications. But nothing could overcome the joy of seeing their families. Keith Stansell was introduced to his five-year-old twin boys, whom he had never met before. "Papa! Papa!" they cried, as they each embraced one of his legs. Their mother had hung Stansell's photo on the wall of the boys' room. They, along with all of the other families, had never forgotten. They kept their faith.

I was privileged to witness several such reunions myself. That night at the Club Militar, I watched as several among the eleven rescued Colombian soldiers and police embraced their loved ones after more than a decade apart. My eyes welled with tears as I thought of all the pain they had endured, and the happiness and relief they must have felt at being able to hold one another once again.

This was a glimpse of the Colombia I had yearned for, the Colombia that I loved, the Colombia that we spent our entire lives fighting to create. A Colombia where families could live together in peace. Where fathers and mothers could embrace their sons and daughters, and never, ever have to let go.

19

Within hours of the raid, we intercepted yet another message from the FARC. It came from the unit that had controlled the hostages, and was intended for the central command. It read simply, *They fooled us.*

For another two weeks, we listened in as the FARC engaged in ever-angrier recriminations, still totally unaware that we had penetrated them to the deepest level, and that we were listening to every word. And then the frequency went silent.

Operación Jaque delivered a catastrophic blow to the FARC. On top of all the other progress we had made in recent years, *Jaque* deprived the FARC of some of their most prized assets and vividly demonstrated the operational superiority of the Colombian security forces, which had been evident for many years already. But we knew that it wasn't the end of the struggle, by any means. We anticipated, correctly, that the FARC would try to recover their reputation by slaughtering innocent people and staging new operations, just as they had countless times in the past. On July 5, three days after we rescued the hostages, our military seized about a ton of explosives at a farm outside Bogotá that we believed was intended for use in a major revenge attack. On July 10, we foiled a raid on the high-security Doña Juana prison in Caldas province, which contained more than five hundred FARC prisoners.

Indeed, our struggle against the FARC would continue to have highs and lows. In the years that followed, other important terrorists would also be neutralized in military operations. We would launch further operations, such as Operation Chameleon, in June 2010, which was in some ways almost as daring as *Jaque*. In that operation, based on intelligence we obtained from a former FARC operative who demobilized, our military rescued three Colombian policemen and a soldier who had been held for more than twelve years. Yet, despite our progress, the FARC and other violent groups would continue to kill and maim innocent people. In 2009, the FARC kidnapped the governor of Caquetá state from his home and slashed his throat, in a disturbing echo of previous tragedies. The terrorists would not simply disappear on their own; the Colombian people needed to remain resolute.

The terrorists' long-term philosophy, and their refusal to fade away, was well articulated by a man who had spent so much time among them: Fernando Araújo. "The problem is that the FARC has no real notion of time," Araújo told an interviewer. "They just think they're going through a difficult moment, and they believe they'll inevitably recover, just as they always have.

"I used to sit in chains and listen to them as they sang their songs," Araújo continued. "They sang, 'If today is bad, tomorrow will be good.' The FARC's main characteristic is perseverance. I don't personally think they'll ever sit down at a negotiating table and give up on their mission. As long as they have economic funds—drugs, that is—and support from foreign governments, they'll have a chance to continue to exist."

20

I shared Araújo's assessment of the challenges that still faced us, as well as the underlying causes. Until the final day of my presidency, we continued our efforts to deny the terrorists a safe haven in other countries. I regret to say that, despite our good faith, our task never got any easier.

One example was in 2009, when I discussed with President Chávez the matter of a notorious terrorist, Luciano Marin Arango, a.k.a. Iván Márquez, of the FARC. Márquez was the leader of the FARC's Caribbean bloc, a kingpin responsible for the murder of several hundred Colombians, and we had intelligence showing that he was in Venezuela. We also had intelligence proving the presence of several other illegal armed camps in Venezuelan territory. I passed all the relevant information to President Chávez. A short time later in a meeting, he told me he had dispatched the Venezuelan army, but they hadn't found a trace of the terrorists.

"*Presidente,* you need to use your intelligence assets," I urged, "because if you just send the army, the terrorists have people who will tip them off, and they will flee."

President Chávez sighed and changed the subject. He then circled back and said that, if his government fought the "guerrillas," then Venezuela would never be helpful as a moderator for peace in Colombia. I replied that as long as the terrorists had a hideout in Venezuela, they would never be *interested* in peace, because they would be comfortable in "exile" and cling to their hopes of one day returning to Colombia to resume their criminal activities.

"Very well," President Chávez replied crisply. "I'll think of a solution and then I'll get back to you."

Shortly thereafter, we both gathered in Trinidad for the Summit of the Americas. It was the first occasion on which President Barack Obama met with leaders from around the region. Following the conclusion of the plenary session, I walked up to President Chávez on the floor of the assembly hall.

"Mr. President," I said, "do you have that solution you promised me with respect to Iván Márquez?"

President Chávez leaned in close to my ear. "Here's the situation," he said quietly. "If you're able, you can go get Marquez, just like you got Granda. But you can't say I gave you permission. If you do, I'll say it's a lie."

I was utterly disturbed by these words, and I immediately voiced my concern to Foreign Minister Bermúdez and Carolina Barco, our ambassador to the United States. We continued to try to address our differences with dialogue and goodwill. But with the partners we had, stopping the activities of the FARC and the ELN in neighboring countries was a constant challenge.

The urgency of this task only increased as the *narcoterroristas* entered their new, more vulnerable phase. I studied how groups such as ETA, the Basque terrorist group, were able to continue operating for many years after they had lost popular support and most of their operational capacity. In ETA's case, the group's leaders were able to find relative refuge for many years in France. Not long ago, Spanish officials told me that the group's deathblow came when France began permitting Spanish police to enter French territory in pursuit of the terrorist leaders. Before long, ETA announced the end of its armed campaign. I believed that, in order to trigger a similar chain of events that would cause the FARC and the ELN to cease their armed activities, one would have to eliminate their ability to be comfortable abroad.

In mid-2010, with just weeks to go until the end of my presidency, we received new satellite photographs and recent short-range videos made by informants proving the presence of FARC camps in Venezuela. We considered three options: One was bombardment, similar to what we had done with Raúl Reyes—but we decided that it was too late in my government to pursue this strategy and deal with the likely consequences. The second option was to remain quiet. But that would have been inconsistent with everything we had done for the previous eight years, and detrimental to Colombia's security. I dreaded the idea of being asked, once my presidency was over: *If you knew something, then why didn't you act?* Whenever the authorities confirmed the information given to us by the community information on an offender, I myself denounced the person in public. My vision was that by losing anonymity, the criminal would also lose impunity. This parallel had lodged itself in my mind and it was thus impossible for me to stay silent. Therefore the final option was to denounce the existence of the terrorist camps before the Organization of American States. This was the best path available under the circumstances, and we took it.

Predictably, this course of action prompted a final round of international confrontation during the final months of my government. Yet again, I was portrayed by some critics as the aggressor—as if I were somehow seeking attention, or spoiling for one last fight as I left the global stage. As if it were somehow *my* fault that we possessed satellite images showing the clear presence of terrorist camps on Venezuelan soil. As if I were supposed to just remain silent and allow this charade to continue. This was another example of the double standard that, even after so many years spent articulating our goals, still confronted Colombia in our quest for security. Should the United States have crossed its arms and done nothing when it discovered Osama bin Laden hiding in Pakistan? Or, to take an example from history, was it President John F. Kennedy's fault when he discovered the presence of Soviet nuclear missiles in Cuba? Did anyone think that President Kennedy should have simply ignored such an existential threat, or that a solution could be reached by cozying up to Fidel Castro?

No, we would defend the security of Colombia at all costs, no matter the consequences. That was the way it had always been; under my government, it would always be so.

Shortly before the end of our presidency, a summit of leaders was held in Cancun, Mexico, in order to advance the creation of a unifying body of Latin American and Caribbean countries. After listening to the President of Haiti and examining the case of our sister nation, almost entirely destroyed by an earthquake, I asked to speak. My hope was to respectfully talk about our situation with Venezuela, in addition to the fact that the Venezuelan government had stopped trade relations between our two countries. President Chávez complained that he had been "thrown out" of the provision to seek the release of the FARC hostages and concluded that he would no longer listen to me and he was leaving. I said, "Mr. President, these meetings are to solve problems." He insisted on leaving, so I said: "Mr. President, you throw insults from over a thousand miles away but when we come face to face, you don't give us the change to overcome our difficulties," My words were useless. He continued to threaten us with leaving, and at that point I rose from my chair and, I must confess, slammed my fist on the table saying: "Be a man and stay." My mind raced. On the one hand, I was worried that I was violating the rules of diplomacy—I was there as a representative of my country. On the other, I thought that for the sake of dignity, it's important to move forward when faced with the cowardice of tyrants.

These confrontations were recurrent right up to the very end. But they were confined to an extremely small number of countries. We enjoyed positive relations with an overwhelming majority of countries in Latin America and around the world. I never understood the people who said that our government's actions had somehow isolated Colombia; through our myriad trade deals, investments, and other measures, my presidency ended with Colombia more economically integrated than ever with the rest of Latin America and the world. Our ties with Europe improved noticeably. During the final year of our presidency, Canadian prime minister Stephen Harper extended me a special invitation to address the summit of G8 nations, composed of the world's biggest economies, and discuss the advances made in Colombia.

In January 2009, I was honored to receive the Medal of Freedom from President Bush—the United States' highest honor for a civilian. The ceremony took place in Washington, and I stood alongside former British prime minister Tony Blair and former Australian prime minister John Howard as they also received the medal. I was pleased that, when President Bush turned his attention to me that day, he honored the strength and perseverance of the Colombian people, congratulating the entire country for our great progress. "Early in this decade, the Republic of Colombia was near the point of being, at best, a failed state," President Bush said. "In those conditions, it took more than ambition and ideals to run for political office—it required immense personal courage and strength of character.

"President Uribe has formed a powerful bond with his people," President Bush continued. "They've met their president in town halls across the country. They've seen him deliver results. . . . By refusing to allow the land he loves to be destroyed by an enemy within, by proving that terror can be opposed, and defeated, President Uribe has reawakened the hopes of his countrymen, and shown a model of leadership to a watching world."

In the years that followed, I also enjoyed a very warm relationship with President Obama and the senior members of his administration. When Secretary of State Hillary Clinton visited us in Colombia in June 2010, she marveled over how she had been able to meet up with her husband, who was in town separately to perform philanthropic work for his wonderful foundation, for dinner at a Bogotá steakhouse. Obviously, a public meeting of such high-profile global figures would have been unfeasible in Colombia just a few years earlier due to security issues. "We talked about how remarkable it was that such a common event could take place," Clinton told reporters the next day. "My heart was filled with the hope that I know fills the hearts of so many Colombians at what has been accomplished." She added that the Obama administration "embraced fully" Plan Colombia, and wanted to "build on the success of recent years as we look forward to a future of even greater sustainable peace, progress and prosperity for the people of this beautiful country."

I saw President Obama on several occasions, including the summit at Trinidad and Tobago. That day, over a lunch we shared with President Alan García of Peru, I found President Obama to be warm, intelligent, and very interested in Colombia. We discussed at some length the triangle of confidence, which I sketched out on a sheet of paper. President Obama smiled, said he agreed wholeheartedly with all three points, and offered to autograph the paper for me. I accepted. *To President Uribe—with admiration!* the dedication read.

I enjoyed overwhelmingly good ties with leaders around Latin America—people such as President Felipe Calderón of Mexico, whom I found to be extremely courageous. Alan García of Peru was an admirable figure. Before him, President Toledo strongly supported us in our efforts to defeat the Amazonian faction of the FARC. I have enormous gratitude and respect for the presidents of Chile, of the Dominican Republic, and countries throughout Central America and the Caribbean. I also owe special thanks to the presidents of Panama: Mireya Moscoso, Martín Torrijos, and the very effective Ricardo Martinelli.

To the surprise of some observers, I also enjoyed warm relationships with many regional leaders who nominally leaned to the ideological left: President Tabaré Vásquez of Uruguay, Fernando Lugo of Paraguay, and many others. I respected Luiz Inácio Lula da Silva of Brazil, finding his personal rise from poverty admirable and his pragmatic policies to be a positive example for others who had once embraced hard-line socialism. I saw him extend the social policies that his predecessor, President Fernando Henrique Cardoso had explained to several Latin American leaders in order for us to implement them in our countries. President Lula was in Colombia for our independence day in 2008, when hundreds of people again took to the streets to repudiate the FARC. The demonstrations took place in cities around the world—in places such as Madrid, Toronto, Sydney, and Paris, where Ingrid Betancourt addressed the crowd and led chants of "No more hostages!" President Lula, President García and I were in Leticia, Colombia, an Amazon town near our border with Brazil, where we were joined by Shakira, the Colombian musician who has done so much good for her country. President Lula wholeheartedly supported our cause that day, proclaiming relations between our countries to be "excellent" and supporting our fight against the terrorists. It's impossible to name all the presidents I was able to spend time with. I will always remember and admire the strength of José María Aznar, the pragmatism I perceived in my talks with Felipe González, the good relationship I enjoyed with President Rodríguez Zapatero and with His Majesty Don Juan Carlos, King of Spain, as well as my good friend the British Prime Minister Tony Blair.

Even those who were initially wary of me, whether because of my interactions with President Chávez or because of other reasons, often came around. I remember sitting down for one meeting with José Mujica, the president of Uruguay who had been a guerrilla leader during the 1970s. I could tell he was looking at me skeptically. I began our conversation by smiling at him and saying, "Oh, the things you must have heard about me!"

President Mujica dissolved into laughter, and thus commenced a solid and constructive relationship. For the countries that supported us in our quest for security and peace, we had only the best sentiments of brotherhood and respect.

21

Among the myriad challenges that still face Colombia, perhaps none concerns me as much—or is as critically important—as the scourge of drugs.

As long as Colombia is a significant producer of narcotics, there will always be the risk of *narcoterroristas*. Fernando Araújo was right: Drugs alone could still sustain the FARC and other groups for many years to come. As my presidency ended, the FARC was still earning about $200 million a year from drug trafficking. This was despite all of our efforts to beat back the narcotics producers—an effort that experienced some success. By the end of my government, the area of Colombia under cultivation by coca plantations fell to about sixty-eight thousand hectares. By comparison, the area under cultivation in 2000 was at least a hundred and seventy thousand hectares—and possibly as many as four hundred thousand hectares, if modern measurement techniques had been used at the time. In any case, the reduction in cultivation in recent years has been incomplete, but significant.

In addition to aerial fumigation and manual eradication, we tried to implement innovative programs as well. One such program was named *Familias Guardabosques,* or "Forest Guard Families." Under this initiative, almost a hundred thousand families throughout Colombia who had been engaged in coca cultivation signed agreements with our government. They agreed to monitor the forest or jungle areas near their homes, keep them free of coca plants, and supervise the recovery of the native ecosystem for the sake of environmental protection. In return, once the United Nations certified that they were fulfilling their obligations, they received cash payments equivalent to about $2,000 every eighteen months. In addition to offering the cash reward, we also worked to provide the citizens with education, health care, and public utilities.

We also worked to dismantle the cartels themselves, both those that worked with organizations such as the FARC and the paramilitaries and the so-called pure drug-trafficking groups. During our government, we extradited approximately 1,140 drug traffickers to the United States, and many others to different countries. During the final three years of our administration, we confiscated fifteen thousand illicit goods in the application of our law that allows for the confiscation of illicit wealth.

And yet, Colombia's efforts haven't been enough. We need to reduce global consumption. Many governments are making efforts; others turn their back on the problem; and yet others refuse to take on the struggle by favoring legalization—the easy way out. It is just as bad to try to leave the problem in the exclusive hands of the state, as it is to ignore the issue under pretense that it should be considered a family issue.

I don't believe in the legalization of narcotics, not only as a father, nor because of our struggle, but because I don't see the logic in the arguments that support it. There is no need to legalize drugs to avoid putting the consumer in jail and offer him medical treatment. Legalization isn't necessary to treat addicts and offer them a decreasing doctor-prescribed dose either. The law does not deny the realm of science.

Experts anticipate that legalization would stimulate social consumption to such an extent, especially during the early years, that there would be no way of removing income to crime, or collecting taxes at reasonable rates and in amounts sufficient to pay for the rehabilitation of the growing number of consumers.

Free will cannot endanger others. With freedom of drug consumption, the individual would lose his own freedom by alienating himself and endangering those around him. He also loses control over his own will, the very essence of freedom and that which distinguishes him from the animal kingdom.

In many countries, including ours, most assassins caught committing a crime have been found under the influence of drugs, often combined with alcohol.

With the increased production in the north and consumption in the south, the old division between producers and consumers has started to blur and the facts reinforce the need for a global effort.

The environmental issue is key, and for Amazonian countries like Colombia, it's of great importance. No matter how much they lower the price as a result of an eventual legalization, drug crops would continue to be a major threat to the forest: a lower price could discourage plantations in California and increase them in the Amazon.

For many scientists the division between soft drugs and hard drugs is euphemistic, the former are vectors that lead to the latter.

When a student asked me why it was ok to legalize alcohol and not marijuana, I replied, "Be prepared to answer why it's ok to legalize marijuana and not cocaine."

The drug economy goes against the productive economy; drug trafficking consists of speculation and crime.

I believe in a correct policy: consumer rehabilitaton without prison, public health policies and community prevention, and prison for drug dealers.

When tourists began to flock to Colombia, an international video accused one of our cities of being a drug user destination. We tried to catch the dealers but were unable to do so. They were only carrying a personal dose. Many of those who denounce these facts are in favor legalization. We can not accept it. More pertinent than the discussion on whether or not to legalize drugs would be whether every country should be held accountable for its actions in regards to consumption, the capture of drug traffickers, the seizure of illicit goods, control of chemicals, and so forth.

22

As my presidency drew to an end, I was faced with one final question. It was a matter that cut to the heart of much of what we had accomplished during the previous eight years. The difficult issues involved were perhaps best reflected by a trip I made to a place just sixty miles from the Caribbean Sea, but so high in the Andes that it often snows nearby: a tiny indigenous village named Kankawarwa.

The people in Kankawarwa wear native dress: long white robes flowing to the ground. Their tribes are directly descended from the Incas, and some of the elders do not speak Spanish. Their isolation throughout most of history was near total—as recently as the 1950s, some residents still believed that Spanish kings ruled the surrounding country. To this day, it is possible to arrive in the surrounding area only by foot, by mule, or by helicopter. A haunting fog enshrouds the peaks of the Sierra Nevada region, where Kankawarwa lies. When it rains there, many villagers ignore it, believing that water cleanses the soul.

The Sierra Nevada is a beautiful, deeply spiritual place. But for too many years, it was a microcosm of the worst tragedies of Colombia. According to tribal elders, white men mostly stayed away from the area until the beginning of the twentieth century. Believing the Indians to be weak, they brought in blacks from the coast to rape their women, in the name of creating a hardier race for manual labor. In the 1950s, refugees fleeing *La Violencia* took the good farmland for themselves, forcing the natives to higher, crueler ground. By the 1970s, some of Colombia's first marijuana crops appeared on the mountains' slopes. Soon thereafter, the FARC and ELN appeared, followed by the paramilitaries, fighting over control of the drug trade and murdering countless innocent indigenous people in the process.

During our government, we worked with the indigenous tribes to restore a level of security that had not existed for nearly a hundred years. We built several new villages from the ground up, including Kankawarwa, whose inauguration I attended in 2009. The people there said much had changed. While the violence had not completely disappeared from the area, tribal elders said the transformation was dramatic. Our high mountain brigades had driven out many of the *narcoterroristas* that had operated there for decades. We had built new schools. There were jobs. Ecotourists from around the world were beginning to discover the Sierra Nevada's charms.

"The change is like night and day," one of the tribal elders, Danilo Villafañe Torres told a visiting journalist. "Things are nothing like they were before."

"When exactly was 'before'?" the journalist asked.

Villafañe thought for a moment. "Two thousand seven," he replied. "In 2007, things were still bad here."

The elder's words were another testimony to our progress as a nation. But they also reminded me of something else—how recent, and fragile, our progress was in many areas of Colombia.

During a *consejo comunitario* that took place early in our government in Nabusimaque, a population of the Sierra Nevada, the indigenous elders told me that three weeks before, some men dressed in uniforms had stopped by, claiming that they were paramilitaries. A few days later, another group of men, with identical uniforms, came by and said they were guerillas. And then the night before we had arrived, a third group had showed up and identified themselves as governments soldiers. That day, we gave an army colonel the mission of liaising with the populace, in order to build trust within the community. We replicated this scheme in several different places. There is something that still continues to weigh on my mind: Trust needs to be forever.

As my second term as president neared its end, I worried that we had not had enough time to implement a lasting and permanent change. In swaths of the country such as the Sierra Nevada, security was improved but still extremely tenuous. Even in areas that we had been focusing on since the beginning of my presidency, such as greater Medellín, outbreaks of killings still erupted with disturbing regularity. I remembered again how, in two centuries of history, Colombia had experienced only forty-seven years of peace. We were dealing with deep issues that were as old as the country itself. I wasn't sure that eight years had been enough time to definitively address those issues and transform the country in a lasting way.

Meanwhile, some of my supporters began discussing the possibility of allowing me to run for a third term as president. Polls showed that more than half of Colombians wanted me to run for president again. More than

85 percent of likely voters said they would vote "yes" to a popular referendum that changed the constitution and allowed me to seek a third term, according to a poll published by *El Tiempo* in January 2010.

Faced with this situation, we had deeply conflicting feelings—what I referred to on many occasions in public as an *encrucijada del alma,* or a "crossroads of the soul." On the one hand, I did not believe in the idea of perpetuating the presidency, for I have spent my entire life promoting democracy. For this reason, the possibility of a third term made me deeply uncomfortable. But I was also concerned by the possibility that our government's policies might not endure, and that the progress we had made was still reversible. I saw in my mind's eye all of the faces of the friends and loved ones we had lost over the years to violence. I also saw those whom our policies had helped, such as the rescued hostages, or the people of Kankawarwa. In that light, I understood the popular desire for our government to spend another four years guarding against any setbacks, and ensuring that there would be more victories.

I believed that Colombia needed to make its decision based on its own particular needs, its own circumstances, and its own laws. But I also noted that, throughout recent history, some democratically elected heads of state in other countries had spent more than a decade in power in order to see through the transformations they had started. Franklin Roosevelt was the president of the United States for thirteen years. Margaret Thatcher was the prime minister of Britain for eleven years. Felipe González had fourteen years as the prime minister of Spain. None of these leaders caused harm to their country's democratic institutions by staying in office for such a long period. All of them took advantage of their extended time to ensure that their governments marked a definitive "before" and "after" in their country's histories.

As the debate intensified, I was intensely criticized for remaining noncommittal—for not clearly announcing my intentions one way or the other. In retrospect, I believe it may indeed have been an error for me not to have halted the popular efforts to allow a possible third term. I could have simply said no. However I took advantage of the debate not to talk about the reelection, but of the need to maintain the policies of the triangle of confidence.

Ultimately, I believed that the best strategy was to show deference to our democratic institutions, and to let the issue run its proper course through the Congress and the courts. So that was what I did.

Soon enough, they delivered their verdict. On February 26, 2010, the Colombian Constitutional Court ruled against the legality of efforts by my supporters to hold a popular referendum on a possible third term.

I was in Barranquilla at a public event where we were discussing problems and solutions in healthcare, when the court's decision was formally announced. Immediately, reporters came charging through the door. They began shouting: What was my reaction to the decision? I asked them to please wait until our meeting had concluded; the business of state always came before politics. Once we finished, a few minutes later, I addressed the nation.

"I accept and I respect the court's decision," I said. "All of us citizens have to respect the law, but especially the president." I spoke briefly about my respect for the separation of powers, the importance of democracy, and the need for popular opinion, to be subjugated to the democratic institutions of our country, in this case the constitutional court. Naturally, I talked about the importance of the triangle of confidence one more time. Then I concluded by vowing that I would "serve Colombia from any trench, under any circumstance, until the last day of my life."

And then I did what I always do: I got back to work.

23

During the final months of my presidency, I made one last visit to the town of Urrao, which had played such a unique, recurring role in my life and in my presidency. This was the town that during my childhood had been the base for Captain Franco and his squadron of liberal guerrillas. Later, it was the staging ground for the FARC kingpins who killed Guillermo Gaviria Correa and Gilberto Echeverri. Urrao was just down the road from Salgar, the little village near the farm where I grew up, and its tradition of coexisting violence and sublime beauty dated back as far as the nineteenth century. General Rafael Uribe Uribe, one of my heroes, whose portrait I hung in my office as president, once referred to Urrao as a "paradise lost."

And a paradise it truly is—gorgeous green hills tapering into a valley that leads west toward the Atrato river and then toward the Pacific. Orchids bloom everywhere, in deep reds and pinks. The marvelous Colombia, the one that my mother and father taught me to love, is in full view for everyone to behold. Yet, despite its natural gifts, shortly after I took office in 2002 the population of Urrao had shrunk to about thirty thousand people because of the bloodshed, according to Luis Ernesto Vélez, the town's mayor. Most businesses closed at five p.m. because the merchants feared attacks, he said. Just two miles outside of town, signs read, WELCOME, FARC. When the terrorists became agitated, the people of Urrao often had to spend three or four consecutive days inside until the mayhem passed, Mayor Vélez told me.

When I arrived in Urrao to hold one of our government's final *consejos comunitarios,* the population of Urrao had recovered, and was back up to about forty-five thousand people, according to Mayor Vélez. The FARC had, for the most part, been chased out of town. Jobs had returned. The state's presence was deeply felt. Urrao's transformation was so thorough that Urrao was best-known not as a terrorist stronghold, but as one of the world's best places for hang gliding, because of its strong winds and gorgeous peaks. Tourists from Europe and the United States were flooding the area, stunned by its natural beauty. The demand was so strong that Mayor Vélez and other people often rented out his own house so that both Colombian and foreign visitors could have a place to stay.

Upon landing in Urrao, I saw a sign that the town residents had put on a nearby mountain. It read, PRESIDENTE URIBE, POR SU CULPA URRAO ESTÁ EN PAZ, or, roughly translated, "President Uribe, it's your fault that Urrao is at peace." It was a message of gratitude with a touch of irony, reflecting the contentious currents that accompanied my time in office, right until the very end. The people gathered that day for our *consejo*, and we talked about the challenges that still faced our country. There were many matters to discuss. But the problems that Urrao was grappling with, the problems that were mentioned at the *consejo* that day, were now closer to those of many other countries—issues such as public utilities, roads, and schools. I noticed how people's attitudes also had changed. When we took office, Colombians suffered violence in silence; victims made no demands; and in the first community councils, claims were expressed with a vehemence that bordered on anger. In the end, this attitude had, for the most part, changed: people made the same claims, or perhaps even more, they were conscious of demanding what they needed from authorities, but most of these claims conveyed confidence. I often bore the brunt of these demands, but I believed that the change was enormously positive. People now trusted their government enough to expect change; it was a remarkable transformation. Instead of being a government that begged for dialogue with the terrorists, we were engaged in a profound dialogue with the Colombian people.

There were precious few moments during my government when I remember feeling happy, or even satisfied. For me, there was always something more to do, another group of people to be rescued, another challenge to our prosperity to be overcome. Yet that day in Urrao, I do recall feeling a strong sense of Colombia's past, present, and future. I could appreciate just where Colombia stood in the "film" that President Clinton had once mentioned to me in front of a large group of people. Several generations in Urrao, including my own, had once been tormented by roving gangs of criminals. Now, while the criminals had not disappeared, life had clearly improved in terms of both security and the economy. And as I prepared to leave office, I was hopeful that Juan Manuel Santos, my former defense minister who had been elected to succeed me as president, would carry on with our work in the future, on behalf of the Colombian people.

Around that same time, I was traveling through a rural area and met a *campesino* who thanked me for the dramatic improvements in our country.

"This is still not a land of milk and honey," I replied.

"Ah yes," he said, "but at least the rivers no longer run red with blood."

That was the Colombia we left for our successors: a Colombia that was not a paradise, a Colombia that still had many serious problems, but a Colombia that was moving in the right direction.

Along the way, we made our share of mistakes. I take responsibility for them, as I always have. Yet I am confident that, on balance, we did things the right way. We stood up to the violent ones and defeated many of them, while maintaining our respect for democracy, human rights, and the cohesion of our society. We did so in a way that earned the support and respect of the vast majority of the Colombian people—as we left office, our government enjoyed approval ratings between 74 and 84 percent.

I look around the planet now, at events in the Arab world, in Afghanistan and Pakistan, and in the rest of Latin America, and I see these countries facing challenges similar to the ones that Colombia faced a decade ago. I hope that leaders in those places can learn from our triumphs, as well as our many failures. The desire for security and prosperity is universal, and there is no system but democracy that can guarantee the sustainability of both.

For future generations of Colombians, and for young leaders around the world, I hope that our story serves as proof that *any* situation, no matter how bleak it may seem, can be addressed. Colombia's story demonstrates that all human problems have a human solution. Where there is love, there is surrender and effectiveness, and therefore it can be said that there truly is no such thing as a lost cause.

EPILOGUE

On the evening of November 29, 2011, fifteen months after the end of my presidency, I was sitting in my office in Bogotá with the journalist Brian Winter, who assisted me with the writing of this book. We were snacking on milk and cookies, and discussing the final days of my government. Our conversation turned to Urrao, and its remarkable turnaround. We decided to telephone Urrao's mayor, Luis Ernesto Vélez, so he could provide us with details about the town's recent progress. He told us the story that serves as the last anecdote in the final chapter.

"Thank you for everything, Mr. President!" Mayor Vélez said before he hung up. "Colombia has forever changed, thanks to the work of your government."

Two hours later, I received a panicked phone call. It was from Mayor Vélez.

"The FARC has set my ranch on fire!" he exclaimed, distraught. The very same residence that he had been renting out to European tourists was now alight.

Only providence prevented further tragedy. Mayor Vélez told me that, if he hadn't waited for my phone call that evening, he probably would have returned to his ranch just as the terrorists were burning it to the ground. "I would surely have been kidnapped or murdered," he said, his voice trembling. He soon discovered that his other ranch had been torched as well.

As this episode illustrates, Colombia's progress remains fragile. We dealt the *narcoterroristas* many crushing defeats, but they have not yet disappeared or given up. The serpent is still alive. Stories such as Vélez's are proliferating in number. In some regions of Colombia, it appears that the government may be losing ground to the violent ones. While I believe that President Santos has a strong determination to defeat the terrorists, I fear that some individuals within his administration have taken the progress of the last decade for granted. They are changing direction and creating new and greater risks. For the sake of our democracy, we must remain resolute. We cannot try to appease the terrorists or those who shelter them. If we fail, there is a possibility that a dark era may yet return to Colombia.

From the moment I went back to being a regular Colombian citizen on August 7, 2010, I have maintained a constant workload. I was honored to serve as the vice chairman of the United Nations' Panel of Inquiry, investigating the May 2010 Gaza flotilla incident. I have served as a visiting scholar at more than a dozen academic institutions. I have defended the legacy of our government, and defended those who have faced unjustified persecution in the years since. I have reconnected with my love of the countryside, and now I am helping to create the dream of a non-profit university that will be accessible to Colombians who live in remote villages.

I continue to be involved in politics. I love Colombia and am thankful for the fact that my fellow citizens allowed me to lead our country for two terms. My critics confuse my political involvement with personal aspirations. I like campaigning without having to be a candidate. I defend a thesis but I am strongly opposed to the lack of connection between a candidate's promises and a leader's actions. I fully understand that ideas cannot remain stagnant, but I hate seeing them left adrift or simply replaced by the applause of the moment. Leadership is knowing how to swim against the current that others want to impose and persevering to change it.

I believe in the Pure Democratic Center that defines the balance between Security, Investment and Social Cohesion. In order to overcome poverty and inequality in Colombia, we need both security and resources.

I hate to think that we are going from security that was making progress to security that does only half the job to general insecurity.

God willing, for my love of Colombia, I will continue to debate until my last day with the sole intention of honoring the countless human beings who sacrificed their lives in this struggle and committed to offering our future generations the right to live in a country of rectitude, well-being and equality.

ACKNOWLEDGMENTS

Everything worthwhile that I have accomplished in my life has been the result of teamwork. This book is no exception.

I would like to express my gratitude to Brian Winter. He has helped me compose a book that covers my government and my life with both detail and emotion. Brian's talent as a writer, his empathy as an interviewer, and his eye for compelling anecdotes have been critical throughout the two years that we worked together on this project.

The sage assistance and counsel of my adviser Iván Duque Márquez were equally instrumental throughout this process. Iván is wise well beyond his years, and I am certain that he has a brilliant future ahead of him.

Many other close friends have provided deep reflections and suggested many ways to improve this book, including Francisco Santos; Generals Oscar Naranjo, Freddy Padilla, and Mario Montoya; Alicia Arango, Luis Guillermo Plata, Jaime Bermúdez, Luis Alberto Moreno, Fernando Araújo, Cecilia María Vélez, and César Mauricio Velazquez. Beatriz Delgado, my personal executive assistant, and Carolina Escamilla, a young and talented aide, have also provided invaluable support,

Lina María Moreno, my wife, and Tomás and Jerónimo Uribe, my sons, have been the most insightful and demanding readers of this book. Their advice and contributions have enriched virtually every page. I love you all.

For Jan Miller, my agent, and Ray Garcia, Mark Chait, and the team at Penguin, I am also very grateful. Thank you also to Leticia Bernal for her immesurable help in the revision of the book. Because of their vision and faith, we have been able to tell Colombia's story to the world in a way that was comprehensive and serious. For this opportunity, I feel enormously privileged.

Any income that I receive from this book will be used for the purposes of funding a nonprofit university that we've working to create. The university will initially have a focus on technology and engineering, and will be as virtual as possible—so that young Colombians distant from large cities will have access to a high-quality education. I have noted with great joy that the publication of this book coincides with the birth of our first grandchild, born to Tomás and Isabel Sofia, and with the marriage of Jerónimo and Shadia. As I grow older, I hope to devote my soul entirely to the new generations of Colombians so that they, including our grandchildren, can live happily in this noble land of ours. That way, my parents and grandparents can be happy in heaven.

I would like to thank, one more time, the members of the armed forces who have provided security to my family and me. I will forever be grateful to Generals Flavio Buitrago and Mauricio Santoyo, Admiral Rodolfo Amaya, Colonel Eduardo Ramírez, and all of the loyal and committed men and women who have dedicated themselves to this difficult and risky task.

Finally, and most importantly, this book would not have been possible without the sacrifices and hard work of the anonymous heroes who endeavored to make a better Colombia. Whether they were members of the armed forces, the police, the judicial system, the various ministries, or just everyday Colombians who were trying to make our country a little bit better, the turnaround of recent years simply would not have been possible without all of their efforts. I am awed and humbled by their contributions. My story is their story; their story is mine. Together, we will all continue working for a better Colombia.

A WORD ON SOURCES

Memory, like all human attributes, is imperfect. We endeavored to provide as rich and layered an account of my life and presidency as possible in this book, so we worked hard to extract background, context, and corroborating information from a variety of sources. The main source of this book's content was four weeks of interviews that Brian Winter conducted with me between May 2010 and November 2011 in Washington, D.C.; Bogotá; Rionegro; and at El Ubérrimo, my farm in Montería. These conversations were supplemented with interviews with roughly two dozen other people, including members of my family, officials from my government, and officers from the Colombian security forces. Brian used reputable media outlets to help fill in context for key dates and events. These outlets included Colombian sources, such as *Semana* magazine and the newspapers *El Tiempo*, *El Colombiano*, and Medellín's El Mundo, as well as well-known international publications such as Reuters, *The Economist*, and *The New York Times*.

Brian and I have done our best to verify the information contained in this book with multiple reputable sources when possible. Inevitably, despite our efforts, there may be mistakes in this book stemming from erroneous or incomplete media accounts and academic works. Any errors of memory are mine alone.

SOURCING BY SECTION

SECTION ONE: The account of Guillermo Gaviria Correa's capture, and the events leading up to it, is drawn from Colombian media accounts as well as a piece published in the *Times of London* by Glenn D. Paige, an American academic who studied the governor's life in detail and nominated him for the Nobel Prize. Descriptions of Governor Gaviria's captivity come from letters he wrote to his wife, many of which were published posthumously. The retelling of the events that led to my father's death is based almost entirely on an account written by my brother Santiago Uribe, which was published in 2002 under the title *El día que las FARC mataron a mi padre*. Ricardo Galán and General Mario Montoya helped us reconstruct many details from the aftermath of the military operation to rescue Governor Gaviria and the other men. The details of the military operation against El Paisa in 2008 are based on an interview with Colombian police officials, and internal documents.

SECTION TWO: My description of Colombia's recent history is based on numerous academic accounts listed in the bibliography below. The deep historical archives of *Time* magazine were also useful for descriptions of events during both *La Violencia* and the troubled 1980s in Medellín and throughout Colombia. Lina helped me remember details of how we met, and our lives together in Rionegro, at Cambridge, and elsewhere. Robin, who is still a trusted hand at El Ubérrimo, provided us with some details from the attempted assault on our farm. Local news accounts provided context regarding the bombing at the Hotel Orquidea Real.

SECTION THREE: The archives of *Semana* magazine and *El Tiempo* newspaper, in particular, helped us reconstruct events during my governorship. A wide variety of international media, including the *Los Angeles Times*, *The Guardian*, and the Associated Press provided the details for the account of Werner Mauss and his history. Any Vásquez helped fill in many of the empty spaces in my memory from the governorship, as well as the attack on Vegachi. News agencies, particularly Reuters, helped provide context for the mounting chaos of the 1990s, including the violence of the 1997 regional and mayoral elections. The story of the descent of the FARC and other armed groups into drug trafficking was told by many sources, including the book by Corporación Observatorio para la Paz, Michael Reid's book, and accounts within Juan Manuel Santos's memoir as well. A 2001 survey of Colombia by *The Economist* supplied some of the data on both the economy and empirical measures of violence prior to my presidency. Jaime Bermúdez helped fill in the blanks on the Oxford years, as well as many of the turning points of my presidential campaign. Ricardo Galán also provided a great deal of color and other detail from the campaign. Lina's collaboration in this section was critical as well.

SECTION FOUR: Ricardo Galán, Francisco Santos, and Admiral Rodolfo Amaya helped us recall some of the details from the inauguration day, and our efforts to keep everyone safe. Vivid accounts by *El País* and *El Tiempo* supplied much of the color from that crucial first day of my presidency in Valledupar and Florencia. Ingrid Betancourt's memoirs supplied her thoughts on her capture and subsequent captivity; a memoir by the three captured American contractors played a similar function for their story. The American academic Harvey Kline compiled useful data, as well as key moments, regarding the Justice and Peace Law and other key moments from my first term. Alicia Arango's collaboration was instrumental in reconstructing my presidency, from the early days onward.

SECTION FIVE: The reconstruction of Rodrigo Granda's capture, and the ensuing events, were taken in part from Jaime Bermúdez's book. Quotes from President Chávez and other players came mostly from international media, including BBC, Reuters and *The New York Times*. Fernando Araújo himself provided us with the full account of his imprisonment and his escape. Luis Guillermo Plata was gracious enough to supply many facts regarding our trade negotiations and the overall performance of our economy. Francisco Santos helped with critical context for our efforts to improve human rights. We depended largely on media accounts, particularly wire services, for descriptions of our day-to-day negotiations with the armed groups, and for casualty figures on terrorist attacks. Some details regarding the incident with the boy Emmanuel came from an interview with General Montoya, while others were taken from Juan Manuel Santos's book.

SECTION SIX: The information regarding the intelligence operations targeted at alias Raúl Reyes came from private interviews with Colombian officials. A book by the American journalist John Otis provided some helpful context for the operation, as well as general descriptions of the FARC's tactics during the second term of my presidency. Much of the data used to provide the final balance for our economic, social, and security policies came from a book that my government produced as our second term drew to a close, called *Uribe: Trabajo, Hechos, y Corazón*. Official transcripts and media accounts helped reconstruct my meetings with foreign leaders, including President Bush and President Lula. The detailed account of *Operación Jaque* came largely from the interview with General Montoya, as well as from a book written by Juan Carlos Torres. Other details of *Operación Jaque* came from a memorable fireside conversation just outside Bogotá with General Freddy Padilla, General Óscar Naranjo, Brian Winter, and myself in May 2010, the day before the first round of the election to choose my successor.

PARTIAL BIBLIOGRAPHY

Bermúdez, Jaime. *La audacia del poder.* Bogotá: Editorial Planeta Colombiana, 2010.

Bushnell, David. *The Making of Modern Colombia.* Berkeley: University of California Press, 1993.

Carpenter, Frank G. *South America: Social, Industrial and Political.* Boston: Geo. M. Smith & Co., 1900.

Cepeda Ulloa, Fernando, ed. *Strengths of Colombia.* Bogotá: Editorial Planeta, 2004.

Coghlan, Nicholas. *The Saddest Country: On Assignment in Colombia.* Toronto: McGill–Queen's University Press, 2004.

Corporación Observatorio para la Paz, et al. *Guerras inútiles: una historia de las FARC.* Bogotá: Intermedio Editores Ltda., 2009.

Davies, Howell, ed. *The South American Handbook 1948.* London: Trade and Travel Publications Ltd., 1948.

Gaviria Correa, Guillermo. Edited by James F. S. Amstutz. *Diary of a Kidnapped Colombian Governor.* Tenford, Pennsylvania: DreamSeeker Books, 2010.

Gonsalves, Marc, et al. *Out of Captivity.* New York: William Morrow, 2009.

Izquierdo, María. *Álvaro Uribe: con la patria en el corazón.* Bogotá: Panamericana Editorial, 2004.

Kline, Harvey F. *Showing Teeth to the Dragons: State-building by Colombian President Álvaro Uribe Vélez.* Tuscaloosa, Alabama: The University of Alabama Press, 2009.

Martin, Franklin H. *South America.* New York: Fleming H. Revell Company, 1922.

Otis, John. *Law of the Jungle.* New York: HarperCollins, 2010.

Policía Nacional de Colombia. *DIPOL: 15 años contra el crimen.* Bogotá: Panamericana Formas e Impresos S.A., 2010.

Reid, Michael. *The Forgotten Continent: The Battle for Latin America's Soul.* New Haven: Yale University Press, 2007.

Robinson, James, and Urrutia, Miguel, eds. *Economía colombiana del siglo XX.* Bogotá: Fondo de Cultura Económica, 2007.

Roldán, Mary. *Blood and Fire: La violencia in Antioquia, Colombia, 1946–1953*. Durham: Duke University Press, 2002.

Santos, Juan Manuel. *Jaque al Terror: los años horribles de las FARC*. Bogotá: Editorial Planeta, 2009.

Torres, Juan Carlos. *Operación Jaque, la verdadera historia*. Bogotá: Planeta, 2008.

Vincent, Frank. *Around and About South America: Twenty Months of Quest and Query*. New York: D. Appleton and Company, 1890.